THE ECONOMICS
OF POVERTY
AND
DISCRIMINATION

THE ECONOMICS
OF POVERTY
AND
DISCRIMINATION

THIRD EDITION

BRADLEY R. SCHILLER
American University

Prentice-Hall, Inc., Englewood Cliffs, N.J.   07632

Library of Congress Cataloging in Publication Data

SCHILLER, BRADLEY R   (date)
    The economics of poverty and discrimination.

    Includes bibliographical references and index.
    1. Poor—United States.   2. Poverty.   3. Discrimination—United States.   4. Economic assistance, Domestic—United
States.   I. Title.
HC110.P6S27   1980   331.5'4'0973   79-25746
ISBN   0-13-232025-8

Editorial/production supervision and interior design by Kim Gueterman
Cover design by Miriam Recio
Manufacturing buyer: Edmund W. Leone

Printed in the United States of America

10 9 8 7 6 5 4 3 2

PRENTICE-HALL INTERNATIONAL, INC., *London*

PRENTICE-HALL OF AUSTRALIA PTY. LIMITED, *Sydney*

PRENTICE-HALL OF CANADA, LTD., *Toronto*

PRENTICE-HALL OF INDIA PRIVATE LIMITED, *New Delhi*

PRENTICE-HALL OF JAPAN, INC., *Tokyo*

PRENTICE-HALL OF SOUTHEAST ASIA PTE. LTD., *Singapore*

WHITEHALL BOOKS LIMITED, *Wellington, New Zealand*

CONTENTS

INSTITUTIONAL FORCES

PREFACE

A first glance, the subjects of poverty and discrimination appear to have changed very little in the last few years. According to Census Bureau estimates, approximately 25 million Americans have been poor in each of last ten years. In each of those years, our expenditures on welfare and other antipoverty programs have grown. And "welfare reform" has been hotly debated each year, without evident resolution.

The same sensation of timelessness is easily experienced on the subject of discrimination. Minority children are still segregated in our schools. Minority and women workers still suffer higher unemployment and lower incomes. And the U.S. Supreme Court is still trying to decide the limits of "affirmative action" and mandatory school busing.

But appearances are deceptive. The constancy of the official poverty count, for example, masks an intense controversy about the dimensions of poverty in America. Many people no longer believe official poverty estimates. Indeed, some critics argue that the War on Poverty has been won. According to them, the income *not* counted by the Census Bureau (e.g. food stamps, public housing) is enough to pull most "poor" people out of poverty. The true size of the poverty population may be only 3 million, not the 25 million counted by the Census.

The debate on discrimination has intensified as well. Ten years ago, discrimination was discussed in terms of black vs. white. Today, other minority groups and women also demand their fair share of schools, jobs, and income. Moreover, they have compelled the government and the private sector to begin responding to their demands. In addition, the Supreme Court is now grappling with the limits to "reverse discrimination" (a remedy) not the legality of initial discrimination (the problem).

This third edition tries to convey these important developments in poverty and discrimination. As in earlier editions, this book offers an initial statement of the problem, a detailed analysis of possible causes, and a review of present and potential policies. Also like earlier editions, the book provides no quick and easy solutions to either poverty or discrimination. Instead, the complexity of these socio-political-economic problems is emphasized. In response to this complexity, a variety of different and reinforcing policies is required. This text attempts to identify the potential of and limits to these many separate approaches. What emerges, hopefully, is a multidimensional view of both the problems and appropriate policy responses.

In pursuit of a multidimensional view of poverty and discrimination, it must be recognized that neither phenomena is purely economic. While the title of the book is intended to convey a particular perspective on the ensuing discussion, it is not meant to imply a strict disciplinary exclusiveness. On the contrary, frequent, and often extended, explorations are made into other disciplines, most notably sociology. These will be most apparent when the cultural and racial aspects of poverty are considered.

Finally, it must be clear from the outset that poverty and discrimination are related, but separate concerns. Not all poor people are victims of discrimination. Nor are all victims of discrimination poor. Hence, we must recognize that the elimination of either poverty or discrimination does not imply the elimination of the other. While antidiscrimination and anti-poverty policies may be mutually supportive, they are only rarely identical.

The ultimate objective of this book is to lay the foundations for a clearer understanding of poverty and discrimination and for a keener perspective on related public policy. The human and economic cost of both phenomena are greater than Americans need or want to bear.

BRADLEY R. SCHILLER

Part 4

THE SCOPE
OF
POVERTY

1 THE NATURE OF POVERTY

Most Americans no longer accept the existence of poverty as inevitable. Indeed, most of us are surprised to learn that millions of Americans remain inadequately fed, clothed, and housed. As a nation we desire and sometimes strive to relieve the material hardships of those who are poor. We also deplore the waste of resources that poverty engenders—especially in the areas of welfare, crime, and civil disorder. Two questions remain, however: (1) Why are so many Americans poor? and (2) What policies will eliminate their impoverishment?

In seeking to answer these questions, we must recognize their interdependence. What we believe to be the dimensions and causes of poverty will have a determining influence on the policies we pursue. If we believe, for example, that people are poor because they cannot find decent jobs, our antipoverty efforts are likely to focus on the creation of more and better jobs. On the other hand, if we believe that people are poor simply because they are lazy, we are likely to provide fewer jobs and services.

Our perceptions of poverty not only influence our policy decisions, but also our ultimate success or failure in eliminating poverty. If people cannot find decent jobs because they lack basic skills, then the provision of more and better jobs will not eliminate much poverty. In this case, misperceptions of the causes of poverty would result in an expensive failure for antipoverty policy. Hence, it is important that our public antipoverty policies be based on informed perceptions of the nature and causes of poverty.

Different historical phases of antipoverty activity in America illustrate this interdependence of causal perspectives and policy prescriptions. In colonial times poverty was viewed as a curse on those of disreputable character. Impoverishment was seen as the companion to and punishment for vice. Accordingly, early antipoverty prescriptions focused on religious training, corporal punishment (to drive out sin), and physical expulsion. Very little was done to help the poor become more self-sufficient or even to alleviate their suffering.

It was not until the depression of the 1890s that many people seriously began to question the proposition that poverty resulted from sin and slovenliness. The march of unemployed and poor men—Coxey's Army—on Washington, D.C., in 1894 helped stimulate fresh perspectives on the origins of poverty. But it was not until 15 million Americans simultaneously experienced unemployment in the depths of the Great Depression that a really new perspective on poverty took hold. Only as millions of otherwise responsible and industrious individuals fell abruptly into joblessness and poverty did the American public begin to speak of poverty as being outside the control of the individual. Awareness grew that poverty might be the consequence of social and economic forces rather than of immorality and vice.

From one point of view, our experience with depressions and poverty may have been too brief. With the passage of time and the return to prosperity, poverty lost its middle-class constituency. With this loss, views toward those who are poor have become less generous. There has been a tendency to return to theories of poverty that characterize earlier eras. Thus, many observers again question the ambitions, motivation, ability, and the entire cultural orientation of those presently poor. To some extent the character of the poor is again being interpreted as different and apart from traditional American mores and ethics. This interpretation has acquired particular significance in discussions of the nation's continuing welfare "crisis." An editorial from the Tulsa, Oklahoma, *Tribune* typifies the residual hostilities and resentments that persist:

> *Relief is gradually becoming an honorable career in America. It is a pretty fair life, if you have conscience nor pride. The politicians will weep for you. The state will give a mother a bonus for her illegitimate children, and if she neglects them sufficiently she can save enough of her AFDC payments to keep herself and her boyfriend in wine and gin.* [1]

A more recent Gallup poll of the general population reflects the same undercurrent of hostility to people dependent on public assistance. Asked to guess what proportion of persons on welfare are collecting more than they are entitled to, 36 percent of the population guessed that at least half of all welfare recipients were "cheaters".[2] An NBC poll showed that only 30 percent of the American public believe welfare recipients really need help.[3] Yet, most Americans still report that they favor help for the poor!

[1] Quoted in Edgar May, *The Wasted Americans* (New York: Harper & Row, 1964), p.7
[2] Gallup survey of May 1979
[3] NBC News Poll of August 1977

The implication of these conflicting views is that poor people do warrant assistance, but once they are provided with it they somehow become unworthy. As Professor John Tropman has observed, most Americans view acceptance of welfare as tantamount to "giving up." Welfare implies a lack of independence and individualism. Accordingly, those who accept welfare are felt to deserve punishment in the form of hostility and stigma.

Current American attitudes toward the poor, then, are best described as ambivalent. "On the one hand, government and individuals alike decry poverty and devise programs geared to eradicate or eliminate it. On the other hand, the poor are disliked and perhaps feared."[4] The disquieting suspicion that external social and economic forces are at the root of poverty continues to stir the public conscience. At the same time, however, the egocentric conviction that the poor are less deserving still lingers close to the surface. Only as unemployment rates reach crisis proportions—as in the mid-1970s— does the former perspective clearly gather significant strength.

Against this background of uncertainty about the dimensions and causes of poverty, it is not remarkable that public policy often appears contradictory and ineffective. Until we reach a consensus on the dimensions of the problem, we cannot muster the necessary political support for public action. Where the causes of poverty remain the subject of intense debate, we cannot expect our efforts to meet with success. Accordingly, a serious effort to do something about poverty must begin with certain fundamentals. We must first decide precisely what we mean when we refer to so many Americans as being *poor*. Then we must determine how many persons fall into this category and why they are there.

POVERTY AND INEQUALITY

It is useful to begin a discussion of poverty with a broader view of the distribution of incomes. We all know that incomes are not distributed equally, that some people have less while others have more. The problem we confront is to determine how *much* less distinguishes a person as being "poor."

Figure 1.1 provides a quick summary of the actual distribution of income in the United States. In 1977, the *median* income of American families was $16,000. But not every family received $16,000. On the contrary, the bell-shaped curve in Figure 1.1 indicates that although many families had incomes at or near the median (the top part of the bell), many families had incomes significantly higher or lower than $16,000 (the lower "tails" of the bell). Indeed, closer scrutiny reveals that nearly six percent of all families (3 million families) enjoyed an income in excess of $40,000 in

[4]John E. Tropman, "The Image of Public Welfare: Reality or Projection?," *Public Welfare* Winter 1977.

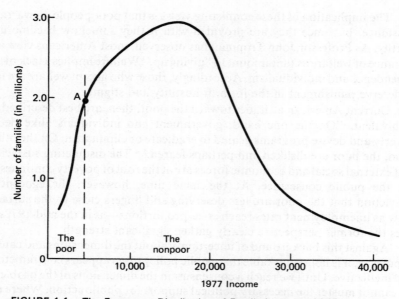

FIGURE 1.1   The Frequency Distribution of Family Incomes, 1977

Source: Approximated from the U.S. Bureau of the Census, *Consumer Income: Money Income in 1977 of Families and Persons in the United States* (Washington, D.C.: Government Printing Office, January 1979).

1977, while a few thousand of these families received over $100,000. At the same time, one out of five families received less than $8,000, many of them much less.

Were all incomes equal, the frequency distribution depicted in Figure 1.1 would narrow to a vertical line, positioned at the average (or mean) income level. But clearly, we are a long way from such complete equality. As a result many people below the average—as well as a good many above it—feel that they are "poor," that they don't have enough, especially in comparison to others. Our initial task is to provide a sounder basis for defining poverty, in other words, to identify a level of income—like point A in Figure 1.1—that distinguishes those who are poor from everyone else. We start out the search with only the conviction that somewhere along the left side of the graph there are families who are truly poor.

ECONOMIC DEFINITIONS OF POVERTY

Despite all the time that has been spent on poverty research, no concensus has been reached on the appropriate location for point A. That is to say, we have not yet agreed as to what we mean by the term *poverty*.

It is facile and perhaps satisfying to reply that poverty is simply a lack of money. And, of course, such a response is essentially correct; poverty *does* mean a scarcity of money. But when we examine this definition more carefully we must recognize a certain vagueness about the nature of poverty. Exactly what is meant by a *lack of money*? Do we mean no money, no income, no assets, and no credit, that is, a complete and devastating inability to acquire the basics of life? Or do we mean simply a shortage of cash? And if any one or all of these criteria, then how do we measure and define each one? Do we speak of a scarcity of money with reference to certain goods we think should or must be obtained, or do we mean scarcity relative to the amount of money, assets, income, or credit that others have? Clearly, there is room for a great deal of ambiguity and discussion even if we can agree that poverty is, in essence, a lack of economic resources.

The Absolute Approach

To achieve a workable and acceptable definition of poverty, we may begin by noting that there are two basic economic approaches to the concept of poverty. The first of these is the absolute approach, which deems some particular amount of goods and services as essential to an individual's or a family's welfare. Those who do not possess the economic wherewithal to obtain these goods and services are considered poor. In the least humanitarian strain of the absolute approach this bundle of economic goods and services consists of the minimum caloric intake essential to human existence, and perhaps some form of shelter. Additional frills are tacked onto this basic diet according to the generosity of the analyst.

This, of course, is the fundamental problem with the absolute approach to defining poverty. Once the bare-bones, life-sustaining minimum caloric diet has been exceeded, there is no agreement as to how many additional frills can be included in the definitional bundle of basic goods and services. In the 1890s no one felt particularly poor if he did not possess electric lights, yet today a family without electricity is most likely considered poor. Thus, we include a provision for electricity in our minimum poverty-defining budget. But consensus is far more difficult to achieve on a table lamp, much less on a television, a car, or a six-pack of beer. How many of these items will we include in a poor family's budget? Our answer will determine where point A is to be located.

How different opinions can be on this subject is illustrated by the continuing controversy over "minimum" needs. Public-opinion polls indicated that people felt $11,600 per year was the minimum amount of income a family of four "needed" in 1979. Yet, the official (government) definition of poverty in 1979 was an income of less than $7,400. Even more extreme, the state of Mississippi indicated that a mere $1,440 per year would suffice.

These differences serve to focus attention on the most perplexing issues of who is to determine the basic needs of individuals, and on what basis that determination is to be made. Quite obviously, each person's conception of what a family "needs" will be conditioned by his or her own economic position and one's familiarity with the poor. Faced with these dilemmas, some observers have suggested an alternative approach to defining poverty, one that depends on *relative* standards.

The Relative Approach

As a practical matter, we have seen that the absolute approach to defining poverty is vague and subject to the views of those formulating the yardstick. The relative approach is simply more explicit about this subjectivity. In essence, it states that a person is poor when his or her income is significantly less than the average income of the population. For example, we might say that a person or family with less than one-half of the average income is poor. By defining poverty in these terms, we not only avoid the need to define absolute needs, but also put more emphasis on the (in)equality of incomes. This broader perspective helps underscore the relationship between our views of poverty and our perspectives on the "fairness" of the entire distribution of incomes.

There are, of course, just as many relative measures of poverty as there are absolute ones. Perhaps the most extreme version of relative measures is one that defines poverty as the low end of the income distribution; for example, anyone in the lowest fifth (or tenth, or third) of the distribution is regarded as poor. From this perspective, poverty will persist as long as inequality does: If the frequency distribution depicted in Figure 1.1 were to move to the right— thus making everyone better off—point A would move along with the curve.

Table 1.1 illustrates the basic distinction between absolute and relative definitions of poverty in another way. Note, for example, that 1.6 percent of all American families earned less than $1,000 in 1970, 4.6 percent less than $2,000, and so forth. Only 4.6 percent of Amercian families earned more than $25,000. Note also that incomes were much lower in the 1935 to 1936 period, even after adjusting for inflation (expressing amounts in 1970 dollar values). In the middle of the Depression 13.4 percent of the population earned less than $1,000, and nearly a third survived with less than $2,000 per year.

Suppose we wanted to compare the number of Americans who were poor in 1970 with the number who were poor in 1936. Franklin Roosevelt spoke of one-third of the nation as being "ill-housed, ill-clad, ill-nourished." Apparently he regarded an income of about $2,000 as a threshold of poverty (see Table 1.1). By Roosevelt's definition, only 4.6 percent of the American population was poor in 1970. From an historical perspective, then, we could conclude that the incidence of poverty in the United States had declined markedly over a period of thirty years.

TABLE 1.1 CUMULATIVE FAMILY INCOME DISTRIBUTION, 1970 AND 1935–1936

Income in 1970 dollars	$1,000	$2,000	$3,000	$4,000	$5,000	$10,000	$15,000	$25,000
Percentage of families with incomes less than specified amount								
In 1970	1.6	4.6	8.9	13.9	19.1	50.9	77.7	95.4
In 1935-36	13.4	31.3	47.3	65.3	77.8	94.6	—	—

Source: U.S. Bureau of the Census.

But what would we conclude about the course of poverty between 1936 and 1970 if we had instead applied the relative concept of poverty to the comparison? If we were consistently to regard the lowest fifth of the American income distribution as poor, then by definition we would find that 20 percent of the population was poor in 1936 and continued to be so in 1970.

This example illustrates the basic weaknesses of the relative measure of poverty. First, it perpetuates poverty in the statistical sense that some fixed proportion of the population is always regarded as poor. If the lowest fifth of the income distribution is regarded as poor, then the poor will certainly be with us always because the income distribution will always have a lowest fifth. Second, a relative measure of poverty by itself tells us nothing about how well or how poorly the people at the bottom of the income distribution actually live. Yet we want to know not only how many people are in poverty but also how desperate their situation is. In a similar vein, we may want to know how much money poor families need to bring their incomes up to an acceptable standard of living.

An improved measure of relative poverty, which has been suggested by Victor Fuchs, meets at least the first objection to relative definitions of poverty. By his definition, those with incomes less than half of the national median are poor. In 1970, for example, the median family income was just under $10,000 (see Table 1.1). Thus, according to the "Fuchs point," families with less than $5,000 (half of the median) should have been considered poor. The advantage of the Fuchs point over simpler relative definitions is that it distinguishes the elimination of poverty from the elimination of inequality. Whereas the simpler relative definition precludes the elimination of poverty until *complete* equality of incomes is attained, the Fuchs points envisions the elimination of poverty occuring with a *reduction* in inequality, that is, a *narrowing* of income differences (and thus a narrower distribution for Figure 1.1).

There is nothing sacred, of course, about the use of one *half* the median as a relative standard of poverty; we could just as easily have chosen to define poverty in relative terms as one-fourth, one-third, or three-sixteenths of the median income. That is, there is as much subjectivity involved in defining the Fuchs point as there is in defining absolute "minimum" standards of poverty. In reality, one's choice of an appropriate Fuchs point is likely to be influenced by the absolute standard of living implied, just as the choice of an absolute standard is likely to be affected by the degree of inequality and the general standards of living we observe.

In view of the conflicting measures of poverty, it is tempting to abandon the search for a poverty line. But this is neither necessary nor appropriate. We need an acceptable definition of poverty in order to identify people we desire to help and to measure our success in helping them. The search for a poverty line is analogous to the search for highway speed limits. No one really believes that all speeds in excess of 55 miles per hour are somehow dangerous and all speeds less than 55 miles an hour are somehow safe; the realities of highway driving are much more complex. Yet, we use 55 miles per hour as a convenient gauge of highway safety. The same is true of our poverty line. On the continuum of misery and human happiness, we cannot pretend that there is some point below which people are unhappy or poor and above which people are in a much better position. But, like highway speed limits, we do have to come to grips with a cutoff point—a poverty line.

In searching for a poverty line, we cannot conclude that one approach to defining poverty is inherently better than the other, or even maintain a rigid distinction between them. Instead, we will simply note that the contrast between relative and absolute measures of poverty highlights a basic policy issue. Is our primary policy concern with the misery of those who command low incomes, or are we concerned with the unequal distribution of incomes? Though income distribution and poverty are intrinsically related, they can be approached separately. Because absolute definitions of poverty maintain this distinction—and because they are the official basis for government policy—we shall utilize them throughout the remainder of the book. Thus, we allow for the possibility of eliminating poverty without altering the relative distribution of incomes, a goal that could be achieved by making *everyone* better off. But we also recognize that direct redistribution of incomes from rich to poor could speed the elimination of poverty and might be a goal in itself.

NONECONOMIC MEASURES OF POVERTY

The distinction between absolute and relative measure of poverty does not exhaust the list of potential definitions: To some observers poverty is just as much a state of mind as it is a state of one's pocketbook. In this most subjective of views a person is not poor unless he or she *feels* poor. The Kentucky backwoodsman is sometimes seen not as impoverished but as enjoying the rich benefits of a bountiful and uncluttered natural world. He is not to be pitied, but rather idealized. To lift him out of financial destitution would be to corrupt him.

Although Henry Thoreau forcefully expressed this distinction between monetary and spiritual richness, his views are not easily translated into statistical or policymaking terms. Short of surveying all destitute persons as to their spiritual contentment and materialistic anxieties, Thoreau's distinction permits no census of the poor. That is not to say that his perspective does not merit reflection, but rather that it does not provide an adequate guide to policy formulation. Accordingly, we are led to use other criteria for identifying the poor and to conclude from their political agitation that the poor are not wholly content.

More recent observers from other social disciplines have construed similar definitions of modern poverty. Generally they focus on the hopes, expectations, and aspirations—the entire "culture" in some cases—of those without material means. To these observers, poverty is to be without money, without spirit, without hope for a better life. Poverty is thus understood to be complete material and spiritual deprivation. Although these concepts have considerable merit in their own right, they are not easily observed, much less quantified. They may contribute to an understanding of poverty in many cases, but they add little to its definition or measurement. Moreover, they are likely to create more disagreement on poverty measures than already exists. Accordingly, we will rely on economic and strictly observable criteria in defining and measuring poverty.

THE OFFICIAL POVERTY INDEX

As noted above, the government has chosen to use the absolute approach to defining poverty. Naturally, this has required the government to identify the minimum amount of money required to sustain a family, a minimum estimated to be $7,400 for a family of four in 1979. But before we look at just who is poor according to this definition, or what conditions give rise to such poverty, we shall take a closer look at how that figure was obtained. One of the problems with not being poor is that it is difficult to comprehend just what it means to be poor. Hopefully, a short review of our current definition of poverty will help increase that comprehension.

The Concept of Minimum Needs

In order to state that a specific amount of money income is required to keep a family out of poverty, one must have a firm notion of just what that much money will buy. That is, the identification of a poverty measure denominated in dollars logically begins with a standard of living demoninated in "essential" goods and services. That task is not easy, particularly in view of the very different opinions people have about just what goods and services are essential. But let us suppose that we really could be coldly scientific and single out such goods.

We may begin to assemble an inventory of "minimum needs" by determining what are the absolutely basic ingredients of human subsistence; presumably everyone will agree that our poverty measure should include at least these components. Such a list will include minimum food, clothing, shelter, and fuel requirements as determined by appropriate experts. To this list of basic minimums we may choose to include means of transportation, some recreation, and whatever additional goods and services we deem appropriate, if not absolutely essential. The sum total of our efforts, assuming consensus can be achieved, will be a shopping list of what we consider to be basic goods and services. Those persons who cannot obtain all the items on our list we will consider poor, those who can as not poor.

Suppose for the moment that nutritionists, physiologists, and other assorted scientific experts could actually detail the minimum subsistence requirements we have outlined. Such a list might be like the one in Table 1.2. Note that each functional requirement is expressed in its generic measure. To this list of social and biological minimums we might add additional food, clothing, or entertainment, depending on our sense of generosity. In this way we could construct a complete specification of what we deem to be the minimum acceptable (or poverty) standard of living.

TABLE 1.2   HYPOTHETICAL MINIMUM HUMAN NEEDS

Category	Amount
Minimum food requirements	2,471 calories
Minimum fuel requirements	37 kilowatt-hours
Minimum shelter requirements	60 board feet
Minimum clothing requirements	4 pounds
Minimum transportation requirements	7 miles

But consider carefully the list we have complied. To begin with, how are we to translate 2,471 calories into more familiar staples, such as peanuts, bananas, and chewing gum? As anyone who has ever dieted well knows, there are an infinite number of ways in which a person can consume the requisite number of calories. Or, consider the clothing requirement. The specification "4 pounds" tells us nothing at all about the appropriate type of clothing or even whether we should shop at Saks Fifth Avenue or a Salvation Army store. Similar problems arise with every item on our list.

As if this vagueness of detail were not a serious enough problem, let us return to the generic specifications. Though there is some conceptual foundation for speaking of "minimum" food, shelter, clothing, or fuel requirements, there is admittedly no firm basis for specifying what these minimums are. People do survive on varying amounts of calories; the warming and protective value of clothing cannot be adequately gauged in pounds; and the need for shelter varies enormously. Consequently, any claim to scientific precision, even in the generic specifications of our poverty standard, is pretentious and misplaced.

While the specification of a poverty standard is an imprecise endeavor, it is not necessarily useless. The achievement of consensus as to the components of a poverty standard may be a formidable task, but it is not necessarily impossible. If we can achieve some sort of reasonable compromise, our basic objective of specification will have been attained.

We return, then, to our position that an absolute standard of poverty can be defined in terms of a shopping list of goods and services. Poverty is thus understood as the inability to obtain the goods and services sufficient to meet socially defined minimum needs. Momentarily sidestepping the issue of specification, our only remaining conceptual problem is to consolidate that list of goods and services into more convenient and observable units.

Units of Measure

In a market economy the ability of an individual to obtain needed goods and services is determined by his *purchasing power*. The producers and sellers of goods require some form of payment before they willingly yield up their wares. Accordingly, we may be able to simplify our poverty standard by expressing that measure, not in terms of a list of necessary goods and services but instead in terms of the purchasing power required to obtain those same goods and services. This simplification will greatly enhance the usefulness of our measure, as we will be able to inquire merely whether a person has a specific amount of purchasing power rather than a cumbersome list of essential commodities.

The obvious and familiar measure of purchasing power in a market economy is money, so it should come as no surprise that we express our poverty standard in dollars and cents. The necessary conversion requires that we price all the goods and services in our list, then sum to determine the total amount of money involved. That total is our gauge of poverty, for its represents command over the goods and services we have specified.

Not only is such a summary measure convenient but it also facilitates the compromise that produced the standard itself. Suppose, for example, that Mr. Blixen believes that 1,437 calories and 1.57 pounds of clothing are the absolute daily minimum needs of one person. You, on the other hand, contend that 2,113 calories and 0.86 pound of clothing are necessary (a difference equivalent to giving up your shirt for a banana split). Given your respective resolutions, you and Mr. Blixen are unlikely to reach a compromise on the generic specifications of minimums needs. However, what if current market prices indicate that your "needs" require $4.37 to fulfill, while Mr. Blixen's budget is $4.35 per day. In *monetary* terms, it is obvious that you are not far away from a potential compromise and that agreement on the *generic* components of a minimum budget might be postponed indefinitely.

While we do need the food, shelter, and other items on our shopping list daily, it is not necessary to have the right amount of cash every day. To shop each day for that day's minimum requirements of shelter, fuel, clothing, and food would be extraordinarily inconvenient at best and downright impossible at worst. Our real interest lies in ascertaining that a person has an adequate flow of cash so that he or she can acquire the basic necessities as the need arises. Hence, our poverty standard will incorporate the basic needs of an individual for some particular span of time and will be expressed in terms of the amount of money needed during that period of time to make the required purchase. Whether that individual then elects to shop monthly, weekly, or daily is immaterial to our concern with poverty.

The best single indicator of a person's purchasing power over a period of time is one's *income* during that period. Income is the flow of cash to a person over time, and thus it represents what he or she will have available to acquire goods and services. But here, too, there are complications. While income does represent purchasing power, it is not the sole determinant of purchasing power. Two other factors, assets and credit, can render a person's command over goods and services much larger than his or her current income. Where credit is available goods and services can, in effect, be borrowed. No current income is necessary, just a promise to make repayment when time and circumstances permit (or the creditors demand).

A similar situation holds true with assets. Here again, a person may acquire goods and services without an income, in effect by trading one good for another. In the most common instance, a person may sell a particular asset to acquire a desired commodity. Or he or she may trade the asset for the commodity or even combine the features of credit and wealth at a nearby pawnshop.

Finally, many people obtain goods and services *directly* without payment of cash or even a promise to pay (credit). In the last ten years or so, the government has assumed an increasing responsibility for providing basic goods and services to people, even if they have insufficient income or assets. Food stamps, for example, allow one to "buy" groceries with coupons ("stamps") rather than money. Hence, food-stamp recipients need less cash income to achieve any particular "minimum" standard. Likewise, families that live in public housing or receive free medical care enjoy a standard of living higher than their money income suggests. Hence, money incomes have become a less reliable index of living standards, especially at the low end of the income distribution.[5]

Despite these limitations, money incomes continue to be used as the single best index of a family's living standard, and we shall follow this practice in our own discussion of poverty standards. However, we will later reexamine

[5]In-kind income is not limited to poor families: middle-class families benefit from subsidized public schools, job-related fringe benefits, special tax advantages, and an array of other noncash ("in-kind") forms of income. If all in-kind benefits were added up—not just those the poor receive—the poor might actually appear relatively worse off than their money incomes imply. The rapid *growth* of in-kind benefits for the poor in recent years—not necessarily their aggregate share—is what complicates poverty measures.

the limitations of this approach, after we have looked at the actual incomes of poor families.

Poverty Thresholds

We are now in a position to identify what may be called a *poverty* line. We have established the process by which that line may be formulated; all that remains is to apply the process. But lest we become too complacent about our theoretical achievements, it should be noted that a nearly identical procedure was formulated at least as early as 1890. At that time Charles Booth, an English sociologist, estimated the goods and services necessary to maintain a family in what he called a "state of chronic want." He then priced those commodities and concluded that a weekly income of approximately twenty-four shillings or less was necessary to achieve the condition he described. At about the same time American economists estimated that from $400 to $600 per year was necessary to attain this condition in the United States.

Since Booth's time our standards of living have grown enormously. So also have the number of proposed poverty lines, each varying with the circumstances of the time and the perspectives of the architect. While it is not necessary to review the history of those lines, each of which had significance in its own time, it is of interest to examine two of the most recent formulations.

The CEA Line

In 1963, the president's Council of Economic Advisers (CEA) officially sanctioned a poverty line of $3,000 per annum for a typical American family. While their estimation effort itself was an important step in the development of poverty statistics and policy, we shall see that their estimate was not without serious faults.

The rationale behind the council's poverty line estimate was similar to that which we have already outlined. The council accepted the notion that food requirements constitute the foundation of any poverty budget. Accordingly, they set out to determine the minimum nutritional requirements of a typical American family. These requirements had been estimated by the Department of Agriculture for the Social Security Administration, which was already developing a poverty measure. The estimates indicated that three minimally adequate meals a day would cost the typical family of two adults and two children exactly $2.736 a day. Now, the very precision of that nutrition estimate should be suspect. We have already suggested the difficulties inherent in specifying minimum nutrition requirements, converting those requirements into real commodities, and pricing those goods in the market. To pretend that this process could yield an estimate as $2.736 a day is to strain one's credibility.

The council adopted a more pragmatic approach to arrive at the *total* budget for a poor family. You will recall that the frills added to a starvation diet were the prime source of arbitrariness in the budgetary process. Some people said ice cream was essential, others insisted on beer and pretzels. These problems were circumvented by simply observing how much money low-income families actually spend on such frills. Consumer studies indicated that such families spend approximately two-thirds of their incomes on nonfood items—hence, on commodities that include clothing, shelter, fuel, and goods that might be considered as less than essential to human subsistence. Using this observation as a benchmark, the council then multiplied their basic food budget by three to determine how much total income a poor family needs. The results of their calculation are depicted in Table 1.3. The council then rounded off the total budget estimate to the $3,000 figure. Using this measure, the council found that there were 33,400,000 poverty-stricken persons in America in 1963.

TABLE 1.3   THE CEA POVERTY BUDGET (1963)

Food budget	$2.736 per day $\times$ 365 days = $ 998.64
Nonfood budget	2 $\times$ food budget = 1,997.28
	Total budget = $2,995.92

Michael Harrington has warned us "not to allow statistical quibbling to obscure the huge, enormous, and intolerable fact of poverty in America."[6] This is a warning we must take seriously, especially when over 9.5 million families may be involved. Accordingly, we would do well to overlook some of the imperfections in the council's estimation procedures and concentrate on the mass of poverty they identified. Whether the "true" size of the poverty population in 1963 was then 33 million, 33.5 million, or even 35.23 million would not seem to be of much consequence.

But one glaring error in the council's estimation procedure prevents us from accepting their results. To appreciate the nature of the council's error, let us look at three families from the 1963 income distribution:

The husband in Family 1 is thirty-seven years old and supports six children and a pregnant wife on his income of $3,200 a year.

Family 2 consists of a soon-to-be-retired couple, both in their mid-sixties. The wife does not work and the husband's earnings amount to $2,800 per year. They own their home, having made the final mortgage payment last Christmas.

[6]Michael Harrington, *The Other America* (New York: The Macmillan Company, 1962), p. 10.

Family 3 consists of a struggling graduate student, his working wife, and their three-month-old child. They both work at the college carryout store in their spare time. Their combined earnings, including overtime and tips, amounts to $2,400 a year.

How did these three families place in the council's census of poor Americans? Family 1, consisting of eight and one-half persons, was officially classified as nonpoor. Families 2 and 3 were counted as poor, as their incomes were under the $3,000 limit. But how many people would be willing to accept the council's classification of these families? Family 1 is clearly desperate, while Family 2 is living a quiet and perhaps comfortable life. Our graduate-student family is not exactly affluent, but they are not desperate on $200 a month.

The source of the council's error should be obvious at this point. The council calculated a poverty budget for a *typical* family of two adults and two children. But not all families consists of four persons, nor do all four-person families have consistently "typical" needs. As our illustration has made clear, the council's definition of a poverty line must *at a minimum* be adjusted for varying family size. A further refinement should take into account gross differences in family needs even among families of the same size.

The SSA Index

These basic refinements of the council's poverty line were undertaken by Mollie Orshansky of the Social Security Administration (SSA). She first adjusted for size of family; then she adjusted for varying family needs based on whether or not the family lived on a farm, whether the family was headed by a man or woman, and how many children there were. Using these four variables, she identified 124 types of families and meticulously calculated an appropriate poverty budget for each one. And while Ms. Orshansky's estimates were not faultless, they represented a significant improvement over earlier estimation attempts.

For the "typical" family of four identified by the Council of Economic Advisers, the SSA poverty budget and the council's own budget were very similar. The SSA adjustments, however, counted many more large families and fewer smaller families as poor due to different family needs. Our earlier examples illustrate the difference. Ms. Orshansky found that Family 3, that of the struggling graduate student, needed only $2,275 for a minimum budget. Hence, they were not counted as poor under the SSA index. Family 2, the soon-to-be-retired couple, required a minimum of only $1,855 and was living quite comfortably on their income. Family 1, however, with eight persons, needed at least $5,100 per year to meet essential needs and were classified as poor by the Social Security Administration index.

The Current Poverty Index

Despite the considerable sophistication of the 1963 Social Security Administration poverty index, it was not presented as either perfect or static. It was recognized that, as prices and our standards of living continued to rise, the SSA poverty lines would require repeated upward adjustments. Over time our concept of what is essential to modern-day living will be enlarged, and the necessary ingredients will also cost more.

The official poverty index now in use has been revised to account for the rising prices of goods and services, but not for our steadily increasing standard of living. According to Ms. Orshansky's earlier calculations, an average nonfarm family of two adults and two children required a minimum of $3,130 in 1963. In 1977, after fourteen years of inflation, that index stood at $6,191. We are saying that it cost $6,191 in 1977 to buy those goods and services that cost $3,130 in 1963. The increased dollar amount of our definition does not imply in any way an increased standard of living for the poor. It adjusts only for rising prices.[7] If we wanted to increase the standard of living of those whom we define as poor—and not many affluent persons are so inclined—then we would have raise the index by more than the inflation adjustment, that is, to a figure higher than $6,191.

A current poverty line that adjusts only for changing prices leaves the standard of living of the poor unchanged. But the income and living standards of the rest of the population will continue to advance as the American economy grows. Hence, poverty lines adjusted only for inflation imply a growing disparity between the status of the poor and that of the rest of the population. If we refuse to raise our expectations of what the poor require, then we will have to confront the consequences of a widening inequality.

Despite the limitations of current poverty line adjustments, we will adhere to present standards. Accordingly, a 1977 income of less than $6,191 will qualify a family of four for inclusion in our head count of the poor. The application of this standard to other family sizes and types is summarized in Table 1.4. It may be seen that poverty lines for farm families are considerably lower than for nonfarm families. This difference is attributable to the fact that the cost of living is less for farm families and that they produce much of their own food.

Enumeration of the persons below either the 1963 or the updated poverty index is a simple and straightforward task and will be undertaken in Chapter 2. Unfortunately, the clinical nature of the statistical operation tends to impress the observer very little with the real impoverishment that

---

[7]Because of very high rates of inflation in 1978 and 1979, the poverty line for a family of four reached $7,400 in 1979. Here again, the higher dollar amount reflects only higher prices, not an improved standard of living for the poor.

TABLE 1.4   POVERTY STANDARDS, 1977

Size of Family	Poverty Standard Nonfarm	Farm
One member	$ 3,075	$2,588
Two members	3,951	3,318
Three members	4,833	4,093
Four members	6,191	5,273
Five members	7,320	6,247
Six members	8,261	7,026
Seven or more members	10,216	8,708

Source: U.S. Bureau of the Census.

the numbers represent. Consequently, it is worthwhile to dwell for a few moments on the standard of living that a poverty budget implies.

The austerity of the poverty budget was well described by B. Seebohm Rowntree, an English sociologist, in 1901. The essence of his description is still valid today:

> *A family, living upon the scale allowed for in this estimate, must never spend a penny on railway fare or omnibus. They must never go into the country unless they walk. They must never purchase a half-penny newspaper or spend a penny to buy a ticket for a popular concert. They must write no letters to absent children, for they cannot afford to pay the postage. They must never contribute anything to their church or chapel, or give any help to a neighbor which costs them money. They cannot save, nor can they join sick or Trade Union, because they cannot pay the necessary subscription. The children must have no pocket money for dolls, marbles, or sweets. The father must smoke no tobacco and must drink no beer. The mother must never buy any pretty clothes for herself or for her children, the character of the family wardrobe as for the family diet being governed by the regulation, 'nothing must be bought but that which is absolutely necessary for the maintenance of physical health, and what is bought must be of the plainest and most economical description.'*[8]

That Mr. Rowntree's description of poverty living remains appropriate can be seen by looking first at the food component of the current poverty budget for a family of four. Our $6,191 budget allows approximately $1.42 per person per day. That is $1.42 for breakfast, lunch, dinner, and any snacks—an amount less than what one lunch costs in most

[8]B. Seebohm Rowntree, *Poverty: A Study of Town Life* (London: Longmans, Green & Co. Ltd., 1901).

places. This means that the homemaker must plan, buy, and prepare a nutritious meal for her family of four for approximately $1.89. When even hamburger cost well over one dollar a pound in urban areas, it is devastatingly clear that this poverty family is not eating either very well or very much.[9] And if they have aspirations to eat out on occasion, their only hope is to save money by eating lots of hot dogs and boiled eggs at home. Then, if they are lucky, they will have enough money to go out and order a hot dog, perhaps in the park.

You may respond that this is a gross exaggeration of how the poor live. You may even know of a poor person who once ate a sirloin steak. And in a sense you are right. We have described how a poor family would act if they spent only their food allowance on food. In fact, poor families do not follow our carefully budgeted allowances. They tend to forego other items and spend some of their nonfood allowance money on better and more palatable meals—maybe even an occasional beer to wash down the grits and pick up their spirits. And it is this process that comes closest to describing what it means to be poor. Every day a poor person or family must choose between an adequate diet of the most economic sort and some other necessity because there is never enough money to have both. Consequently, some of the poor eat steak and walk around with holes in their shoes.

It is interesting to contrast what is officially regarded as a poverty income to what Americans generally believe is required to make ends meet. A Gallup poll taken in May 1977 asked a cross section of Americans: "What is the smallest amount of money a family of four (husband, wife, and two children) needs each week to get along in this community?" Their answers averaged out at $199 a week, or $10,348 a year. Quite clearly, most Americans do not believe that the poverty standard is enough, that is, that families really could get by for long on the government's definition of minimum needs. It is nevertheless true that poor families must find some way to cope. Indeed, most poor families command even less income than the official standard. In 1977, for example, the typical poor family had a cash income (including cash welfare benefits it received) of only $3,292.[10] For these families, even having the opportunity to choose between minute steak and hole-worn shoes would seem like affluence.

If the prospect of existing for a short time on a poverty budget or less is not disquieting enough, consider the prospect of subsisting at that level on into the indefinite future. A poor family must not only adjust to a

[9]Since 1963, the Department of Agriculture has increased its estimate of a minimum food budget, based on revised nutritional requirements and changing food choices. This increased food budget would increase the poverty line; however, no official action has been taken.

[10]The total real income of many poor families is higher than this as a result of receiving noncash income (e.g., food stamps, Medicaid, housing subsidies); this is discussed in Chapters 2 and 12.

subsistence budget but must also be prepared to remain at that standard of living. That is why a more affluent person cannot adequately grasp the significance of poverty by adopting a subsistence budget for a brief time. The affluent person knows that his experiment can and will be terminated shortly. The poor person possesses no such luxury. As was reported on a similar experiment by Tolstoy, "poverty is not the lack of things; it is the fear and the dread of want. That fear Tolstoy could not know."[11]

Let us then be clear about what our poverty index implies. The line we have drawn separating the poor from the nonpoor does not indicate what is enough—it only asserts with confidence what is too little. As Robert Hunter observed in 1904, "to live up to the standard . . . means no more than to have a sanitary dwelling and sufficient food and clothing to keep the body in working order."[12] Those who fall below the line are unquestionably poor by contemporary standards. Nevertheless, many of those who have incomes above our standard cannot be regarded as rich or even as moderately well-off. While we will concentrate our discussion on those persons we have defined as poor, we would do well to remember that there are a great many more people whose standard of living is only marginally higher than that of the poor.

FURTHER READING

COE, RICHARD, "The Poverty Line: Its Function and Limitations," *Public Welfare,* Winter 1978.

COUNCIL OF ECONOMIC ADVISERS, "The Problem of Poverty in America," in *Economic Report of the President,* Washington, D.C.: Government Printing Office, 1964.

HARRINGTON, MICHAEL, *The Other America.* New York: The Macmillan Company, 1962.

HUNTER, ROBERT, *Poverty.* New York: The Macmillan Company, 1904.

KRISTOL, IRVING, "Taxes, Poverty, and Equality," *The Public Interest,* Fall 1974.

PEN, JAN, *Income Distribution.* New York: Frederick A. Praeger, Inc., 1971, Ch 3.

U.S. DEPARTMENT OF HEALTH, EDUCATION AND WELFARE, *The Measure of Poverty.* Washington, D.C.: Government Printing Office, 1976.

[11]Conversation quoted in Robert Hunter, *Poverty* (New York: The Macmillan Company, 1904), p. 1.
[12]Ibid., p. 7.

2 THE POOR

Having established a workable measure of contemporary poverty, we are now in a position to proceed with a census of the poor. In so doing, we will consider several related questions. First, how many Americans are "poor," that is, have incomes below the official budget standards? Second, who are the poor; do they have distinguishing characteristics (other than lack of income)? Have the number or characteristics of the poor changed over time? Finally, how long do people remain poor? Is poverty a permanent condition for some families or do families move in and out of poverty?

These questions are of more than merely academic interest. What we know about the extent of poverty helps to determine the interest and resources we devote to its elimination. If we were to discover that economic want affects only a few thousand individuals in the United States, presumably antipoverty concern would occupy a very low position on our scale of public priorities. On the other hand, if poverty were found to be the condition of a majority of Americans, we can suppose that its eradication would be of foremost public concern. What one considers a "large" or "small" poverty population is essentially a question of individual predilections, of course, but at least a specification of the number of poor persons will provide a common basis for discussion and policy planning.

Unfortunately, estimates of the size of the poverty population vary tremendously. A recent poll of college seniors elicited estimates ranging from 120,000 poor persons to over 60,000,000 poor persons. Even experienced researchers argue about the true size of the poverty population. The official (Census Bureau) estimates of the poverty population hover around 25 million people. Many economists argue, however, that these estimates grossly overestimate the amount of poverty in America. Indeed, they believe poverty has virtually been eliminated in the United States. Clearly, agreement on the importance in America's poverty problems would be difficult to attain in the face of such diverse perspectives.

THE NUMBER OF POOR PEOPLE

The Official Poverty Count

We will begin our own census of the poor with official estimates of the poverty population. These are based on a comparison of a family's *cash* income to its estimated needs. As noted in Chapter 1, 34 million persons—one out of five Americans—were officially counted as poor in 1963. According to our definition of poverty, that is the number of persons whose cash income in 1963 was less than the minimum standard needed for their particular family size and type. This tremendous number of poor persons convinced President Kennedy and President Johnson to start a "war on poverty." As Michael Harrington observed at the time, the number of poor Americans was simply unconscionable.

Table 2.1 updates the official poverty count to 1977 and shows that the prevalence of poverty in the United States has diminished markedly in a relatively short time. In 1977 the number of poor Americans was just under 25 million, one-third fewer than in 1963. At the same time, the incidence of poverty declined from one out of five Americans to one out of nine.

We may also observe in Table 2.1 that the incidence of poverty varies enormously among population groups. For example, more whites experience poverty than blacks but in far smaller numbers than the relative size of the white population would suggest. Accordingly, we may say that blacks face a far greater likelihood (31.3 percent) of being poor, although blacks still comprise a minority of the poor. The same relationship applies to the aged population and, to a lesser extent, all children. We will discuss these inequities in later chapters.

Table 2.1   THE POVERTY POPULATION, 1977

Group	U.S. Population	Persons in Poverty	Poverty Rate (%)
All persons	213,103,000	24,720,000	11.6
White	184,449,000	16,416,000	8.9
Black	24,684,000	7,726,000	31.3
Aged persons	22,468,000	3,177,000	14.1
Spanish origin	12,046,000	2,700,000	22.4
Children (under 18)	72,839,000	10,416,000	14.3

Source: U.S. Bureau of the Census.

The marked decline we have observed from 1963 to 1977 in the number of poor persons is a legitimate foundation for some optimism about America's poverty problems. Before concluding that poverty is disappearing, however, we need to consider Figure 2.1. This figure illustrates the year-to-year changes in the size of the poverty population since 1963. Most of the decline in the size of the poverty population occurred in the 1960s, at the height of the War on Poverty. Since then, the poverty population has apparently not declined further.

FIGURE 2.1   Decline of the Poverty Population

Year

Note: Trend based on official census estimates of the poverty population

Adjustments for In-kind Transfers

Critics of official poverty estimates argue that our apparent failure to win the war on poverty is an illusion. In reality, argues Professor Martin Anderson, of Stanford's Hoover Institution, "The war on poverty has been won, except for perhaps a few mopping-up operations."[1] According to his reading of the data, there are only a few million people still poor in America.

[1] Martin Anderson, *Welfare* (Stanford, CA: Hoover Institution Press, 1978), p. 37.

The major deficiency of the official poverty statistics is that they count only a family's *cash* means. Yet, all families receive some income "in-kind." Many low-income families, for example, receive food stamps, Medicaid or Medicare, or subsidized housing. Instead of giving poor families the cash needed to buy groceries, health care, or housing, the government provides these goods directly.[2] As a result, low-income families don't need as much cash income to maintain a given standard of living; in-kind transfers substitute for cash income.

The Census Bureau ignores all in-kind transfers when it counts the number of poor people. As a result, many of the people who are counted as "poor" may in fact have a total income (cash and transfers) that exceeds our poverty standards. In this case, official estimates exaggerate the size of the poverty population. If all in-kind transfers are added up, the overestimate appears to be substantial. In fact, "corrected" estimates suggest that fewer than eight million people remain in poverty—about one-third as many as official estimates.[3]

The "corrected" estimates are subject to criticism as well, however. Not all in-kind transfers represent an improved standard of living. The amount of medical assistance a person receives, for example, depends on how sick one is. Accordingly, it isn't appropriate to regard a person as "nonpoor" just because he or she receives a lot of in-kind medical assistance (Medicaid or Medicare).

There is no agreement as yet about how many people move from poverty to nonpoverty as a result of in-kind transfers. All we can say with certainty is that official estimates of poverty are too high. Even after all appropriate adjustments, however, there are still millions of poor Americans. It is also important to recall that the official census of the poor takes place *after* the provision of government assistance. Remember that we are defining poverty in terms of a family's total cash income, relative to its needs. Part of this cash income is provided by the government, in the form of Social Security benefits, public welfare assistance, or unemployment benefits. As a result, many families who would be poor in the absence of government assistance are not counted in our census of the poor; the "nonpoor" status of such families depends on continued public assistance. The Congressional Budget Office estimates that the poverty population would *double* if all social security benefits, public assistance, and other government transfers were cut off. If dependence on public transfers is itself a definition of poverty, then America still has a very serious poverty problem.

[2]The in-kind transfers programs are described more fully in chapter 12.

[3]See Morton Paglin, *Poverty and Transfers In-Kind* (Stanford, CA: Hoover Institution Press, 1979); Timothy M. Smeeding, "The Antipoverty Effectiveness of In-Kind Transfers," *Journal of Human Resources,* Summer 1977; and Congressional Budget Office, *Poverty Status of Families Under Alternative Definitions of Income,* (Washington, D.C.: Government Printing Office, 1977).

We should also note that a reduction in poverty is not synonymous with a reduction in inequality. Because we use an absolute measure of poverty, it is possible that the entire distribution of incomes has shifted to the right since 1963, leaving everyone better off, including some families who were formerly poor. This possibility is illustrated in Figure 2.2. In fact, this is exactly what has taken place: relative incomes (the degree of inequality) have remained virtually constant while absolute incomes have risen. Hence, our observation that the number of people officially counted as poor has diminished does not vitiate efforts to reduce inequality.

FIGURE 2.2   A Shifting Income Distribution

A final constraint on our optimism concerns the meaning of the numbers themselves as we have presented them. The numbers we have used to depict the size of the poverty population tell only part, perhaps only a small part, of the poverty story. They fail to tell us how malignant a disease poverty is, or how widespread is the affliction. To understand this failure, we must examine the concept of income mobility.

Income Mobility

Consider again the number of persons who were poor in 1963. Our total indicated approximately 34 million. The number itself is based on a statistical sample undertaken by the Census Bureau. Of course, there are problems with any estimate based on samples. The individuals sampled may not be representative; they may not be willing or able to tell the truth. But these are straightforward statistical problems, and we learn to solve them, or at least live with them. They need not detain us here.

In evaluating our census of the poor, however, we must consider how much poverty qualifies a family for our statistical count. Must a family be in poverty all year long to be counted as "poor," or will more limited exposure to poverty suffice? Suppose, for example, that your family's income was $7,000 in 1963. You had one brother, your mother was a housewife, and your father was a plumber. Based on your father's income, we excluded your family from our count of the 1963 poverty population.

But suppose further that in August your father dislocated his wrist while bowling. He recovered but was not able to turn a wrench for the remainder of the year. Although he earned $250 a week during the first seven months of the year, his earnings dropped to zero after his accident. Moreover, because his accident was not work-related, your father was not eligible for medical insurance benefits. From that point on your family began to taste poverty. Your allowance disappeared, your mother was suddenly doing babysitting and ironing, the family vacation was canceled, and in the fall you and your brother had to drop out of school.

Regardless of whether your family recovers, we are faced with a serious conceptual and statistical problem. Should we restrict our census to those families who were poor throughout 1963, or do we want to include all families who experienced impoverishment at least part of the year? In the extreme, you might even want to include yourself because you were out of money and hungry on Sunday night. In practice, we consider only *annual* income and needs, thus omitting from our poverty count many individuals and families who experience severe economic distress at least some of the time.

Our use of an annual accounting period also obscures another important problem: incomes change from one year to the next. Some families who appear "poor" in one year may enjoy a comfortable income in the following year. Such families are probably less in need of public assistance and services than those families who are in poverty year after year.

Consider again the observed decline in the size of the "official" poverty population.[4] The number of poor people fell from 34 million in 1963 to 25 million in 1977. As important as this decline has been, the numbers themselves do not tell us whether the people who were poor in 1977 are the same people who were poor fourteen years earlier. But it matters a great deal whether poverty is a malignant affliction for some identifiable part of our population or if, instead, it is a communicable disease that strikes different families every year. The one situation implies, for example, the need for a lot of social work and family counseling, while the other argues for improved unemployment insurance.

[4]Hereafter, all poverty statistics refer to the official Census Bureau estimates; no other detailed estimates are available.

Apparently, families do experience significant changes in income from one year to the next. By observing the same families over a period of seven years, Frank Levy (University of California–Berkeley) discovered that one-third of the nonaged families who were poor in 1967 were not poor in 1968. However, many families fall back into poverty in later years. Over the entire seven-year period (1967–73), Levy observed that

> Only 25 percent of the families who were poor in 1967 were nonpoor at least five of the subsequent six years.
>
> 30 percent of the 1967 poor families remained poor about half the time.
>
> 45 percent of the families who were poor in 1967 remained in poverty in almost all years.[5]

How completely one can distinguish between a "permanent" poverty population and a more "temporary" one is a basic policy concern. In later chapters we shall examine this issue more fully, seeking to identify those forces that distinguish one group of poor people from the other. In the remainder of this chapter, we will set the stage for this analysis by reviewing the characteristics of those people presently counted as poor.

CHARACTERISTICS OF THE POOR

While the statistics we have reviewed might justly support the statement that poverty in America is still of massive proportions, we must be cautious in our use of descriptive adjectives. The poverty that we have observed is certainly not like the mass poverty that still exists in most of the world today. Whatever the differences in the depth of deprivation experienced in earlier times and in other countries, an outstanding dissimilarity between modern American poverty and the poverty of India or Sicily is that, in America, to be poor is to be markedly distinguishable from the majority of the population.

If you lived in India, you would not have to make an effort to uncover the poor—they would be everywhere all the time. In America the situation is dramatically different. Except for an occasional panhandler on a downtown street, most of us never come into direct contact with the people we have enumerated in our census of the poor. The poor in America are a minority, albeit a sizable minority, and they are largely unseen and unheard by the affluent majority. As a consequence, very few of us know anything sub-

[5]Frank Levy, "How Big Is the American Underclass?" (Berkeley, Calif.: University of California, 1976). Income mobility among a broader spectrum of individuals and families is described in James Morgan et al, *Five Thousand American Families* (Ann Arbor, Mich.: Institute for Social Research, 1976), and Bradley R. Schiller, "Relative Earnings Mobility in the United States," *American Economic Review,* December 1977.

stantial about the characteristics of the poor—we rely instead on gross generalities and largely unfounded stereotypes.

We have already previewed some of the most salient characteristics of the poor in our census. In this section we continue that examination and attempt to deepen our familiarity with the 25 million poor individuals we have counted. The formulation of intelligent policies to combat poverty demands not only that we know how many persons are poor but also whether they are young or old, infirm or employed, and whether they live in Abbeville, Louisiana, or Winchester, Oregon.

A complete statistical profile of the poor would demand considerable effort and patience. In addition, such an array of statistics would tend to smother any meaning the numbers might possess. Therefore, we will examine the composition of the poverty population only as it relates to three major and policy-relevant characteristics: age and family status; geography and residence; and labor force status. We will observe also the racial makeup within each category.

Age and Family Status

Michael Harrington has said that this is no country for old men—that our society is obsessed with youth and tries to ignore age.[6] Statistics on the number of aged poor confirm his observations. Figure 2.3 shows that the aged comprise a sizable minority of the poor. In 1977 they accounted for one-eighth of the poverty population, and one out of every seven aged persons was poor.[7]

Who are the aged poor? Approximately one-third are couples, many of whom own, or have an equity in, their own modest homes. The other two-thirds are primarily widows, some living in their own homes, but more often living in rented rooms in old hotels and apartment houses. They are just as likely to be found in metropolitan areas as in smaller cities and rural communities. Their income sources are few and consist primarily of public or private retirement payments, such as Social Security. Their savings are negligible.

Although the aged command the barest sort of material existence, poverty is not their only misfortune. Most of the aged poor live isolated and lonely lives and suffer chronic poor health. While we cannot hope to explain the American ethos that has led to the social deprivation of the aged, we should not ignore it.

The second population group depicted in Figure 2.3 refers to nonaged persons without children; that is, without children under the age of eighteen.

---

[6]Michael Harrington, *The Other America* (New York: The Macmillan Company, 1962), p. 10.
[7]We employ the term *aged* here to refer to persons over the age of sixty-five.

Statistically they account for approximately 20 percent of the poor. Although these retired and soon-to-be-retired men and women are slightly younger than the aged poor, the social and material circumstances of the two groups are very similar; the only significant distinction is age. What is perhaps most disheartening about this subpopulation of the poor is that they have so much misery to look forward to. They have no tangible prospect for a better life; they simply get older and poorer.

The aged and aging poor, for whom there are now few alternatives, represent failures of our politico-economic system. The existence of such clusters of poverty serves to underscore the importance of doing something about material deprivation while there are still a variety of remedies available. From now on, while not forgetting the aged poor and their problems, this book will focus primarily on those who are still young and able enough to escape the demeaning poverty of the aged.

A second reason for concentrating our attention on the younger generations of the poor is the sheer size of this group. As Figure 2.3 clearly indicates, families with children constitute the dominant subgroup of the poor population, accounting for approximately 70 percent of the American poor in 1977.

Contrary to a popular impression, approximately half of the families in the younger poverty group have a male head-of-household (father). Nevertheless, families headed by females account for over half of the younger poor population and a sizable majority of the young black poor.

FIGURE 2.3   Age and Family Status of the Poor, 1977

Aged (3.2 million)

Nonaged without children (4.5)

Families with children (17.0 million)

Note: Shaded areas represent black population

Source: U.S. Bureau of the Census

Of the 17 million people in the youngest poverty classification, over 10 million are children under eighteen years of age. Hence, children alone comprise fully 40 percent of all poor persons in the United States. We might well reflect on how equitable such a distribution of poverty is and what kind of preparation for adulthood an impoverished childhood provides. Will poor children later become poor adults? If so, we may confidently predict that poverty has a great future in this country.

Geography and Residence

In an increasingly urban nation, it is not surprising to find a high proportion of poor families in metropolitan areas.[8] In 1977 over one-half of all the poor lived in metropolitan areas, most of them in the central city. In general, the residential distribution of poor families resembles the residential distribution of all families. However, there does exist a tendency for the poor to be overrepresented in large central cities and in rural areas and underrepresented in suburban communities (see Table 2.2).

Table 2.2   RESIDENTIAL DISTRIBUTION OF THE POOR, 1977

	White		Black	
Location	Number (thousands)	Poverty Rate (%)	Number (thousands)	Poverty Rate (%)
Entire United States	16,416	8.9	7,726	31.3
Metropolitan areas	9,265	7.6	5,289	28.6
In central cities	4,762	10.7	4,254	31.2
In suburban rings	4,503	5.9	1,035	21.3
Outside metropolitan areas	7,151	11.2	2,437	39.1
Farm	1,125	15.4	165	39.9

Source: U.S. Bureau of the Census.

The racial distribution of poverty among metropolitan and non-metropolitan areas is very similar; that is, poor whites are just as likely as poor blacks to reside in metropolitan locations. However, a marked racial difference is apparent *within* metropolitan areas. While poor whites are likely to be found in either central cities or suburban communities, poor blacks are confined almost exclusively to the cities. It is important to note, though, that the high number of poor blacks in central cities is a result of the greater degree of urbanization among the black population rather than a higher likelihood of poverty in the cities. Indeed, a black person in a rural area is more likely to be

[8]The term *metropolitan area* essentially refers to cities of at least 50,000 persons and their surrounding communities.

poor than his counterpart in an urban metropolis (poverty rates of 39.1% and 28.6%, respectively).

Nonmetropolitan areas include smaller cities, rural communities, and farms. While nearly one-half of all the poor live in such localities, very few poor persons actually live on farms. Farm poverty is a serious problem in the sense that the incidence of poverty among farmers is very high (over 15 percent for whites and 40 percent for blacks), but because the entire U.S. farming population is relatively small, poor farmers constitute less than 6 percent of all the poor. In this case we must distinguish between the incidence of poverty among a particular group and the prevalence of that group within the entire poverty population.

Because the economic resources and social conditions of different regions in the United States vary tremendously, it is important to know the geographical location of the poor. Slower economic growth or less opportunity in a region is likely to create a regional concentration of poor families and require special programs. Were the poor all concentrated in Appalachia, for example, particular antipoverty policies would be appropriate.

Outside the South, poverty is fairly proportionately distributed across the country for both whites and blacks (see Table 2.3). Thus, a person is as likely to be poor in New England as he is in the Corn Belt or in the West. In each of those areas, the incidence of poverty among whites is around 7 to 9 percent and around 25 to 30 percent for blacks. While there are fewer poor persons in the West than in the northeastern or north-central states, that disparity conforms to general population patterns.

Table 2.3   REGIONAL DISTRIBUTION OF THE POOR, 1977

Region	Number (thousands)		Poverty Rate (%)	
	White	Black	White	Black
Northeast	3,725	1,183	8.5	27.1
North-central	3,938	1,584	7.6	32.1
South	5,735	4,383	10.3	33.3
West	3,018	576	8.8	25.6

Source: U.S. Bureau of the Census.

It is apparent from Table 2.3 that the South[9] contains a disproportionate number of poor persons. Less than a third of the total U.S. population lives in the South, but 40 percent of the poor reside there. This excess of poverty results not only from a high concentration of blacks in the South,

[9]The Census Bureau includes the following states in its definition of "South": Alabama, Arkansas, Delaware, District of Columbia, Florida, Georgia, Kentucky, Louisiana, Mississippi, Maryland, North Carolina, Oklahoma, South Carolina, Tennessee, Texas, Virginia, West Virginia.

but also from the fact that the South is simply poorer and less urban than any other region. Hence, a southern resident, regardless of his color, is more likely to be poor than his northern counterpart, and in both the North and the South, a black person is three times as likely to be poor as is a white person.

Labor Force Status

The geographical and family characteristics of the poor are important considerations in the formulation of antipoverty policies, but their primary value is that they tell us something about the potential of the poor to participate in national employment- and income-generating policies. In a market economy the relationship of a person or his family to the labor market is the prime determinant of his income. Furthermore, the willingness of society to provide for the poor is materially affected by whether the poor are thought to work or at least seek work. Accordingly, the last characteristic we shall observe is the labor force status of the poor.

To be "in the labor force" signifies that a person is either employed or actively seeking employment ("unemployed"). Also included in this category are persons who are temporarily not working because of illness, bad weather, vacation, or a labor-management dispute. All these people are regarded as idle only momentarily, with visible prospects of returning to work. Their regular work may be full-time or part-time (less than thirty-five hours per week), and it must be monetarily compensated. Hence, volunteer work is regarded as activity outside the labor force.

To be "out of the labor force" means essentially that a person does not fall into one of the foregoing categories. These persons are keeping house; attending school; unable to work because of age or disability; or, if otherwise able to work, are not actively seeking employment. The inactivity of the last group may result from a desire to seek leisure or the fact that employment prospects are too dim to merit job-hunting.

It is widely believed that the poor are essentially a lazy lot. While we will examine this contention in considerable detail in later chapters, Table 2.4 provides a preliminary perspective on the employment behavior of the poor. This table indicates what percentage of poor families worked at some time during the year. Nearly three out of four fathers of poor families worked in 1977. So did more than one out of three women who headed poverty families. Although these employment percentages are lower than those of nonpoor families, they still suggest substantial labor force participation. In later chapters we will examine the reasons for these differences, as well as the reasons many working families remain in poverty.

Table 2.4 WORK EXPERIENCE OF POVERTY POPULATION, 1977

| | Percent Who Worked During 1977 | |
	Poor (%)	Nonpoor (%)
Families with children		
Male-headed	73.9	93.4
Female-headed	37.9	64.0
Aged persons		
Males	12.5	26.7
Females	0.6	12.0

Source: U.S. Bureau of the Census

OVERVIEW

The statistical profiles of the preceding section are not intended to dull one's senses nor to obscure the many problems of the poor. Rather, they are offered as a backdrop to the analytical discussions that follow in later chapters. If any general impressions are possible, we might say that the statistical profiles of the poor are not markedly different from those of the rest of the population. For the most part, the poor population is a little older, more southern, blacker, and slightly less attached to the labor force than is the rest of society. Nevertheless, the poor, like the larger society, consist primarily of whites, of younger families with children, of urban dwellers, and of labor force participants. There do exist important distinguishing demographic characteristics, but they must not be allowed to conceal the basic similarities between the poor and nonpoor populations.

The demographic characteristics we have reviewed by no means provide a complete description of the poor. Among the more obvious omissions in our profile are education, family size, and health. These characteristics are discussed in later sections, where a more complete examination of the traits described above is also found. But our profiles are incomplete in another important sense. We deal in this book almost exclusively with measurable, or at least observable, phenomena. Thus, we may report how old, white, or employed the poor are, or whether they live in cities or suburbs. What we are unable to do is relate how oppressed, politically isolated, or hostile the poor may be. In *The Other America,* Michael Harrington argues that today's poor are "more isolated and politically powerless than ever before." Although we are not in a position to evaluate that statement, we must recognize that such forces may be critical considerations in the lives of the poor.

FURTHER READING

CONGRESSIONAL BUDGET OFFICE, *Poverty Status of Families Under Alternative Definitions of Income. Washington, D.C.:* Government Printing Office, 1977.

DANZIGER, SHELDON, and ROBERT PLOTNICK, *Has the War on Poverty Been Won?* New York: Academic Press, 1980.

LEVY, FRANK, "How Big Is the American Underclass?" Berkeley, Calif.: University of California, 1976.

MORGAN, JAMES, et al., *Five Thousand American Families.* Ann Arbor, Mich.: Institute for Social Research, 1976.

PLOTNICK, ROBERT D., and FELICITY SKIDMORE, *Progress against Poverty: A Review of the 1964–1974 Decade.* New York: Academic Press, Inc., 1975.

REIN, MARTIN, and LEE RAINWATER, "How Big is the Welfare Class?" *Challenge,* September–October 1977.

SCHILLER, BRADLEY R., "Relative Earnings Mobility in the United States," *American Economic Review,* December 1977.

SMEEDING, TIMOTHY M., "The Antipoverty Effectiveness of In-Kind Transfers," *Journal of Human Resources,* Summer 1977.

U.S. BUREAU OF THE CENSUS, *Current Population Reports, Series* P-60. Washington, D.C.: Government Printing Office.

THE CAUSES
OF
POVERTY

3 GENERAL PERSPECTIVES

Although it is evident that the number of people we count as poor in America is substantial, the causes of their plight are the subject of heated controversy. Generally, people approach the subject of causation from one of two extreme perspectives. From the first perspective, poverty is regarded as the natural result of individual defects in aspiration or ability. In colonial times, this perspective was aptly summarized by the puritanical Humane Society, which concluded that "by a just and inflexible law of Providence, misery is ordained to be the companion and punishment of vice." In more modern times, theories of sin and immorality have not fared well, and there now exists a general reluctance to ascribe to the laws of Providence the misery of the poor. Instead, we speak in terms of "motivation" or "work ethic": Poverty is thought to result from insufficient amounts of either. Hence, modern poverty originates in Flawed Characters, much as in puritanical times.

The Flawed Character argument comes in many forms. However, an essential ingredient in all such arguments is the assumption of pervasive opportunity. From this perspective, there are abundant opportunities for material advancement; all one need do is pursue them. Anyone who wants to escape poverty can do so.

The Flawed Character argument applies both to jobs and schools. In the labor market, people who do not find good-paying jobs are assumed to lack sufficient initiative or diligence. To the extent that they are less able—as measured by education, skills, or ability tests—their disadvantage is to be explained by earlier lack of motivation in school. Individuals who do not work hard in school end up failing in the job market as well. Thus, the Flawed

Character perspective sees individuals as in full control of their socioeconomic status.

The alternative explanation of poverty proceeds from the perspective that impoverishment may result from forces beyond the control of the individual. According to this argument—the Restricted Opportunity argument—the poor are poor because they do not have adequate access to good schools, jobs, and income, because they are discriminated against on the basis of color, sex, or income class, and because they are not furnished with a fair share of government protection, subsidy, or services. In the face of these socially imposed constraints, no amount of work ethic of effort assures escape from poverty. A basic implication of this argument is that the provision of improved opportunities—such as more and better jobs and improved access to quality education—would alone assure a reduction in the number of people we count as poor.

The following eight chapters examine the substance of the Flawed Character and Restricted Opportunity perspectives in great detail. But before proceeding to that examination, we should recognize potential biases. First, we should note that the Flawed Character argument appeals directly to the psychological needs of the middle-class majority. If the poor are poor because of flawed characters, then the nonpoor must be nonpoor as a result of non-flawed characters. (Otherwise, how are we to explain the superior position of the latter class?) Hence, the Flawed Character argument implies a psychological pat-on-the-back for the nonpoor. Adam Walinsky made note of this same phenomenon when he observed that ego satisfaction requires each of us to ascribe the status of "those above us" to luck and the status of "those below us" to character and ability.[1] Thus, the Flawed Character argument not only explains poverty, but explains and justifies the position and privileges of the nonpoor as well. To deny the Flawed Character argument is tantamount to questioning the status of the middle and upper classes.

There are economic interests wrapped up in the Flawed Character argument as well. A basic implication of this argument is that society is already doing everything it can to help the poor, that we are providing the opportunities necessary for escape from poverty. This view is economically appealing as it implies fewer additional public expenditures, lower taxes, and the lack of any need to initiate structural changes in the way the economy functions. To the harassed taxpayer who equates higher taxes with more money for "the bums on welfare," the Flawed Character argument sounds very convincing.

The Restricted Opportunity argument likewise derives support from unspoken biases. Some people are simply convinced that Society is to blame for *all* social ills, that individuals are forever innocent and blameless. As a consequence, they are not inclined to collect or even examine evidence that might fault individuals for their own plight. This is the kind of bias often

[1] Adam Walinsky, "Keeping the Poor in Their Place," *New Republic*, July 4, 1964.

referred to as "bleeding heart liberalism." Often, this liberalism may be buttressed by economic interests, particularly interests (e.g., university researchers and public employees) that would benefit from expanded social programs and budgets.

Knowing our potential biases does not settle the controversy, of course, or even assure that we will remember them at the right times. But awareness of them may help engender just a bit more objectivity as we proceed through the details of our analysis. At least we know that the deck *may* be stacked before the game begins.

LABOR MARKET FOCUS

Our basic approach for identifying the true causes of poverty begins with a distinction between those who are in the labor force and those who are not. To be "in the labor force" means that a person is either employed or actively seeking a job. Obviously, such persons (and their families) are much more likely to be out of poverty, either now or in the near future. On the other hand, those individuals and families who do not participate in the labor force do not have access to a prime source of income—labor earnings—and are thus more likely to be represented among the poor.

It remains to be seen, of course, just why such people are out of the labor force—whether they are excluded by "flawed characters" or "restricted opportunities." For example, the decision on whether or not to go looking for a job—that is, whether or not to enter the labor force—may itself be influenced by the jobs available. If the probability of finding a job is very low (opportunities are restricted), the incentive to enter the labor force is negligible, and it is misleading to point to nonparticipation (flawed character) as an explanation for poverty. As is true of so many other social problems, the interaction of different forces needs to be examined.

In view of the fact that poor people tend to shuttle back and forth between jobs, unemployment, and welfare, we must also take care not to regard our distinction between participants and nonparticipants as a rigid dichotomy. Nor can we assume that labor force participation alone is a ticket out of poverty. In 1977 over 50 percent of the families in poverty participated in the labor force at some point during the year. Moreover, over 1 million families were poor despite the presence of at least one person who worked full time, all year long. Nearly as many families were poor even though they had at least two family members working. Clearly, we are going to have to look a little more carefully at labor market dynamics to explain such widespread poverty.

The major causes of poverty for labor force participants may be classified into three types: human capital deficiencies, deficient demand for labor, and discrimination.

HUMAN CAPITAL DEFICIENCIES

Human capital refers to the bundle of skills and abilities that a person carries with him into the labor market. In general, the less human capital a worker possesses, the lower is his or her potential productivity on a job. Hence, employers will be less eager to hire persons with little human capital and less willing to pay them high wages once they are employed; such decisions tend to leave a good many workers in poverty as a result of both unemployment and low wages.

The human capital a worker possesses is significantly determined by genetic endowments ("natural ability") and social environment; however, a person can increase his or her human capital by learning new skills. Education and training provide such opportunities, and a worker can effectively invest in his or her own human capital by pursuing them. The "dividends" from such an investment will typically include better jobs and higher pay in the future. Thus, a direct link between educational attainment and income should be apparent. And in fact it is. People with college educations are rarely found among the ranks of the poor, whereas people who fail to acquire as much as a high school diploma are all too often poor.

DEFICIENT DEMAND FOR LABOR

Having the "right" amount of human capital is itself no guarantee of job success, however. Human capital traits such as education merely define the supply characteristics of the labor force, and thus are only the beginnings of an explanation of income status. It is equally important to examine the labor market forces that determine the demand for labor, and thus to ascertain the market value of specific human capital characteristics. To determine how much a person's productivity is "worth," we must know something about the market value of the goods or services he or she produces. This value will be determined by the interaction of market supply and demand forces.

The distinction between supply characteristics and mai :et demand applies even to college graduates. If there is little market demand for the services of college graduates, the attainment of a diploma will add little to an individual's income. In the early 1960s, for example, there was a great demand for engineers, largely as a consequence of our attempts to beat the Russians to the moon. In response to this demand, the value of an engineering degree rose markedly, and thousands of college students eagerly switched majors. Widespread disillusionment set in later, however, when the increased supply of engineers entered the labor market and discovered that the space program and the derived demand for their particular skills had been cut back. The upshot of this little lesson in economics was higher unemployment and lower wages for engineers.

The sad saga of the engineers provides insights for other members of the labor force as well. When the aggregate demand for labor is low, an increased number of people are going to discover that their human capital is "deficient." During the exceptionally high unemployment that persisted throughout the 1930s—official unemployment rates rose as high as 25 percent and never fell below 10 percent during the decade—even Ph.D. degrees were inadequate stepping-stones to secure jobs and income. On the other hand, when the aggregate demand for labor is high, everyone's chances for a decent job and income are improved. Accordingly, we may say that the demand for labor is an important determinant of incomes and, more specifically, that a deficient demand for labor can be an important cause of poverty.

DISCRIMINATION

The third general set of causes are those related to discrimination, both in the schools and in the labor market. Minority groups, women, and the offspring of the poor are generally not given an equal chance to acquire the right set of human capital characteristics nor to use those characteristics in the labor market. Moreover, as long as such institutional barriers remain, poverty may exist even in the presence of abundant human capital and a high demand for labor. Hence, race, sex, and class discrimination may have significant impact on both the distribution and the extent of poverty. As long as discrimination persists, we may predict that children of the poor, blacks, and families headed by women will dominate the ranks of the poverty population.

In terms of our earlier generalizations it is clear that those demographic forces that define a person's human capital are the focus of Flawed Character perspectives, while Restricted Opportunity arguments build on the notions of deficient demand for labor and the institutional barriers erected by discrimination. In trying to identify the relative importance of each, it is important to distinguish between *correlates* of poverty and *causes* of poverty. Everyone agrees, for example, that poor people are generally less educated than the rest of the population, that is, that low educational attainments are *correlated* with poverty. What is debated is the nature of the causal relation. On the one hand, low educational attainments may so constrain a person's productivity that he or she could never earn a decent income. On the other hand, there may not be enough good jobs to go around, with those available being parceled out according to educational attainments. In this case, it would be more reasonable to argue that deficient demand for labor is the *cause* of poverty, with educational attainments determining how that poverty is distributed among us.

The distinction between correlates and causes is perhaps even clearer in the case of race. As we noted in Chapter 2, blacks are much more likely to be poor than are whites; thus being black is correlated with poverty. But what is the *causal* relationship? Is it true, as some argue, that black individuals are so genetically or culturally handicapped that they simply cannot bring enough human capital to the market? Or is it more correct to suggest that a combination of deficient demand for labor and institutional barriers traps them in poverty? Obviously, the heart of the argument is over causes, not correlates.

In assessing the significance of any particular demographic, labor market, or institutional force, we will be interested in two dimensions of causation: with respect to each force, we will inquire as to its effect either on the *extent* or on the *distribution* of poverty. The extent of poverty refers to the particular people who are consigned to impoverishment. Some forces may influence the size of the poverty population without affecting the selection of individuals so included. Other forces may markedly affect the distribution, but not the total extent, of poverty. Therefore, we are asking what forces determine how many individuals will be poor and which determine who is to be included in that total.

4 SUBEMPLOYMENT

We have already suggested that a deficient demand for labor may be a major cause of poverty. One symptom of that deficiency would be high unemployment rates. Another would be large numbers of potential workers outside the labor force, waiting for improved job opportunities to emerge. A third symptom would be large numbers of workers employed at jobs far beneath their actual capabilities. Together all these phenomena consititute subemployment, and can contribute significantly to the number of poor in America. These relationships between the demand for labor and the level of poverty are examined in this and the following chapter.

CAPITALIST IDEOLOGY

It is a basic tenet of capitalist ideology that an individual must contribute to the output of the economy in order to share in its output. All individuals are supposed to share in total output in proportion to their productive effort and the amount of capital (machinery, buildings) or land they contribute to the production process. Individuals who aspire to higher incomes must work or save harder, thereby asserting a claim to more output. In such an economy, an individual who chooses not to contribute to the production process may be denied a share of the goods produced.

In a purely competitive capitalist economy, it is clear that the unemployed will not eat, or at least they will not obtain sustenance by conventional routes. By the same token, among those who are employed, individual productivities will determine how much and how well each person eats. Accordingly, in assessing the relationship between poverty and labor force status, we may conveniently examine two groups of individuals separately, the nonworkers and the workers.

We should not approach our inquiry, however, under the impression that capitalist ideology is rigidly enforced. Adherence to the "no work, no bread" doctrine is by no means complete; in fact, there are more exceptions than non-exceptions. For starters, consider all the spouses who choose to stay at home rather than seek paid employment outside the home. Then there are millions of children, many of whom are legally barred from employment. To this list we may add the aged, whom we often compel to retire; the infirm, who cannot work; and college students, whose productivity is assumed and deferred. Indeed, the number of people eating but not working exceeds 100 million.

Aside from such obvious exceptions as infants and the infirm, we may ask why society allows, even encourages, such widespread dependency. Clearly, maximum production, especially when it is based on desperate incentives, is not the only goal we pursue. Rather, we recognize that other social objectives compete with those of production. While maximum output from maximum labor force participation might seem like an appealing goal, that goal is severely and willingly compromised in practice. Issues that we must reflect on in the course of our analysis are: (1) Who makes the exceptions to society's work ethic? and (2) On what basis are such exceptions made?

SUBEMPLOYMENT AND POVERTY

The Nonparticipants

People who do not participate in the labor force must have an alternative source of support. For most nonparticipants, this support comes from their immediate families; they share the income of a relative who works. A good many others individuals are past traditional working ages and depend on retirement incomes, typically public (social security) or private pensions. But not all families are retired or contain a working member. It is these latter families who are most likely to be poor. Indeed, the median family income, including welfare, of men aged twenty to fifty-four who do not participate in the labor force is less than $500 per month. Very few such men are able to sustain their families above a poverty line.

Why do such men fail to participate in the labor force? Is it because they prefer idleness and impoverishment, or is it because they are physically unable to work or locate a job? A 1967 U.S. Department of Labor study suggested that a good many such persons were "dreamers and drifters who were able to adjust both financially and psychologically to nonworker status." No data were available, however, to support that allegation. More recent studies have shown that very few men with family responsibilities desire to "dream and drift" rather than work. More likely, these nonparticipants are either too sick or disabled to work. A considerable number of others have not looked for jobs because they are convinced that no employment opportunities are presently available for them.[1]

As we observed in Chapter 2, half of all poor families are headed by women. These women typically must fend for themselves to support their families. Yet, only one third of the women who head poor families participate in the labor market in any given year.

The lower labor force participation of women who head poor families is most readily explained by their family responsibilities. A single-parent family simply does not have the capability to keep one parent at work and one at home. Moreover, the jobs available to poor women may not pay enough to provide for nonparental child care, even if the mother would prefer to work outside the home. As a result, the labor force participation of female heads of poor families is restricted by both family and economic forces.[2]

The phenomenon of nonparticipation is not a permanent state. Most so-called nonparticipants do work if and when they are able. As their physical condition, child-care arrangements, and/or the economic outlook improves, nonaged nonparticipants are most likely to resume their search for employment. Indeed, one of the outstanding characteristics of the poor is their extraordinarily high rates of mobility between different labor forces statuses. The poor are constantly moving in and out of the labor force and from employment to unemployment and back again. A poor person out of the labor force one week may well be working or looking for a job the next week.[3]

To note that nonparticipation is likely to be a temporary condition is not tantamount to denying its causal importance for poverty. On the contrary, we have observed that nonparticipation is a condition that many poor heads-of-household experience. In later chapters we shall examine the causes of this nonparticipation in more detail.

The Unemployed

That unemployment, like nonparticipation, might lead to poverty is a chain of causation few people question. After all, to be unemployed means

---

[1]In 1977, for example, of the 3.1 million men between the ages of 25 and 59 who did not work, 1.5 million were sick or disabled; 337,000 were going to school; and 176,000 had retired.

[2]The availability of welfare benefits also discourages labor force participation, as we shall demonstrate in Chapter 12. Because work outside the home necessarily reduces home production (e.g., child care, cooking, etc.), many single-parent families remain poor in a fundamental sense even if their market income exceeds the poverty standard (see Clair Vickery, "The Time-Poor: A New Look at Poverty," *Journal of Human Resources,* Winter 1977).

[3]In fact, there are six times as many prime-age men outside the labor force at some time during the year than there are outside the labor force all year long. Nonparticipation is obviously a temporary condition for the father of a poor family.

that one is out of work and actively seeking employment. Can we assert with confidence, then, that unemployment is a major cause of poverty?

Some seeds of doubt about this association between unemployment and poverty are sown by those who compare unemployment totals with the size of the poor population. In 1977, for example, there were an average of about 6.9 million persons unemployed, while there were nearly 25 million poor persons (see Table 4.1). Moreover, not all of the 6,855,000 unemployed were from poor families. From an aggregate perspective, unemployment thus appears to account for only a small fraction of poverty at best.

To compare the total number of poor people with the average number of unemployed is quite unfair, however. First, the poverty population includes not only heads-of-household but also their dependents. As the unemployment figures do not include dependents, the comparison is obviously unbalanced. Looking more closely at the figures in Table 4.1, we find that only 1,850,000 of the unemployed were nonaged heads-of-household. At the same time, there were only 5,310,000 nonaged poor *families,* and thus that many poor household heads. Accordingly, on this more detailed basis, it appears that unemployment may contribute to the low economic status of as many as 35 percent of all nonaged poor families.

TABLE 4.1   UNEMPLOYMENT AND POVERTY STATISTICS, 1977

Group	Unemployed	Poor
Average, all persons	6,855,000	24,720,000
Average, heads-of-household *	1,850,000	5,310,000
Number of heads-of-household who experience unemployment during year	7,530,000	1,600,000

* Figures for heads-of-household exclude aged population.

Source: U.S. Bureau of the Census and U.S. Department of Labor.

The comparison between unemployed and poor heads-of-household suggests a markedly stronger relationship between poverty and unemployment than do simple comparisons of national averages. Yet even this adjustment is only the beginning of a serious analysis. Just as nonparticipation is likely to be a temporary condition for the poor male head-of-household, so we must recognize that unemployment is likely to be a transitory state for most of the poor. There will be many more persons who *experience* unemployment during the year than there are unemployed at any given time. In fact, the turnover in the ranks of the unemployed approaches 400 percent. This means that nearly four times more persons experience unemployment during the year than are unemployed at any one time. In 1977, for example, at least 20 million persons (of whom 7.5 million were household heads) experienced unemployment even though only 6.9 million (1.9 million household heads) were unemployed at any one time. Hence, there are more heads-of-household who experience unemployment than there are poor heads-of-household. On this basis unemployment begins to look like a dominant explanation of poverty.

Can we say, though, that all of these household heads who experience unemployment are poor? No, a great many of these unemployed persons enjoy incomes sufficiently high while working to stave off poverty when jobless. Others are fortunate enough to have other family members in the labor force who can provide alternative incomes. Probably less than one-fourth of those who experience unemployment have family incomes below our poverty standards. While many of the other unemployed may be near our poverty threshold, they are presently counted as nonpoor. Hence, we may conclude that approximately one-third of all nonaged poor heads-of-household, or about 1,600,000 nonaged families, experience a direct income loss as a result of unemployment.[4]

The Process of Economic Deterioration. Just how unemployment leads to poverty is evident when the relationship is viewed over time. Whereas a few days or a week of unemployment will not significantly diminish a family's income, several weeks of joblessness will begin to undermine a family's economic foundations. Accordingly, we expect to see more and more people slip into poverty as the duration of unemployment status lengthens. This process is confirmed by Table 4.2, which portrays the various methods families use to meet expenses as the duration of unemployment increases.[5]

In Table 4.2, the income sources of short-term and long-term unemployed families are compared. It can be seen, for example, that among the

TABLE 4.2   METHODS USED BY FAMILIES TO MEET LIVING EXPENSES, BY DURATION OF UNEMPLOYMENT (PERCENT DISTRIBUTION*)

	Duration of Unemployment	
Method	*5 to 25 Weeks*	*27 Weeks or More*
Used savings	49.1	39.9
Borrowed money	23.7	18.8
Moved to cheaper housing	8.8	12.0
Received help from friends	18.0	22.5
Received public or private charity	14.7	31.9

*Sum of percents is more than 100 because many families resorted to more than one method.

Source: Adapted from Stanley Lebergott, ed., *Men Without Work* (Englewood Cliffs, N.J.: Prentice-Hall, Inc., 1964), p. 144.

[4]The relationship between unemployment and economic hardship is also discussed by the National Commission on Employment and Unemployment Statistics in *Counting the Labor Force* (Washington, D.C.: Government Printing Office, 1979). The Commission's "hardship index" is discussed in Chapter 5.

[5]For a more recent look at the experiences of people unemployed for an extended period of time, see Walter Nicholson and Walter Corson, "Experiences of Unemployment Insurance Recipients During the First Year After Exhausting Benefits" (Princeton, N.J.: Mathematica Policy Research, Inc., 1976).

short-term (up to twenty-six weeks!) unemployed, 49 percent of the families have savings from which to draw in order to meet their everyday living expenses. As the duration of unemployment surpasses 27 weeks, however, the number of families with savings or available credit declines. As unemployment continues and the families become more desperate, they begin to sell their homes, to seek aid from friends, and, most striking of all, to fall back on public or private charity.[6]

Discouraged workers

While it is already clear that unemployment constitutes a direct and increasingly serious threat to a family's economic welfare, we have not yet completely described the dimensions of that threat. So far, we have considered only the immediate income loss to those families who suffer unemployment. There are indirect effects as well, however. These indirect effects further strengthen the causal link between unemployment and poverty and extend the resultant hardships to still more persons.

When unemployment rates are high in a particular area, job-seekers are apt to become increasingly frustrated in their efforts to secure employment. Jobs are scarce and available to only a select few. Faced with one employment rejection after another, job-seekers are likely to give up the search. This erosion of confidence was expressed by a young man who described his search for a job as follows:

> *I'll tell you, man, I go to Catholic Charities, to the youth center, down by the employment people—a couple of weeks ago I try to buy a job—I talk to social workers . . . you go from place to place, you know, and you get tired. I guess you get bored. Guys say no work, no nuthin', and then you say, "to hell with it. Let the job come to me."* [7]

Not surprisingly, this young man is called a "discouraged worker." Because he no longer seeks work actively, he is not counted as among the unemployed; he belongs to the ranks of the nonparticipants previously discussed. Yet it is clear that the two categories are not wholly separable. The extent and likely duration of unemployment in an area has a significant effect on the size of the nonparticipating population. Accordingly, many discouraged workers must be counted among the casualties of unemployment.

No one knows the exact number of discouraged workers among the poor. We do know, though, that a household head cannot maintain both a discouraged status and a family for long. The family must eat, and the head of

[6]In 1977 the average duration of unemployment for *all* the unemployed, poor and nonpoor, was fourteen weeks.

[7]Quoted in Edgar May, *The Wasted Americans* (New York: Harper & Row, Publishers, 1964), p. 60.

the household will be compelled to locate some work, any work, just to keep body and soul together.

Discouragement is not limited to household heads. In families with both a mother and a father present, high rates of unemployment are most likely to affect the mother's labor force participation. Where unemployment is prevalent, a wife's chances for employment are likely to be even smaller than her husband's. Hence, the family may decide that her job search is fruitless and that her productivity will be highest in the home. Unfortunately, in withdrawing from the labor force—giving up the search for paid employment—the wife markedly increases the family's chances of becoming poor: working wives are one of the surest escape routes from poverty.

Considerable statistical attention has been directed recently toward the phenomenon of discouraged workers. As a result, the U.S. Department of Labor estimated that in 1977 there were 1 million persons who wanted a job but were not looking for work because they felt their search would be in vain. Two-thirds of these discouraged workers were women and most of the rest were teenage males or older men. What proportion of these individuals were from poor families we do not yet know, but the impact of this group on the size of the poverty population is potentially sizable.

Underemployment

Another indirect hardship resulting from high unemployment rates concerns the type and amount of work people undertake when jobs are scarce. As we already noted, the head of a low-income family, facing a dismal labor market, may have to accept whatever employment and wages are available. The work may not fully utilize either his or her time or talents and is likely to be menial. But the person accepts the work as a temporary measure while waiting for better employment opportunities to emerge. When a person is in this situation, we may say that he or she is *underemployed*. That is, the person is at work (hence not unemployed) but not working to capacity. Commonly, the underemployed work full time at menial jobs or part time at any job, while seeking more or better employment. In 1977, the U.S. Department of Labor estimated that more than 4 million persons were underemployed in these ways. This group included at least 200,000 poor household heads who were working part time while awaiting better employment opportunities.

Subemployment

The phenomena of unemployment, discouragement, and underemployment combine to form the concept of *subemployment*. Taken as a whole, the distressing impact of subemployment on a family's finances is reasonably clear; very few families have enough economic resources to maintain themselves in the face of these forces for long. What is not so obvious is that the social foundation of the family, as well as its economic foundation, may suffer from the impact of these phenomena. Can we expect the father in a low-income family to gain in self-respect or familial admiration as his employment prospects and income diminish? Do we anticipate a Charles Dickens' kind of increased solidarity as the family begins to sink into impoverishment? It is more reasonable to expect intrafamily tensions to mount along with economic distress. To the extent that economic distress leads to a weakening of the family relationship or even to dissolution of the family unit, we must include family disintegration as one of the consequences of unemployment. While we postpone a more thorough discussion of this relationship to Chapter 7, we note here that the potential exists for family breakup as a result of labor market forces.[8]

Tallying the Losses.   As the list of direct and indirect consequences of unemployment grows, the crushing burden of a loose labor market on the economic status of the poor becomes apparent. The size of this burden can be approximated by asking how much income the poor have lost as a result of each form of subemployment. The total answer represents the amount of income the poor would have received had they been able to participate fully in the economy. The totals, presented in Table 4.3, are striking.

We have suggested that as many as 1,600,000 poor heads-of-households may have experienced direct unemployment in 1977. Given the typical wages of the working poor ($125 per week) and the typical duration of their unemployment (eighteen weeks), we may estimate the income loss to these families as approximately $2,250 per unemployed family. This is the amount of additional income these poor families would have received had they not

TABLE 4.3   APPROXIMATE LOSSES FROM SUBEMPLOYMENT

Source of Loss	Number of Poor Families Affected	Aggregate Income Loss
Unemployment	1,600,000	$3,600,000,000
Discouragement	200,000	800,000,000
Underemployment	200,000	400,000,000
Total	2,000,000	$4,800,000,000
Broken families	?	?

[8]We should also note that an involuntary change in status from employed to unemployed may have serious and long-term effects on a person's self-perception and social behavior; see D. D. and B. M. Braginsky, "Surplus People: Their Lost Faith in Self and System," *Psychology Today,* August 1975, and Harvey Brenner, "Estimating the Social Costs of National Economic Policy: Implications for Mental and Physical Health, and Criminal Aggression," a study prepared for the Joint Economic Committee, U.S. Congress (Washington, D.C.: Government Printing Office, 1976). Other researchers report that the anxieties that accompany unemployment reduce a person's life expectancy by as much as five years.

experienced unemployment. Multiplying the number of affected families (1,600,000) by their average loss ($2,250) tells us that the poor as a group lost approximately $3.6 billion of potential income as a direct result of unemployment.

We estimate the number of poor persons out of the labor force in 1977 due to the erosion of confidence we term discouragement to be about 200,000 individuals, mostly wives and female heads-of-household. Because these individuals were out of work all year long, their implied loss is equal to their opportunity incomes, that is, the incomes they would have received if they had been able to get a job. For poor persons, we may approximate this figure as $4,000 per discouraged worker. Multiplying the number of affected families (200,000) by the average loss ($4,000) indicates that the poor were deprived of another $800 million by labor market discouragement.

The third effect of high unemployment rates, namely underemployment, deprives about 200,000 poor families, each losing on the order of $2,000 per year. Their losses are smaller because they are employed much of the time, but these losses still add up to a significant $400 million for the poor population.

On the basis, then, of some rather conservative assumptions, we may conclude that at least two million poor families are financially stricken by subemployment in one form or another. Moreover, the implied aggregate loss to the poor approached $5 billion in 1977, *enough money to move most of these families out of poverty*! If we include the number of families broken up as a result of subemployment, the total number of affected families would probably reach 40 percent of all nonaged poor families, or 30 percent of all poor families, including the aged. Given the enormity of this loss, we must conclude that subemployment is a direct, and perhaps the dominant, cause of poverty.

THE QUESTION OF CAUSATION

The tremendous significance of subemployment to the extent and depth of poverty is apparent. However, we have not really resolved the question of causation. The evidence we have reviewed thus far only confirms that subemployment is a major correlate of poverty; it does not tell us how all that subemployment came about.

Do the Poor Really Try?

When we seek to explain why so much subemployment exists among the poor, we may fall back to our earlier distinction between the Flawed Character and Restricted Opportunity perspectives. On the one hand, it may be the case that the poor are not serious or persistent enough in their job search activity. They may be unrealistic in their employment demands or simply too lazy to go out and secure available work. On the other hand, the subemployment of the poor may result from no fault of the poor themselves; perhaps it is simply a reflection of the fact that few decent jobs are presently available for them.

The first explanation is more convenient for the nonpoor and enjoys a distinct popularity. If the poor can be shown to be inadequately concerned about their own welfare, then the responsibility of the rest of society for their impoverishment is considerably reduced. Among those who sense a certain irresponsibility on the part of the poor is sociologist Nathan Glazer, who perceives that at "the heart of the crisis is a massive change in values which makes various kinds of work that used to support families undesirable to large numbers of potential workers today."[9] In other words, the jobs are there but the poor simply refuse to take them. Unfortunately, Glazer offers no evidence to support the allegation he made. However, a later attempt by a second observer in New York City yielded the following evidence:

> *No one who rides the subways can fail to see the numerous ads for electrician's helpers (about $7,000 per year), subway patrolmen (around $8,000 per year), Office Temporaries, and Kelly Girls. The New York Telephone Company urges people to join them and be trained by them. No one who walks down Madison, Lexington, or Third Avenue will miss the signs for Help. No one who has had the misfortune of staying in a hospital recently, or even visiting one, is untroubled by the shortage of auxiliary and service personnel. . . . and any one who rides taxis with any frequency is aware of the number of taxis in the garage despite the industry's efforts to recruit additional drivers. . . . One of the fascinating statistics about New York City is that fewer persons were employed in domestic service in 1968 than in 1960. This is surely not the result of diminished demand but of a refusal to accept such employment.*[10]

Despite this catalogue of apparent opportunities, there seems to be little evidence to support the notion that the poor are turning down abundant job offers. At the time Bernstein related her impressions (1970) there were about 5,000 standing job vacancies, including domestic service, for unskilled workers in New York City. Confronting these vacancies were 139,000 unemployed individuals and over 200,000 heads-of-household receiving public assistance. In the light of the enormous number of potential and actual job seekers, the number of available jobs for the poor is hardly significant. Even if a poor person keenly desires to secure a dead-end job, his chances to do so hardly seem encouraging.

[9]Nathan Glazer, "Beyond Income Maintenance," *The Public Interest*, Summer 1969, p. 120.

[10]Blanche Bernstein, "Welfare in New York City," *City Almanac*, February 1970, p. 6.

Another study in Washington, D.C., compared the job vacancies advertised in the local Sunday paper (the *Washington Post*) with the number and characteristics of the poor people in the metropolitan area. At the time of the study, 36,400 people were officially counted as "unemployed," and 28,000 adults were receiving welfare payments. Yet, 3,028 job vacancies were listed in the paper, suggesting that many of the jobless could have found work if they really wanted to. Closer examination of the ads revealed a very different story, however. Most of the jobs required educational attainments or experience that poor people simply do not have. In all, only 354 of the job vacancies—12 percent—were jobs that poor people might get. Phone calls to the employers listing these jobs confirmed that nearly all of the job vacancies were filled, usually in a day or two.[11]

What is surprising, then, about the poor is not that they sometimes appear idle but that they exert so much energy trying to secure employment, despite often negligible job opportunities. We have already seen evidence of this activity in the high turnover rates among the employed and the attendant mobility of the poor between labor market statuses. Even the U.S. Department of Labor acknowledges that "policies aimed at reducing poverty should start from the premise that most poor people are already working unless barred from jobs by labor market or other personal circumstances. Contrary to a widely held opinion, what the great majority of poor people need is not a stronger work ethic but added skills and more employment opportunities."[12] An earlier study by the Labor Department noted that the poor are active in their job search activity, that they seek primarily lower skilled jobs, and that their salary expectations are very low.[13] It does not appear, therefore, that the poor are conspicuously indolent or unrealistic in their employment demands.

Where Are the Jobs?

If the poor are trying so hard to secure regular and decent employment, why are such jobs not available to them? Because we profess the ethic that a person should work for his keep and because the poor apparently do try to find jobs, we must determine what obstacles impede the fulfillment of our ideological objectives and the economic needs of the poor.

[11]Bradley R. Schiller, "Want Ads and Jobs for the Poor," *Manpower* (U.S. Department of Labor), January 1974.

[12]U.S. Department of Labor, *Manpower Report of the President,* March 1970 (Washington, D.C.: Government Printing Office, 1970), p. 119.

[13]Robert Stein, "Work History, Attitudes and Income of the Unemployed," in Stanley Lebergott, ed., *Men Without Work* (Englewood Cliffs, N.J.: Prentice-Hall, Inc., 1964), pp. 130–46; see also John Pucher and Bennett Harrison, "Reservation Wages, Unemployment and Earnings Expectations in Urban Labor Markets" (Cambridge, Mass.: Massachusetts Institute of Technology, 1975).

To visualize the potential impact of labor market demand on unemployment and poverty rates, imagine that all potential workers could be ranked on the basis of their employability. That is, suppose that we could somehow assign everyone a relative position based on the amount of human capital they bring to the labor market. The most productive workers will be at the front of the line, the least productive at the back.

It seems reasonable to assume that employers will seek to hire the most productive workers first, and thus will start filling job vacancies from the front of the line. In many cases, of course, an employer will not be able to determine exactly who is the more or less productive job applicant. But he will try to approximate that distinction, perhaps with the aid of aptitude tests, school records, even racial and sexual prejudices. All we need to note at this point is that employers will tend to start making their selections at the front of the line and proceed toward the back.

The question that concerns us now is how far back in the line employers will go; that is, how many jobs will be available. Clearly, an individual's chances of getting a job depend not only on his position in line (his supply characteristics) but also on how many workers employers decide to hire (demand characteristics). What we want to emphasize here is that deficiencies in demand can overwhelm supply characteristics, leaving otherwise qualified people among the ranks of the unemployed and poor.

The potential of demand fluctuations to overwhelm forces on the supply side of the picture is perhaps most apparent when we compare labor market conditions at different points in time. Consider the years 1969 and 1977, for example. The average unemployment rate in 1969 was 3.5 percent, meaning that 2,832,000 people were out of work and searching for jobs. In 1977, by contrast, the unemployment rate was twice as high (7 percent) and nearly 7 million people were out on the streets at one time. Can anyone reasonably argue that the increased unemployment was due to deteriorating supply characteristics? Had our labor force grown less educated, less experienced, less motivated, less intelligent, or generally less able? Surely not. In fact, we would expect that the supply characteristics of the labor force *improve* with the passage of time, rendering such arguments almost ludicrous. Seen in this context, fluctuations in the demand for labor emerge as a primary cause of unemployment and, by implication, the level of poverty.

The relationship between fluctuations in demand and the extent of unemployment is illustrated in Figure 4.1. Note that we have arrayed all labor force participants according to their skills (human capital), with the most skilled at the top. As we suggested above, the distinction between those who are employed and those who are unemployed depends not on any absolute level of skill development, but on just how far down the line employers choose to go. In 1977 employers stopped far short of where they went in 1969, leaving millions of previously employable (and employed) workers on the jobless side of the line. Hence, we may conclude that the additional unemployment repre-

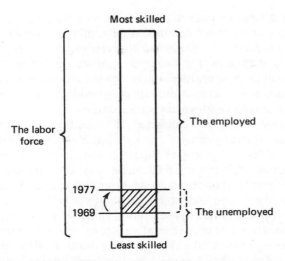

FIGURE 4.1   The Impact of Deficient Demand

sented by the shaded area in the figure was due to a deficiency of demand in 1977.

Although deficiencies of demand clearly emerge as a major cause of unemployment and poverty, we cannot attribute *all* unemployment to demand forces. Instead, economists distinguish between four types of unemployment: frictional, seasonal, cyclical, and structural. Frictional unemployment arises when people move from one job to another with only a slight interval of time in between. People who are frictionally unemployed normally have visible job prospects and are simply in transit, either geographically or occupationally. Likewise, people who are seasonally unemployed often face the sure prospect of renewed employment as the weather or season changes. This is not to say that their unemployment is not serious; we merely distinguish its sources from other types of unemployment.

Aggregate or "cyclical" unemployment is markedly different from the first two types of unemployment. Not only is the nature of later job prospects uncertain, but the causes of this type of unemployment are also distinct. Cyclical unemployment exists when there is less demand for labor in the economy than there is labor willingly available. In this situation, neither a change in the weather nor a change of residence is likely to create employment for the jobless. For this reason the unemployed individual has no certain prospect of later employment. Instead, he must wait, along with others so positioned, for an expansion of the demand for labor. This is the kind of unemployment depicted in Figure 4.1.

Structural unemployment is, in many respects, similar to cyclical unemployment. Here, however, the shortage of demand appears to be confined to only a few occupations or areas. While most people seem able to locate jobs, there may be a large number of pipe fitters, coal miners, or flight engineers seeking employment. There may be a large number of people out of work in the Texas Panhandle and Appalachia but relatively few in other areas of the country. Thus, it appears that localized or structural deficiencies in demand are more at fault than general demand shortages. Job prospects may seem better in this case, as an occupational or geographical move appears to hold promise of improved employment opportunities.

The purely structural character of structural unemployment can, however, be easily exaggerated. Can we maintain that the jobless situation of coal miners and flight engineers is impervious to the state of demand in other occupations or areas? While it is reasonable to expect some hesitancy in moving across geographical or occupational boundaries, it is unrealistic to imagine that the speed and extent of such moves are not conditioned by employment opportunities. When good jobs exist in plentiful supply elsewhere, the structural character of structural unemployment is bound to erode. People will move and change occupations as alternative prospects merit. Even in Appalachia, an area often presumed to exist in economic isolation, unemployment rates follow national patterns. Accordingly, the apparent dimensions of structural unemployment are shaped in part by the state of aggregate demand and, thus, are subject to the social decisions of which we have spoken. As Paul Samuelson has noted, "the alleged hard core of the structurally unemployed is in fact a core made of ice and not of iron. The core of ice can be melted over a period of time by adequate effective demand, or it can be solidified from inadequate over-all demand."[14]

SUMMARY

A positive relationship between an individual's employment status and his economic status is central to the American capitalist ethic. Accordingly, we are not surprised to discover that among those who work little or not at all, poverty is a relatively common occurrence. What is perhaps more noteworthy is the observation that the poor are integral members of the labor force and are constantly shifting from one labor force status to another. Therefore, we may conclude that millions of individuals are poor, not because they never work, but because they do not work as much or as often as others.

The work loss of the poor takes many forms. They may, at any given time, be out of the labor force, unemployed, or underemployed. These conditions are not independent but instead are related, in the market place, by the forces of aggregate demand. Together they constitute a condition of subemployment

[14]Paul A. Samuelson, *Economics*, 8th ed. (New York: McGraw-Hill Book Company, 1967), p. 802.

and may be costing the poor as much as $5 billion a year in lost income. Hence, subemployment appears to be a major cause of American poverty.

Finally, we have seen that the subemployment of the poor cannot be explained by their failure to seek employment. On the contrary, it appears that their subemployment is determined in large part by the decisions society makes regarding the utilization of economic resources. As long as the demand for labor is deficient, we must expect high unemployment rates and the poverty that results therefrom.

APPENDIX: UNEMPLOYMENT AS A SOCIAL GOAL

The deficiencies of aggregate demand that result in increased unemployment and poverty are not the consequence of unbridled market forces. Nor will the required expansion of demand emerge as the work of an "invisible hand" of the kind that Adam Smith described. On the contrary, the level of demand, and hence the level of aggregate unemployment, is now widely recognized as being a component responsibility of government. Fiscal and monetary policies largely determine the number of available jobs. Because these policies are the outcome of conscious activity on the part of a federal administration and not autonomously formulated by an invisible hand, we may say that the level of unemployment is part of society's matrix of goals. Hence, the level of demand we seek and the means by which we achieve it are directly subject to the collective will, as expressed in the political process.[15]

Of course, no one consciously and forcefully promotes a high level of aggregate unemployment for the sheer sense of achievement or Satanic art. Were the level of demand our only social concern, then we could confidently anticipate that aggregate unemployment would disappear. But we must recognize that the goal of aggregate full employment competes with other social objectives for the limited attention and resources of the public. As a consequence, consciously, unthinkingly, or simply by default, a nonzero level of aggregate unemployment may become a social goal.

The goal most often deemed in direct competition with full employment is that of price stability. It is widely believed that we cannot have both price stability and full employment at the same time. This implies that the pursuit of one objective necessarily means the abandonment of the other. Furthermore, because the potential destruction of currency and market functions that might accompany really serious inflation is widely feared, price stability is

---

[15]For an introduction to the fiscal and monetary policies appropriate to the goal of full employment see Bradley R. Schiller, *The Economy Today* (New York: Random House, Inc., 1980).

considered a foremost policy goal. As a consequence, some unemployment is tolerated as part of the cost of maintaining existing price levels.

The seriousness with which this trade-off is regarded by policymakers was evident in the early actions of the Carter administration. Upon taking office, President Carter initiated policies to reduce the rate of unemployment. As the unemployment rate dropped, however, prices began to rise more quickly. Carter responded by designating inflation "our top economic priority" and slowing the progress towards full employment.[16]

THE PHILLIPS CURVE PROBLEM

President Carter's willingness to tolerate higher levels of unemployment was based on the historical relationship between inflation and unemployment. As Figure 4.2 suggests, lower rates of unemployment have generally been accompanied by higher rates of inflation. This tendency, first observed in England by A. W. Phillips (for whom the curve in Figure 4.2 is named), has been found to prevail in scores of countries. Accordingly, the Phillips curve not only summarizes a historical relationship between unemployment rates and inflation rates, but appears to offer policymakers a finite set of choices. As long as the curve is an accurate description of economic performance, then full employment and price stability are not attainable at the same time. Instead, some point on the curve, a distinct compromise between the two goals, must be selected as a policy target. And so it happens that some policymakers choose to sacrifice full employment in the hopes of achieving lower rates of inflation.

Although the Phillips curve appears to present policymakers with a finite set of trade-offs, we must not be too quick in rejecting the goal of full employment. At best, the Phillips curve is a *generalization* of historical experience; in fact, we have experienced scores of inflation-unemployment combinations that lie both above and below the curve depicted in Figure 4.2. Thus, it is certainly *possible* to achieve more desirable combinations of unemployment and inflation than the Phillips curve suggests.

The reasoning behind the Phillips curve is also suspect, resembling as it does certain structural unemployment arguments. Nearly everyone agrees that an expansion of aggregate demand is necessary to reduce high levels of unemployment. The proponents of the Phillips curve theory argue that comparatively few benefits of increased spending actually reach the unemployed, because they have the wrong skills, are too young or old, live in the wrong places, or are simply unaware of new opportunities. Accordingly, demands for new output are met by overworking existing employees rather than by hiring

[16]Council of Economic Advisers, *Economic Report of the President* (Washington, D.C.: Government Printing Office, 1979).

FIGURE 4.2   The Phillips Curve

new workers. Wage rates, and then prices, go up while unemployment rates
change little. The greater the effort to reduce unemployment, the faster the rate
of inflation.

The argument for a trade-off between fuller employment and greater
price stability has a convincing plausibility. Nevertheless, there are grounds
for believing full employment and price stability to be more compatible than
the Phillips curve (and much political discourse) implies. Indeed, both theory
and practice suggest that the relationship between unemployment and inflation is more flexible than current attitudes and policy presume.

In theoretical terms, an expansion of demand for output can be expected
to increase the producer's demand for labor. Producers will have to hire
additional workers or employ their existing labor forces more fully. Other
workers may not be immediately available, however, and they are likely to require training or orientation before they can contribute to output. As a result,
producers probably will have to rely primarily on their existing workers for an
initial expansion of output. Such reliance is expensive, however, as overtime
wages rates are high; productivity is likely to decline with longer hours; and
workers will feel in a better position to demand higher base wages. Hence,
producers will have a large and increasing incentive to locate and train new
workers as expanded output continues. As time passes, producers will substitute new labor for overtime labor, thus reducing costs.

The labor market adjustment process described here implies that expansion of demand will, indeed, lead to higher prices but that the stepped up rate
of inflation may be a temporary phenomenon. As new workers are absorbed

into the production process, the pressure on prices may abate. Hence, what the Phillips curve may portray on an aggregate level is the rate of inflation necessary to evoke the required labor force adjustment. It should not necessarily be understood to mean that the same high rate of inflation will continue once the adjustment is made. Not only may the price rise be temporary, but it is an integral feature of the adjustment mechanism. Hence, we might be able to say that an 8 percent rate of inflation is necessary to reduce the unemployment rate from 6.0 to 5.5 percent, but we have no firm reason for anticipating continued high rates of inflation once the lower level of unemployment is reached.

High rates of inflation could continue, of course, but they would be the consequence of actions other than the initial effort to reduce employment. Inflationary *expectations* are often the source of continued wage-price escalation. When people see prices rising, they may come to expect inflation to continue. Prodded by such expectations, they may themselves demand higher wages and prices, thereby making inflation a more permanent phenomenon.

To the extent that structural factors or expectations create a trade-off between unemployment and inflation, the job of attaining full employment is obviously more difficult. This does not mean, however, that we are stuck with any particular trade-off. Policies that reduce structural bottlenecks or restrain inflationary expectations can *shift* the Phillips curve to the left. In so doing, they make it less costly (in terms of inflation) to reach the goal of full employment.

If, for example, the move toward full employment is slowed by the fact that unemployed workers possess skills in small demand or live in the wrong areas, further expansion of demand might be channeled more specifically in their direction. Hence, the *pattern* of demand, both occupationally and geographically, will affect the speed of adjustment and, thus, the dynamic trade-off. Accordingly, there is no unchangeable relationship of inflation to unemployment, as the relationship depends on the capability and determination of policymakers to alter the pattern of demand as they expand it.

A similar qualification to the Phillips curve emerges when we consider the phenomenon of racial discrimination in the labor market. Even when employers are reluctant to hire black workers, their reluctance will not be impervious to economic forces. An unassisted market adjustment thus implies that more and more racial barriers will be eliminated as the economic incentive for recruiting new and able workers increases. By the same token, the extent and strength of discrimination are among the forces that determine the dynamic trade-off between unemployment and inflation. Accordingly, the government's efforts to overcome or circumvent discrimination can lead to different trade-offs. Again, there is no necessary or fixed relationship between inflation and unemployment.

The upshot of these considerations is that a fixed rate of inflation is not associated with any given level of unemployment or with efforts to reduce unemployment by any given amount. Policymakers have a variety of options available at all times to effectuate an improved trade-off between inflation and unemployment. By changing the pattern of demand or improving the function of the labor market, policymakers can achieve lower rates of unemployment with little pressure on prices. To formulate the goal of price stability as an alternative to fuller employment is to ignore other options and rob the poor.

FURTHER READING

COUNCIL OF ECONOMIC ADVISERS, *Economic Report of the President,* Washington, D.C.: Government Printing Office, 1975, Ch. 3; 1978, Ch. 4.

FINEGAN, T. ADRICH, "Should Discouraged Workers Be Counted as Unemployed?" *Challenge,* November/December 1978.

FISH, MARY, "Income Inequality and Employment," U.S. Department of Labor, R & D Monograph 66, 1978.

GARRATY, JOHN A., *Unemployment in History: Economic Thought and Public Policy.* New York: Harper & Row, 1978.

LEVITAN, SAR, MARTIN REIN, AND DAVID MARWICK, *Work and Welfare Go Together.* Baltimore, Md.: Johns Hopkins University Press, 1972.

NATIONAL COMMISSION ON EMPLOYMENT AND UNEMPLOYMENT STATISTICS, *Counting the Labor Force.* Washington, D.C.: Government Printing Office, 1979.

"THE STRUCTURE OF LABOR MARKETS: DIVERSE VIEWS (A SYMPOSIUM)," *Challenge,* May/June 1978.

U.S. DEPARTMENT OF LABOR, *Employment and Training Report of the President.* Washington, D.C.: Government Printing Office, annual.

5 THE WORKING POOR

If deficient demand for labor and the resultant unemployment is a major cause of poverty, it would seem that we could eliminate most poverty if we could provide everyone with a job. According to this line of reasoning, employment emerges as a sure route to at least some degree of economic security. We have already learned, however, that this route is not so certain. We know, for example, that many poor people whom we think of as "unemployed" do work a great deal. In fact, a salient characteristic of the subemployed poor is that they are repeatedly engaged in part-time or part-year work. Hence, we can quickly reject the naive assumption that employment automatically lifts a person out of poverty.

A slightly more sophisticated view of the relationship between employment and poverty would suggest that the attainment of economic security depends not on whether one works but rather on how much one works. By and large, economic security will be reserved for those individuals and their families who work full time throughout the year. In this chapter, we examine this expectation in greater detail. In so doing, we focus on those individuals who fail to meet our expectations—the working poor.

WORK EXPERIENCE AND POVERTY

The expectation that increased employment improves one's chances of escaping poverty is fully supported by available data. As Figure 5.1 shows, there is a distinct inverse relationship between the number of weeks a household head

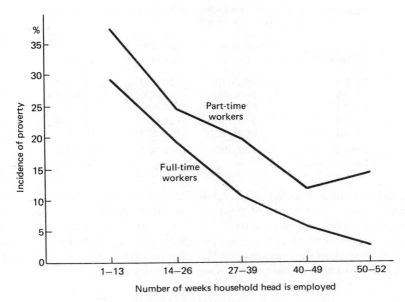

FIGURE 5.1   Poverty and Employment, 1977

Source: U.S. Bureau of the Census.

works and the likelihood of poverty. As the duration of employment increases, the incidence of poverty progressively drops. Among household heads who typically work full time (thirty five hours per week), those who are employed less than half the year have a one out of six chance of being poor. By contrast, household heads who work full time all year round have a one out of forty chance of being poor.

The same relationship between the duration of employment and poverty is true for part-time workers, as Figure 5.1 also indicates. The only exception to the rule occurs among part-time workers who work all year round. Their noticeably higher rate of poverty reflects the fact that this group of workers is comprised primarily of female heads-of-household, who have large family responsibilities and few income sources.

The relationships depicted in Figure 5.1 are likely to instill the comfortable feeling that there are few full-time, year-round workers among the poor. But this impression is dispelled quickly when the numbers are examined more closely. Because year-round workers in the economy vastly outnumber part-year workers, the incidence rates do not adequately reflect the work experience of the poor. Once again, numbers and proportions convey very different impressions.

Table 5.1 summarizes the work experience of the poor in absolute numbers. It shows that there are 850,000 poor families whose heads work full

Table 5.1 WORK EXPERIENCE OF THE POOR (HEADS-OF-HOUSEHOLDS), 1977

Weeks Worked	Full-time Workers	Part-time Workers	Total
50–52	850,000	190,000	1,040,000
40–49	200,000	43,000	243,000
27–39	240,000	80,000	320,000
14–26	325,000	134,000	459,000
1–13	284,000	197,000	481,000
Total, 1–52 weeks	1,900,000	644,000	2,543,000
Did not work	—	—	2,745,000

time all year round. Another 190,000 poor family heads work part time all year round. In fact, the number of poor year-round workers nearly equals the number of poor part-year workers. From another perspective, we may observe that one-fifth of *all* poor families are headed by a year-round worker, while one-fourth of the nonaged poor families are so headed. In short, extensive work effort and experience is characteristic for the poor.

THE HARD-WORKING POOR

If we include the dependents of these household heads in our calculations we find that there are over 4 million persons in families headed by individuals who worked all year round at full-time jobs. Why, we may ask, are so many people poor if their families work so much? Doesn't the existence of this paradox violate the very same principles that comprise our capitalist ideology? If we cannot guarantee economic security to those individuals who contribute their maximum work effort, what sort of admonitions or incentives can be directed to those who work less?

We may entertain two general explanations for the status of the hard-working poor. The most obvious suggestion is that their wages are unusually low. At poverty wages, very few people can work hard or long enough to attain economic security. But low wages are not the only possible explanation for the plight of the working poor. Poverty refers to the relationship between a family's income and its needs. Thus, it might also be the case that the poor simply have above-average needs, due to either larger families or special expenses, for example, medical bills. In this situation, even standard wages would tend to leave the family financially destitute. The distinction between income and needs is vital for policy concerns. The one situation implies the need for labor market intervention of some kind, while the second implies the need to address nonmarket phenomena, such as family planning or health insurance.

To the extent that the poor do have larger families, they require, of course, higher wages. The full-time working head of a family of four required wages of $3 per hour in 1977 to attain our poverty standards. The head of a five-person family needed $3.50 an hour to reach the same level, while families of six required $3.95. Still larger families would have to command nearly $5 an hour to maintain a poverty budget. With average blue-collar and clerical wages only slightly higher than this, it is clear that heads of large families will have to be fairly productive workers.

While it is obvious that the incidence of poverty will be aggravated by the wage requirements of larger families, it does not follow that the poor are impoverished because of their above-average needs. We still must inquire whether the hard-working poor command high-enough wages to support even an average (four-person) family. If they do not, then the above-average needs of larger families simply deepen their poverty rather than explain it.

Poor Wages

There is abundant evidence that the hard-working poor do not command wages high enough to assure economic security for an average-size family or, for that matter, for any family. Very few full-time working poor earn as much as $4 an hour, and virtually none earn more than $5 an hour. On the contrary, the typical wage of a poor head-of-household who works all year round at a full-time job is between $2.50 and $3 an hour.

To work long hours all year round and still remain in poverty must be tremendously frustrating, and yet many of these families supply even more work effort. Among poor families with full-time working heads, close to half send other family members into the labor market also. Not only is the head of the family unable to provide financial security as a result of his or her own efforts, but even the contribution of working spouses and children leaves many families in poverty.

The total incomes of families with full-time working heads are given in Table 5.2. Note that these incomes include not only the full-time earnings of the head-of-household, but also the earnings of any other family members who work, plus any income from other sources (including welfare). When viewed from this perspective, it is evident that the wages of poor workers are extremely limited. Especially disheartening is the high concentration of working families with incomes of less than $4,000 per year.

The hard-working poor are not the only workers to command low wages. While the poor are slightly more visible than other low-wage workers, nearly 10 million workers earned hourly wages of less than $3 as recently as 1977; millions of these earned less than $2.25 an hour. Although increases in the minimum wage since 1977 have reduced the number of people earning low wages (exact figures are not available), in 1978 there were still millions of *year-*

TABLE 5.2 INCOMES OF THE WORKING POOR (TOTAL INCOME OF FAMILIES WHOSE HEAD WORKED FULL TIME YEAR ROUND), 1977

Total Income	Percent of Families
Under $2,000	28
$2,000–3,999	24
$4,000–5,999	27
$6,000–7,999	16
$8,000 or more	5
Total	100
Number of families	853,000

Source: U.S. Bureau of the Census.

round, full-time workers earning less than $7,000 a year and many part-time workers earning still less. Accordingly, we can conclude that low-wage workers are still in abundance. What keeps these persons out of poverty is the fact that they have slightly smaller families or none at all, or keep more family members in the labor force for longer periods of time. Many, too, are dependents of workers who command more substantial incomes. Nonetheless, these workers are not very far removed from poverty; they and their families have incomes very close to our poverty standards. In the best of circumstances, they are referred to as the near-poor. In less favorable times they become part of the poverty population.

Poor Jobs

If there is any moral to be gleaned from the foregoing figures, perhaps it is this: a poor janitor who works hard stands a very good chance of becoming a hard-working, poor janitor. There seems to be little prospect of economic security for the poor as a result of their own efforts. Too many people earn too little. Elliot Liebow has summarized the prospects for the working poor:

> ... the man does not have any reasonable expectation that, however bad it is, his job will lead to better things. Menial jobs are not, by and large, the starting point of a track system which leads to even better jobs for those who are able and willing to do them. The busboy or dishwasher in a restaurant is not on a job track which, if negotiated skillfully, leads to chef or manager of the restaurant. The busboy or dishwasher who works hard becomes, simply, a hard-working busboy or dishwasher. Neither hard work nor perseverance can conceivably carry the janitor to a sit-down job in the office building he cleans up.[1]

[1] Elliot Liebow, *Tally's Corner: A Study of Negro Streetcorner Men* (Boston: Little, Brown and Company, 1967), p. 63.

Not all the poor, of course, are janitors. Most middle-class persons, in fact, probably think of janitors as low-income workers, but not poor. More likely to come to mind—if it is acknowledged at all that the poor do, in fact, work—are bellboys, busboys, and nonunionized street cleaners, plus a small army of aged farmers and stooping sharecroppers. Once again, however, the preconception departs considerably from the reality of everyday poverty. The working poor are likely to be found in all broad occupational categories. Table 5.3 depicts the actual occupational distribution of the poor. While it is true that nearly 25 percent of all farmers and farm workers are poor, these two occupations account for only one-sixth of the jobs held by the poor; as many poor work as operatives or service workers. Even white-collar jobs do not guarantee financial security, as more than 500,000 people depicted in the table testify.

It is just as easy to overstate the occupational status of the poor as it is to understate it. The occupational profile of Table 5.3 includes very broad employment categories and may lead to erroneous impressions. While there are 83,000 poor professional and technical workers, there are very few poor scientists, dentists, or even college professors among them. More likely to be poor within that occupational classification are hospital technicians, recreation and social workers, and evangelist healers. Similarly, in other occupational categories, the poor tend to hold the least desirable, most marginal kinds of jobs. They are dishwashers, loggers, theater ushers, porters, tailors, shoe repairmen, and laundry workers. Accordingly, while it is true that the working poor are distributed throughout the labor market and in all industries, they will always be found in the lowest-ranking, least noticeable jobs. They constitute what might be called a phantom labor force.

TABLE 5.3   OCCUPATIONS OF THE POOR (HEADS-OF-HOUSEHOLDS), 1977

Occupation	Number of Persons
Professional and technical	83,000
Managers, officials, and proprietors	167,000
Clerical workers	197,000
Sales workers	111,000
Craftsmen and foremen	316,000
Operatives	509,000
Private household workers	99,000
Other service workers	446,000
Unskilled laborers	206,000
Farmers and farm managers	261,000
Farm laborers and foremen	149,000
Total	2,544,000

Source: U.S. Bureau of the Census.

The Significance of Secondary Workers

We have already drawn attention to the fact that poor families often send wives and other family members into the labor force to supplement the low wages of the family head. These secondary workers contribute a great deal to family incomes and are often able to help lift the family above the poverty standard. What must be emphasized is that these secondary workers are often the only available bridge between poverty and near-poverty. Poor families, however, are often prevented from sending secondary workers into the job market by the presence of young children in the household. Younger children tend to keep their mothers out of the labor market, and younger families have fewer older children available for part-time work. Consequently, a major distinction between poor families and near-poor families is that the former are slightly younger and less likely to contain secondary workers. One implication of this distinction is that many of the near-poor passed through poverty in the natural course of family development. Later chapters will consider how and why they return to that status.

A Hardship Index

The President's Commission on Employment and Unemployment Statistics attempted to summarize the effects of low wages, secondary workers and repeated unemployment on low-wage workers and their families. To do so, the Commission formulated an index of "economic hardship," which relates a worker's earnings to his or her family income. A person is counted as a "hardship" case if he or she (1) participates in the labor force at least 40 weeks during the year, (2) earns less than the poverty threshhold, and (3) is a member of a household whose total income is less than twice the poverty standard. The hardship index thus encompasses all the working poor, many of the subemployed poor, and many others who are close to our standards of minimal need—despite extensive labor force participation. The Commission counted over 7.5 million such persons in 1976. From this perspective, labor market participation is clearly no assurance of nonpoverty status.

WHY ARE WAGES SO LOW?

While poverty and employment might seem incompatible, there is no shortage of available explanations for the low wages of the working poor. Predominant among these are that the poor are undereducated, inexperienced, underskilled, trained in the wrong occupations, and geographically handicapped.

There exists abundant evidence to support each of these explanations, and we cannot deny their importance in holding down the wages of the poor. What we must also recognize, however, is that these explanations focus almost exclusively on the supply side of the labor market. They tell us what qualities an individual brings to the labor market but do not provide a complete explanation of why those particular qualities are paid so little. To understand the process by which wages are determined, we must also ask what the demand side of the labor market looks like.

In the most general terms, we say that a worker's wages are determined by the contribution he or she makes to output, that is, by his or her marginal product. But what is it that makes the output of a pipe fitter less valuable than the output of an advertising executive? Clearly, what most differentiates the incomes of these two people is not the physical output that each produces, but rather the value that society attaches to their products. If society were suddenly to become disenchanted with the wares of advertising executives and find increased value in fitted pipes, then the incomes of pipe fitters would exceed those of advertising executives, regardless of their respective physical outputs. By the same reasoning, if society were to attach more value to the kinds of ouput that the poor can and do produce, then we could expect the incomes of the working poor to rise.

The notion that the extent and structure of demand are significant determinants of the wages of the poor does not constitute a revolution in economic thinking. On the contrary, economists have long taken credit for the discovery that prices, and thus wages, are determined by the interaction of supply and demand. In the realm of policy formulation, however, the impact of the demand side of the market on the economic position of the poor is easily neglected. To do so is to ignore tremendous potential for eliminating poverty.

During the 1940s, there was a tendency for wage rates and incomes at the bottom of the occupational ladder to rise faster than those at the top, due to an upsurge in demand for unskilled, semiskilled, and operative kinds of labor needed for war production. The structure of demand since the 1940s, however, has primarily benefited workers with higher education and more technical expertise. Accordingly, we find the unskilled, semiskilled, and operative workers heavily represented among the poor. What must be acknowledged in this development is that the distribution of wages and incomes is partly a reflection of collective social decisions regarding the merits of particular kinds of output. Sociopolitical decisions to expand the educational system, to arm for peace, and to explore the moon have all had a profound impact on the structure of demand for labor. Had we decided instead to dredge more rivers, to build more houses, or to clean up our cities, the extent and nature of poverty might now be markedly different. Without attempting to predict those changes here, we may at least take note of the fact that the poor now suffer from some of society's past and current labor utilization decisions and stand to benefit if and when society decides to place higher value on the available services of the poor.

SUMMARY

In Chapter 4, we observed that labor market forces have a substantial impact on the rate of employment for the poor. In particular, we observed that, in 1977 approximately 2 million poor families suffered income losses as a direct or indirect consequence of unemployment. We noted further that this unemployment was beyond the control of the poor and largely determined by labor market forces. We may add to that analysis now by observing that the level and structure of demand also helps determine what incomes the poor will command when they do work. Relatively low levels of aggregate demand will restrain all wages, while particularized demand shortages may, and do, depress the wages of the working poor.

We suggested earlier that about 40 percent of all nonaged poor families were affected by unemployment. We have now counted another 850,000 poor families whose heads work full time but whose wages are too low. Because these wages are themselves influenced by the same variables that determine unemployment rates, we may reasonably, and probably conservatively, conclude that labor market forces are responsible for substantially more than half of today's poverty among nonaged families.

APPENDIX: DUAL LABOR MARKETS AND THE TRICKLE DOWN

A major implication of the last two chapters is that the poor would benefit substantially from an expansion of aggregate demand—in particular, that the poor would benefit in the form of more jobs and higher wages, thus making possible their escape from poverty. But the link between aggregate demand expansion and the plight of the poor is not always apparent. Indeed, there are many observers who argue that the poor will benefit little, and perhaps not at all, from traditional increases in demand; that they are largely excluded from the jobs and higher wages such expansions create. The purpose of this brief appendix is to examine more carefully the relationship between demand expansion and the status of the poor.

The Trickle Down Perspective

Rarely does the government use its fiscal and monetary powers to expand aggregate demand in a form that is designed to help the poor *directly*. Instead, demand is expanded for those goods and services deemed to be of intrinsic worth to society (say, transportation or weapons systems) with the underlying conviction (hope?) that the poor will share in the benefits of the *generalized* demand expansion that follows. The expectation is that some of the benefits of increased demand will ultimately "trickle down" to the poor.[2]

Will the trickle really occur? In what forms?

To evaluate the validity of the trickle down hypothesis, suppose that the federal government decides to build a moon shuttle, capable of taxiing busloads of scientists and tourists back and forth to the moon. Obviously, such an undertaking would require the expenditure of tens of billions of dollars and the employment of highly skilled labor and capital equipment. The question is whether and how the poor folks back in the ghetto would benefit from this excursion into space.

It is possible, of course, that some of the poor would be employed directly in the moon shuttle program, say as grounds sweepers, gate attendants, or in other low-skilled jobs. But the potential for such *direct job creation* is apt to be small. A far likelier source of jobs are the *multiplier effects* that will take place once the program gets under way. The aerospace workers will want to spend their increased incomes, and in so doing will add to the demand for more conventional goods and services, such as houses, hot dogs, beer, gardeners, and maids. As the production of these goods and services expands, more jobs and incomes will be created, thereby increasing the chances that some needy souls from the ranks of the poor will obtain better jobs and wages. Such multiplier effects will continue to reverberate through the economy as the income spent by the aerospace workers is passed from hand to hand.

Although multiplier effects provide the best hope of jobs and income for the folks in the ghetto, there are other ways in which the poor might benefit from the moon shuttle program. The people who obtain jobs directly in the moon shuttle program will probably vacate positions that offered lower wages or benefits, jobs which then are available to others, including the poor. Such *substitution effects* may continue all the way down the occupational ladder, ultimately resulting in job vacancies for the poor. In addition, employers faced with a sudden shortage of labor will have an economic incentive to *train* the poor and unskilled, thereby further enlarging the size of the trickle.

The Dual Labor Market Perspective

Although the trickle down hypothesis seems plausible enough (even if somewhat remote), not everyone shares the expectations it generates. In particular, it is argued that the poor do not really participate in the mainstream economy, that they are excluded from the jobs and income that a moon shuttle program would create. In effect, it is argued, the poor participate

[2]The expression "trickle down" was coined by W. H. Locke Anderson in "Trickling Down: The Relationship between Economic Growth and the Extent of Poverty among American Families," *Quarterly Journal of Economics*, November 1964.

in a separate and distinct labor market, a *secondary labor market,* which is distinguished from the mainstream or *primary labor market.* From the perspective of the dual labor market hypothesis an expansion of demand that occurs in the primary market—such as in a moon shuttle program—will not benefit workers in the secondary market.

A variety of barriers are alleged to exclude the poor from the primary labor market, in effect creating the secondary market. Outright discrimination against minority groups or the poor, for example, would exclude the poor from the trickle. So, too, would recruiting practices that emphasized skill, experience, and stable work histories, prerequisites that the poor job-seeker can rarely satisfy. Institutional barriers like strong labor unions could have the same effect, especially if unions opted to maximize the earnings of their current members rather than to expand employment and union membership.

It is unlikely, of course, that these barriers would be so great as to exclude all poor job-seekers from the benefits created by a moon shuttle program (or any other form of demand expansion). It is much more reasonable to expect that *some* additional jobs and income will in fact trickle down, thereby reducing the number of people we count as poor. But the dual labor market hypothesis serves to remind us that the really critical issue is *how much* actually "trickles down." And it also suggests that public policy can be used to increase the size of that trickle by reducing the barriers that separate the poor from the jobs and incomes we create.

FURTHER READING

CAIN, GLEN G., "The Challenge of Segmented Labor Market Theories to Orthodox Theory: A Survey," *Journal of Economic Literature,* December 1976.

DOERINGER, PETER, and MICHAEL PIORE, "Unemployment and the 'Dual Labor Market'," *The Public Interest,* Winter 1975.

GARFINKEL, IRWIN, and ROBERT HAVEMAN, "Earnings Capacity, Economic Status, and Poverty," *Journal of Human Resources,* Winter 1977.

GORDON, DAVID, *Theories of Poverty and Underemployment.* Lexington, Mass.: D. C. Heath and Company, 1972.

HARRISON, BENNETT, "How American Households Mix Work and Welfare," *Challenge,* May/June 1978.

LEVITAN, SAR, and ROBERT TAGGART, *Employment and Earnings Inadequacy: A New Social Indicator.* Baltimore, Md.: Johns Hopkins University Press, 1974.

NK, "How Big Is The American Underclass?" Berkeley, Calif.:
sity of California, 1976.

COMMISSION ON EMPLOYMENT AND UNEMPLOYMENT
TICS, *Counting the Labor Force.* Washington, D.C.: Government
g Office, 1979.

6 AGE AND HEALTH

Although it is clear that deficiencies of aggregate demand explain much of the poverty we have observed, we cannot regard labor market forces as a complete explanation for poverty. As noted earlier, income-earning opportunities may be limited by supply-side characteristics as well, by demographic forces that result in human capital deficiencies. Moreover, as we also noted, most non-poor observers are predisposed to explain the existence of poverty on the basis of such forces (the Flawed Character argument). Accordingly, this chapter begins a detailed inquiry into the demographic characteristics of the poor and the potential that such characteristics possess for explaining poverty.

AGE

We have already counted among the poor 3,177,000 individuals over the age of sixty-five. Our purpose in reexamining the situation of the aged poor is not to remind ourselves how desperate they are but to investigate the link between their age and their economic status. What we seek to determine is whether there is something in the process of aging itself that leads to poverty.

The very size of the aged poor population creates a strong presumption that a causal link exists between age and poverty. Not only are 14 percent of the aged poor, but such individuals comprise one-eighth of the total poverty population. Moverover, the economic problems of the aged will be of increasing importance over time as the number of people living past the age of sixty-five continues to grow. The extension of life expectancies from forty-nine years in 1900 to seventy-three years in 1977 is reflected in the fact that the number of aged has increased by nearly 700 percent since the start of the century. And the aged population can be expected to continue to grow at a faster rate than the rest of the population for several decades, as a result of the maturing of the "war babies" and the decline in birth rates. Continuing discoveries in medical science may expand the aged population still further.[1]

These considerations have led Michael Harrington to observe that "the poverty of old age in America is rooted in a biological revolution."[2] We must take care, however, not to attribute to biology the economic ills of the aged. Changing fertility patterns and medical advances are responsible only for the fact that so many more people live to old age. They do not explain why so many of these people live in poverty. To understand more fully the forces that lead to economic destitution, we begin by reviewing the sources of support that the aged command.

Sources of Economic Support

The most obvious constraint on the incomes of the aged is the fact that so few older individuals remain in the labor force. Only one-fourth of all aged couples have at least one member in the labor force. Among aged individuals living alone (mostly women) labor force participation is even lower—about 12 percent. Accordingly, earnings from employment account for less than one-third of the incomes of the aged and provide little income at that. The poor among the aged are even less likely to work (see Table 2.4), and this absence of employment income is a major determinant of their economic status.

Low labor force participation among the aged reflects a continuing trend in American society. At the beginning of the century, more than two-thirds of all men over the age of sixty-five were in the labor force; today, only one out of five older men work. The reasons for this decline in labor force participation are many but surely do not include increased physical requirements of labor or diminished health status of the aged. More likely to have contributed to the decline are an increased desire for leisure, an abatement of the economic necessity to work, and a reduced demand for the skills of the aged.

There is considerable evidence that many of the aged are involuntarily out of the labor force due to forced retirements and prolonged unemployment. If an older worker is laid off for any reason, for example, plant shutdowns, production slowdowns, or forced retirement, he faces little opportunity of

[1]The U.S. Census Bureau estimates that persons aged 65 and over will comprise 30 percent of the total population by the year 2000, and over 50 percent by the year 2050. See Joseph J. Spengler, "Population Aging and Security of the Aged," *Atlantic Economic Journal*, March 1979.

[2]Michael Harrington, *The Other America* (New York: The Macmillan Company, 1962), p. 102.

finding another job. He is likely to have developed highly specialized skills in an occupation that is on the decline. Moreover, because of his advanced age, other employers see little benefit in retraining him or redirecting his skills. Other employers also anticipate increased costs as a result of higher disability rates and imminent retirement. Simple economics thus militate against the older job-seeker. Because his employment prospects are so unpromising, the older job-seeker is likely to drop out of the labor force earlier than he wants to, thereby closing a prospective income source. Of those older persons already "retired," over one-third report they were forced to retire. Nearly half of those older persons in poverty report forced retirements.[3]

There are alternatives to employment income, of course. One of the commonest substitutes for employment income is income from savings, assets, and various retirement plans. If the aged are generously provided with these, then the loss of employment income may not be so serious. Indeed, the availability of alternative sources of income could actually encourage retirement, with no implied loss of individual welfare. The question is, are the aged adequately provided with nonemployment retirement income?

A potentially important source of income for the aged is the savings they accumulated during their working years. Unfortunately, such savings are typically inadequate. Because the aged live longer today and retire earlier, they must accumulate greater savings than families once did. The unfortunate but simple economics of this relationship is that the longer one lives, the greater are the chances of destitution: Savings are depleted at the same time as one's employment capabilities and opportunities disappear. Hence, the aged of today must command considerable assets and savings if they are to experience a comfortable retirement.

At present, the aged poor clearly do not possess such savings, and many of the nonpoor aged do not fare much better, either. A recent (1977) survey indicated that only half of all aged families hold at least $100 in a savings account. The average value of an aged family's total assets is only $15,000 or so, and most of this value is tied up in home ownership. The average value of liquid assets (that is, assets that can be readily sold or converted into cash) of aged families averages much less. In fact, a substantial percentage of aged families possess *no* liquid assets. Hence, accumulated savings provide little antipoverty protection for the aged. Moreover, there is abundant evidence that the near-aged, that is, people fifty-five to sixty-five years old, have no greater savings. It appears, then, that the presently aged poor are only a small fraction of those who will follow.

Two more questions arise with regard to the savings of the aged: first, did the aged ever possess enough resources to save for old age; and second, did

---

[3]National Council on Aging, *The Myth and Reality of Aging in America,* (Washington, D.C.: National Council on Aging, 1977), p.87.

they save what resources they had? The distinction is important for policy purposes because many observers still believe it is necessary to distinguish the deserving poor from the undeserving poor, even among the aged. From this perspective, an impoverished older individual may simply be experiencing the consequences of an earlier decision to make merry while the sun was shining.

An examination of the previous experiences of the aged poor offers no evidence that they enjoyed an especially lascivious or spendthrift past. A study by the University of Michigan suggested that the aged poor had never earned enough income to provide for retirement or, for that matter, a comfortable living prior to retirement. Among those aged poor whose incomes were known, over 40 percent had never earned as much as $2,000 per year. Such statistics have led at least one observer to conclude of the aged poor that "the misery of their old age is simply the conclusion of a life of misery. They are the ones who have grown up, lived, and will die under conditions of poverty.[4] Many, and probably most, of the aged poor were always in or on the margins of poverty.

Some individuals do experience impoverishment for the first time, however, as they grow old. Just as few people think about dying, few ever plan to get old and retire. Despite the statistical expectation of extended retirement and diminished incomes, only a small number of people make provisions for old age. People's essential optimism is revealed in consumer surveys, such as the one that disclosed that families who have not had as much as $500 in the bank during the last five years confidently anticipate a comforable retirement. Confidence appears to fade with age, however; among younger families, only 9 percent foresee hard times after retirement; among middle-aged families, 16 percent sense trouble ahead. But when they reach old age, at least 25 percent of these individuals end up in poverty.[5]

Aside from their own savings, aged persons may draw income either from private pension plans or social security, but these sources usually provide much less income than most persons anticipate. Pension plans are often a great disillusionment. Many workers who confidently subscribe to company pension plans find that they have no pension rights upon retirement. If a worker is laid off or disabled before working, say, ten years with the same firm he or she may not be eligible for *any* pension payments. Presently, only 20 percent of all aged people receive private pensions, and these payments are primarily available only to those who had better jobs and higher incomes earlier.[6]

[4]Harrington, *Other America*, p. 105.

[5]The substantial discrepancy between actual saving rates and those required to support post-retirement living standards is illustrated in James A. Schulz and Guy Carrin, "The Role of Savings and Pension Systems in Maintaining Living Standards in Retirement," *Journal of Human Resources,* Summer 1972.

[6]Some of the abuses of the private pension system were eliminated by the provisions of the Employee Retirement Income Security Act of 1974; however, pension benefits remain the privilege of those with better earnings histories.

Moreover, even those who receive private pension benefits are often disappointed to learn that private pensions are typically not adjusted for inflation. As a result, the real value of private pensions diminishes with age.

Social security payments reach far more of the aged— nearly 90 percent of the aged now receive or are eligible for benefits— and constitute the single most important source of income for the elderly. Moreover, social security retirement benefits *are* adjusted for inflation, thereby retaining their real value. Nevertheless, social security benefits alone do not assure an adequate income. Because the amount of monthly benefits depends in large part on the amount of prior earnings, individuals who are poor while working are likely to be poor after retirement as well. The Social Security system is discussed at length in Chapter 12, along with other income transfer programs.

A final source of potential support for the aged may be found in their own families. The extended family unit has long represented the most dependable source of social and economic security for many people. However, continuing industrialization and urbanization have tended to disintegrate the extended family, leaving each core family unit to fend for itself. Despite whatever material and social benefits this development has yielded for others, it has deprived the aged of a source of support, immediate companionship, and, in many cases, a roof over their heads. Today, less than a third of the aged live with relatives, and of those that do not, less than 3 percent receive any income support from their offspring. Accordingly, relatives rarely constitute a source of economic security for the aged and cannot be expected to provide an escape from poverty.

Even when the aged are supported by their families, such support may be regarded as a mixed blessing. Many aged people live with relatives simply because they cannot afford to live by themselves. Moreover, they may not be counted as "poor," because the income of the household in which they live exceeds poverty standards. Yet, these older people are truly dependent if their living arrangements are dictated solely by economic necessity. The basic issue is not whether the aged live with their relatives or not, but whether the aged command enough economic resources to make a free choice of their own.

The income sources of the aged are summarized in Table 6.1. Related in the table are two distinct kinds of information. The middle column depicts the proportion of aged households that receive any income at all from the sources discussed above. Thus, an aged couple earning only $4.32 interest on their bank savings is included among those with asset income. If they receive social security payments too, then they are also included in that category. As the table shows, very few elderly persons receive any monetary assistance from relatives or friends (included in " other sources").

The last column of Table 6.1 depicts the relative importance of each income source; social security and employment earnings are clearly the most significant. It is interesting to note how the importance of asset income

TABLE 6.1   INCOME SOURCES OF THE AGED

Source of Income	Percent of Aged Households Receiving Such Income	Total Share of Income Provided by Source (%)
Wages and salaries	32	24
Self-employment income	10	6
Private pensions	20	7
Social security	87	33
Other public pensions, inc. veteran's benefits	19	7
Public assistance	9	2
Asset income	66	18
Other sources	32	3

Source: U.S. Senate, Special Committee on Aging, *Developments in Aging: 1978* (Washington, D.C.: Government Printing Office, 1979.)

diminishes as we move from column two to column three: while 66 percent of the aged receive some asset income, that source accounts for only 18 percent of all income for the aged, implying that most asset holdings are quite small. If, in fact, a small minority of the aged have very large asset holdings, which include savings, bonds, stocks, and property, then the rest of the aged own virtually nothing.

Expenses of the Aged

The serious decline in the sources and amounts of income that the aged command creates enough momentum to impoverish a high proportion of these individuals. But dwindling incomes are not their only burden; the aged also confront very large, and often rising, expenses. The interaction of these two forces is a virtual guarantee that a still higher proportion of the aged will experience material want before they die.

Everyone realizes that the aged are likely to experience high rates of sickness and disability. Often forgotten, however, is the tremendous financial burden that such disabilities impose. In 1977, for example, the average health bill for a person sixty-five or older was $1,745, including the expenses of hospital care, physician's services, and all drugs. This is a bill the average aged person cannot afford to pay. These health costs are equal to one-third of an aged individual's annual income and over 50 percent of his yearly income if he is old and poor.

Even these average expenses understate the burden of illness for those actually most sick. Hospitalization expenditures, for example, are incurred by only a portion of the poor, and these individuals pay all the costs, not just the "average" cost (which amounted to $769 in 1977). Furthermore, most likely to be sick or disabled are those who have endured impoverishment and hard labor the longest and are thus least able to afford the costs of sickness. Accordingly, many individuals who manage to fend off poverty during their working years are likely to succumb to fiinancial impoverishment when illness strikes. For those who have always been poor, illness in old age represents one more burden and indignity.

Medicare and Medicaid have done a great deal to reduce the threat of impoverishment among the aged due to illness. By providing subsidized medical insurance (Medicare) and the purchasing power required to buy needed medical services (Medicaid), the government has effectively removed a major financial burden of the aged. However, the financial protection provided by Medicare and Medicaid is not complete. Medicare does not pay all medical costs; there are limits on the type and extent of coverage. Moreover, Medicare users must pay premiums and deductibles that many poor people cannot afford. As a result, Medicare ends up paying less than half the health expenses of the aged.

Medicaid pays a larger share of the medical expenses of aged recipients. However, an individual must be poor to receive Medicaid benefits.[7] Typically, this means that an aged individual must exhaust most personal income and assets before becoming eligible for Medicaid assistance. Poverty is a prerequuisite for Medicaid protection. Moreover, neither Medicaid nor Medicare provide preventive health care. As a consequence, all too many older poor people are burdened with both discomfort and poverty, sometimes even relegated to unsympathetic and inadequate institutions to wait idly for death.

In many areas of the country, the aged are also burdened by taxes, particularly property taxes. For most of the aged, their homes represent the only significant asset they possess and embody a lifetime of savings. But because local property taxes continue to rise, many of the aged find themselves unable to maintain their investment. Property taxes alone may consume as much as 30 percent of the incomes of aged persons living just above the poverty line. As a result, the U.S. Senate Special Committee on Aging reports that hundreds of thousands of aged persons are being driven from their homes by mounting property taxes. Still more are being forced to liquidate other assets to pay their taxes. Thus, the only visible economic security of many of the aged may itself contribute to their improverishment.

Home ownership often imposes another unforeseen cost. Many of the aged purchased their homes in central cities at a time when inner city locations seemed most attractive. As the years have passed, however, inner city neighborhoods have deteriorated. Younger families have sought the freshness

---

[7]Income and asset limitations for Medicaid eligibility are determined by the states, and are typically somewhat higher than federal poverty standards. For a summary of how health expenses of the aged are paid, see Robert M. Gibson and Charles R. Fisher, "Age Difference in Health Care Spending," *Social Security Bulletin*, January 1979.

and space of the suburbs, while racial segregation and hostility have contributed to a general depreciation of inner city property values. As a consequence, the aged are apt to find themselves socially and racially isolated in neighborhoods they once thought attractive. They cannot afford to sell because the value of their homes has fallen while suburban values have skyrocketed. Hence, they can only hold on until the burden of property taxes leads them to rented quarters or nursing homes.

Making Do

An aged person with diminishing income and mounting expenses has little hope for economic security. An aged person's chances have simply run out; past labors and thrift are able only to postpone impoverishment in most cases. The question arises, then, as to how the aged actually manage in the face of such imposing circumstances. The most succinct answer came forth in hearings before a committee of the U.S. Senate:

> *"How do you manage?" I asked. A lady replied, "It's hard, Pat, oh, it's hard." "Well, what do you do?" "We don't do," someone replied, "That's how we manage!"*

> *"I don't" is a most accurate description of the older adult living in retirement. I don't entertain. I don't go out with friends. I don't eat in restaurants. I don't go to movies. I don't buy new clothes. I don't ride subways and buses. I don't buy cake. I don't eat a lot. I don't take care of my health like I should. I don't, I don't, I don't.[8]*

For the aged, then, growing older means giving up one thing after another until there is nothing more to forsake. When that time comes, they can only wait for death; sometime before that, they are unquestionably poor.

Assessing Causation

Poverty among the aged is not a natural product of biological development. Rather, it emerges from a diminution of income sources, a lack of accumulated resources, and the imposition of frequently rising expenses. Maintaining income sources or providing financial relief from taxation and illness will effectively prevent many aged individuals from falling into poverty. For others, however, poverty does not emerge in old age but is, instead, a continuing condition. The causes of poverty for these people must be sought elsewhere and earlier. Identifying and eliminating the causes of poverty for the nonaged will help to prevent later poverty among the aged.

[8]Special Committee on Aging. *Economics of Aging: Toward a Full Share in Abundance,* U.S. Senate, 91st Cong., 2d sess., 1970 (Washington, D.C.: Government Printing Office, 1970), p. 34.

One way to assure individuals greater prosperity and security in old age is to maintain their good health in younger years. Better health contributes to economic security in two important ways: by permitting persons to earn more income; and by reducing financial expenditures arising from health needs. All other things being equal, a person with good health is likely to accumulate greater financial reserves when he is young and to need them less when he is old.

It is not difficult to surmise the potential poor health has for undermining a family's economic security. A sick or disabled father not only fails to earn a full income; he also increases household expenses. To appreciate how expensive illness can be, we may observe recent income losses and health expenditures. In 1977, for example, illness and disability imposed an income loss in excess of $50 billion on American workers, and more than $160 billion was spent for health maintenance and care. This works out to an average income loss of $650 per worker and average health expenses of $740 per person. Even if the poor experienced only an average amount of illness and disability, their incomes would be severely depleted by poor health.

The relationship between health and income status is not simple enough, however, to permit the use of averages in ascertaining the cost of illness to the poor. Just as illness may tend to deplete a family's resources and leave it poor, so may poverty itself increase the likelihood of getting sick. Poor families suffer notoriously from chronic malnutrition and unsanitary environments, both of which nurture ill health. As a consequence, they are apt to be ill or disabled more often than the nonpoor. Poor families have markedly higher disease and mortality rates and miss more than twice as many days of work due to illness than do the nonpoor.

Poverty and illness, then, interact in a reciprocal relationship. As shown in Figure 6.1, illness leads to poverty and poverty leads to poor health.

FIGURE 6.1 Illness and Poverty

However, the relationship is not necessarily equally strong in both directions. We may still inquire as to how many families or persons actually fall into poverty as a result of illness or disability; that is, we may still ask to what extent poverty is actually *caused* by ill health. Many persons were poor before they were sick, so we cannot claim that illness caused their poverty. At most, we may say that illness maintains their poverty or that it makes poverty more miserable.

The search for causal significance thus centers on the question of how many nonpoor persons sink into poverty as a result of illness. The answer, of course, depends on how far above the poverty line families begin and how much illness they contract. Also important is the extent to which families are protected by insurance from the impositions of work loss and medical expenses.

A family need not be far above the poverty line to have an adequate margin against the burdens of ill health. Our 1977 poverty line for a family of four is just over $6,000. Average yearly medical expenses for a family this size are around $1,400 per year. Hence, for the typical family, an income of over $7,500 would easily prevent slippage into poverty as a result of illness. Moreover, as we have already suggested, the incidence of illness falls as income rises, further immunizing the nonpoor against poverty. Families with higher incomes also have more private health insurance. As Table 6.2 reveals, 70 percent of high-income families have private major medical insurance coverage, whereas only 16 percent of low-income families have such coverage. Higher-income families can better afford to safeguard their health and to protect their economic position when illness strikes. Consequently, for families with some margin of income above the poverty standard, only severe and protracted illnesses represent a real threat to economic security. Illness is still painful and may even lower standards of living for these families; it is unlikely, however, to lead to poverty.

Families on the margin of economic security are not so well fortified against the onslaught of illness. With an income of $6,000 to $7,000, a family

TABLE 6.2 PRIVATE HEALTH INSURANCE, BY FAMILY INCOME

Family Income	Percent of Persons with Private Major Medical Coverage
Under $5,000	16
$5,000–9,999	45
$10,000–19,999	61
$20,000–29,999	57
$30,000 and over	70

Source: Congressional Budget Office, *Catastrophic Health Insurance* (Washington, D.C.: Government Printing Office, 1977).

has little financial reserve. Such families are likely to be ill more often and less likely to be protected by insurance (Table 6.2). Consequently, they are prone to fall into poverty when illness strikes. Near-poor families do, in fact, move back and forth across the poverty line with great frequency. In part, this movement is due to the sporadic occurrence of illness. Economic security for these families is, at all times, vulnerable to any kind of setback, be it illness, increased unemployment, or other misfortune. We cannot say exactly how much poverty is caused by illness and disability, but it is safe to conclude that very few people fall into poverty from any significant height as a result of ill health.

The intergenerational links between health and poverty are more discouraging. Up to now, we have considered only the impact of health on an existing family's economic status. But the illness bred by poverty may leave scars that last for generations. A child born to a poverty-stricken mother is likely to be undernourished both before and after birth. Furthermore, the child is less likely to be cared for properly after birth, to be immunized against disease, or even to have his eyes and teeth examined. As a result, the child is likely to grow up prone to illness and poverty, and in the most insidious of cases, be impaired by organic brain damage. A 1976 study by the U.S. Department of Health, Education, and Welfare reported that poor children

- Suffer 23 percent more hearing impairment.
- Do not grow as tall as other children.
- Are more likely to have low hemoglobin values during their years of growth.
- Suffer a higher incidence of impetigo, gastrointestinal diseases, parasitic diseases, and urinary-tract infections.
- In urban areas, are more often the victims of lead-paint poisoning and insect and rodent bites.[9]

To what extent do these childhood health impairments affect later educations, job skills, or income? No one knows for sure. However, there is a strong suspicion that poverty in one generation may result in illnesses and disabilities that become a significant cause of poverty in the next generation.

Mental health, as well as physical health, is an important dimension of poverty. The issue here is the same as before: does mental disability lead downward to the slums, or does slum life accentuate tendencies toward mental illness? The former question embodies a popular "drift" hypothesis. According to this thesis, failures from all walks of life drift into the slums, creating our present poor population. The available evidence, however, once again shatters the popular myth. One of the few detailed studies undertaken on

[9]U.S. Department of Health, Education and Welfare; Office of Child Health Affairs, *A Proposal for New Federal Leadership in Maternal and Child Health Care in the United States* (Washington, D.C.: Government Printing Office, 1976), pp. 9–10, 15.

this subject traced the socioeconomic histories of schizophrenic individuals. The results were unambiguous: 91 percent of such patients were in the same socioeconomic class as their parents.[10] There was no evidence of substantial drift. Instead, the results suggest that poverty is more likely to lead to ill health than result from it.

SUMMARY

Age and illness are highly visible correlates of poverty and, because of this, are often assumed to bear a causal relationship to economic impoverishment. The reasoning behind such an assumption is simple and appears eminently plausible. As reasonable as such a conclusion is, however, there are several reasons for attaching only limited causal importance to the impact of age and illness. Many of the aged poor, for example, were always poor, so that aging itself causes little change in their economic status. Similarly, poor persons are more prone to illness, and illness for them represents no sudden loss of well-being. Even for those who are driven to poverty for the first time by age or illness, the loss of economic status is occasioned by a variety of forces, none of which is inseparable from the natural processes of aging and illness.

It is not possible to attach exact quantitative significance to the amount of poverty caused by age and illness. Given the data reviewed in this chapter, however, we may tentatively estimate that no more than 10 to 15 percent of the poor are impoverished as a result of age or illness. This assumes that only one-half of the aged poor experience poverty for the first time in old age and that only 5 to 10 percent of the poor have been destituted by the effects of ill health.

FURTHER READING

Age

CLARK, ROBERT, JUANITA KREPS, AND JOSEPH SPENGLER, "Economics of Aging: A Survey," *Journal of Economic Literature,* September 1978.

U.S. DEPARTMENT OF LABOR, *Employment and Training Report of the President, 1978.* Washington, D.C.: Government Printing Office, Ch. 4.

U.S. SENATE, Special Committee on Aging, *Developments in Aging.* Washington, D.C.: Government Printing Office, annual.

[10]Rodger L. Hurley, *Poverty and Mental Retardation: A Causal Relationship,* (Trenton, N.J.: New Jersey Department of Institutions and Agencies, April 1968).

Health

CONGRESSIONAL BUDGET OFFICE, *Catastrophic Health Insurance*. Washington, D.C.: Government Printing Office, 1977.

RODGERS, HARRELL R., JR., *Poverty Amid Plenty*. Reading, Mass.: Addison-Wesley Publishing Co., Inc., 1979, Ch. 6.

7 FAMILY SIZE AND STATUS

There are two persistent accusations leveled against the poor: one is that the poor do not limit their family size; the other is that they do not maintain stable families. The implication in both cases is that the poor exhibit too little self-control and are thus responsible for much of their own plight. The purposes of this chapter are to examine more closely the relationship between poverty and family size and status and to determine the extent of responsibility that the poor themselves must bear for their own deprivation.

The central questions of this chapter are much like those of Chapter 6. That is, we inquire whether either large family size or family instability preceded economic impoverishment. If so, then there may be some validity to the claim that the poor caused their own poverty by creating conditions that make it difficult or impossible to hold a job that pays an adequate income. If not, then there exists a basic presumption that poverty was not caused by either phenomenon. Indeed, in such circumstances, we may be led to ask whether the sequence of causation is reversible, that is, whether poverty itself may lead to family instability or excessive procreation.

FAMILY SIZE

Large numbers of children clearly constitute a sizable drain on family resources. Not only are the physical needs of the family increased, but the mother is likely to be restricted to the home for more years than the mother of a smaller family. If the mother chooses not to stay at home, she must pay

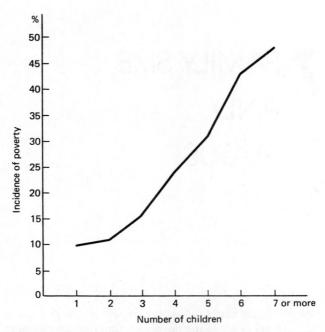

FIGURE 7.1   Incidence of Poverty by Family Size, 1977

Source: U.S. Bureau of the Census.

someone else to tend the house while she works. Childbearing and rearing thus make it either physically impossible or economically unrewarding for many mothers to participate in the labor force. Confronted with more needs and fewer resources, many large families are unable to fend off poverty.

Figure 7.1 depicts the actual incidence of poverty for different family sizes. The incidence clearly rises as the number of children increases, first slowly, and then quite sharply after the third child. Clearly, there are a disproportionate number of families among the poor who have a large number of children. Over 20 percent of all poor families with children have at least four children; among nonpoor families, only 10 percent have that many children.

To grasp the implications of larger family sizes among the poor, we may ask how many larger poor families would move out of poverty if they had fewer family members. For example, we know from Table 1.4 that five-member families are considered poor if their 1977 incomes were under $7,320, but the same poverty standard for a family of four was $6,191. Hence, any family of five whose income was less than $7,320 but more than $6,191 would no longer be counted as poor if it could somehow eliminate one family member. Or, to put it slightly differently, we may say that such a family would not have fallen into poverty if it had bred one less child. By counting the total number of such families, we may estimate the potential of family planning as a means for reducing poverty.

The statistical exercise required to make such an estimate is summarized in Table 7.1. The exercise is carried out on two levels: the first calculation tells how many larger poor families (of five or more persons) would move out of poverty if they had one less member. Among poor five-person families, we look for all those whose current income could support four persons; among six-person families, incomes that will support five people, and so on. Based on these calculations, we observe that 289,000 poor families, a total of over 2 million individuals, would no longer be counted as poor if each family had one person less.

The second calculation summarized in Table 7.1 imposes an even stricter constraint on family size. Rather than trim all larger poor families by one person, it reduces all such families to the standard four persons. Hence, six-person families statistically lose two members, and their poverty line falls from $8,268 to $6,197. This kind of standardization creates an astounding reduction in the size of the poverty population. On these assumptions, over 500,000 families (3.3 million individuals)—nearly one-seventh of all the non-aged poor—would no longer be counted as poor.

Our statistical exercise leads us to the conclusion that mild restraints on family size (one person less) would reduce the nonaged poverty population by some 9 percent, while severe limits on family size (maximum of four) would effect a 14 percent reduction in the number of poor. Such results underscore the potential importance of the causal link between family size and poverty. Before turning to a discussion of causality, however, it is necessary to subject our statistical results to some critical scrutiny.

TABLE 7.1   THE POTENTIAL IMPACT OF FAMILY PLANNING

A. QUESTION: How many families and persons would no longer be counted as poor if each larger poor family were reduced by one person?

ANSWER:	From 7-person or Larger Families	From 6-person Families	From 5-person Families	Total
Families	110,000	44,000	135,000	289,000
Persons	815,000	264,000	675,000	2,043,000

B. QUESTION: How many families and persons would no longer be counted as poor if each larger poor family were reduced to four persons?

ANSWER:	From 7-person or Larger Families	From 6-person Families	From 5-person Families	Total
Families	241,000	128,000	135,000	504,000
Persons	1,857,000	768,000	675,000	3,300,000

Source: U.S. Bureau of the Census.

First, our statistical exercise tacitly assumes that there is no positive relationship between family size and family income. The statistical elimination of one family member is presumed to have no effect on family income. But this is not necessarily true. Among families dependent on public assistance, for example, family income usually rises with additional children. Thus, if we were to eliminate one family member, we would also have to adjust the size of the welfare grant. One less child would mean less income and continued poverty. Accordingly, few, if any, welfare families—who constitute one-half of the population of poor families with children—can be included in our calculations.

Family income may also rise with family size for other reasons. The father of the family may be impelled to work overtime or at a second job as his family responsibilities expand; hence larger families may constitute a special kind of incentive to work. Larger families may also enable other family members to work; they may have a greater number of older children who can contribute directly to family income by working part time or who enable the mother to work by assuming child-care responsibilities. Hence, the statistical reduction carried out above may, in fact, diminish sources of family income.

Further consideration must also be given to those families and persons whom we suppose statistically to escape poverty by our calculations. Some family members are constrained by our arithmetic to disappear, and we can ignore them for the moment. Surviving family members, however, improve their economic status only marginally, and we must recognize that their statistical "escape" is, therefore, not very impressive. Almost all such families remain within a few hundred dollars of our poverty standards, even after they manage to leave the poverty population.

These qualifications to our earlier calculations reduce the impact of family size as a cause of poverty; unfortunately, there is not enough information about the poor to make a meaningful estimate of its true impact. We can observe, however, that even if we envision only limited birth control (one less child in each larger family) and consider the foregoing qualifications important enough to reduce our estimates by at least half, then large family size still accounts for 4 to 5 percent of the nonaged poverty population. Under stricter family size controls, the reduction would amount to 7 percent.

The Causal Relation

Even when reduced by cautious skepticism, family size still appears to possess some potential for explaining the existence of poverty. Given the obvious association between these two phenomena, it would not seem necessary to pursue the subject of causation further. But the direction of causation is an important ingredient of policy decisions and must be examined. If the poor are mindlessly, even willfully, propagating beyond their financial means, policy intervention will be more difficult and less available; but if the poor are excluded from access to birth control, intervention is easier and more broadly acceptable. The former case comes closest to the position that excessive family size leads to poverty, while the latter case implies the reverse.

There is no evidence at all that presently large poor families ever enjoyed a more comfortable economic status. Larger families do have an effect on the dimensions of poverty to the extent that continued procreation may lengthen a family's stay in the poverty population rather than cause it to fall from nonpoverty to poverty. Large family size thus retards the flow of people moving out of poverty and contributes over time to an expansion of the poverty population. By itself, however, it creates very little new poverty.

Against this background, we must also ponder the accumulation of evidence suggesting that the poor continue to have little access to birth control information. Public schools, especially in low-income areas, are still reluctant to provide birth control information, while public welfare authorities are, in most cases, prohibited from providing it. As a consequence, poor families end up with more children than other families, not because they want them, but because they are unable to prevent them. One study by the National Academy of Sciences indicated that over one-third of the least-educated families had unwanted children, and a survey of welfare mothers in New York yielded similar findings. Even more revealing are recent studies that indicate the extent to which unwanted births increase at lower income levels; 17 percent of all nonpoor families report unwanted births, compared to 26 percent for near-poor families and a whopping 42 percent for poor families.[1]

Given the high incidence of unwanted births among the poor, it is evident that improved access to birth control information and contraceptive devices would lessen the amount of poverty, although not by a great amount. From this perspective, poverty is more a cause of excessive family size than the other way around, at least so long as access to birth control is conditioned on economic status. And there is evidence that this is the case. In addition to the statistics above we need only remind ourselves that the most reliable source of birth control information is the private family doctor, by and large an inaccessible luxury for the poor.

We must conclude that excessive family size is not an important cause of poverty on the basis of our earlier observation that poor families were, by and large, once smaller poor families rather than smaller nonpoor families. If causation were to be specified here, we would have to surmise that lack of access to birth control is one of the ways in which poverty itself creates more poverty. Eliminating family size as a significant independent cause of poverty should not, therefore, divert attention away from the potential of greater family planning efforts to alleviate the conditions of

[1]"Why the Poor Get Children: Findings of Two Major Studies," *Newsweek,* June 19, 1972. See also James Cramer, "Births, Expected Family Size, and Poverty," in James N. Morgan, ed., *Five Thousand Families: Patterns of Economic Progress* (Ann Arbor, Mich.: Institute for Social Research, 1974); Larry Bumpass and Charles F. Westoff, "The 'Perfect Contraceptive' Population," *Science,* September 1970.

the poor. The fact remains that greater availability of birth control would help reduce the number that are poor.

FAMILY STATUS

One-parent families, especially black ones, have long attracted the attention of social scientists, politicians, and the general public. They have been regarded with pity, with scorn, and even with a sense of fear. Single-parent, or broken, families do not fit easily into traditional American patterns and are often regarded as a threat to community morality, not to mention the whole institutional character of marriage. Recently, added concern over the existence of broken families has emerged from the observation that they tend to become financially dependent on the public purse. Within the confines of this chapter, there is hardly room for a thorough examination of the economics and sociology of one-parent families. Instead, the subject of family status, as of all other demographic characteristics, is treated with a focus on the existence of possible causal links to poverty.

In virtually all cases where only one parent resides in the family, that parent is the mother. Accordingly, the census classification "female-headed families with children" refers to nearly all those families whose social and economic life has been ruptured by the loss of a parent. Broken families actually arise from two different contingencies: either a previously two-parent family is literally broken up by the death or separation (by divorce, legal separation, or desertion) of one parent; or the parents never formed a stable union, legal or otherwise. While the net effect in either case is to leave only one parent in the family, the economic and social ramifications of each situation may be quite distinct. A twenty-six-year-old widow, for example, may command more social support and economic resources than an unwed mother of the same age.

A one-parent family is severely handicapped in the effort to attain economic security. The loss of one potential breadwinner is a large and obvious constraint on economic stability. Potential family income is reduced by *more than half* with the departure of one parent. Where two parents exist in the family, one parent can devote full time to labor market activity while the other is free to combine household and labor market activity. When only one parent resides in the family, such flexibility is diminished. The single parent is unable to devote all time to labor market activity, at least not without paying someone else to assume household responsibilities. Hence, the potential net income of a one-parent family is often closer to one-third rather than to one-half of a two-parent family's income. If women's employment opportunities in the labor market are further constricted by conventional sexual stereotypes, their potential income will be lower still. Accordingly, one-parent families bear an extraordinarily high risk of economic impoverishment.

While the potential of family breakup (or nonformation) for impoverishment is clear, the direction of causation is not necessarily so apparent. We need evidence that family breakup *leads* to poverty, and not the reverse, or at least that it effectively acts as an independent barrier to economic security.

Historically, there has seldom been any reluctance to "explain" the existence of one-parent families among blacks. As late as the 1920s, allegations of "animalism," "moral putridity," and "primitive sexualism" were often advanced as explanations for the great incidence of broken families among American blacks. The latent implication was always that blacks were responsible for their own destitution, because they were morally, physically, or culturally unable to stabilize family relationships. Such explanations for black family instability and poverty have never fared well under scholarly examination. Among others, E. Franklin Frazier, an outstanding expert on the black family, has shown that family patterns are comprehensible only in the context of existing social and economic forces. Moreover, the fact that there are as many poor white female-headed families as poor black female-headed families would tend to undermine purely racial explanations of the link between family status and poverty.

There is strong evidence against racial theories of causation between family status and poverty, but the theories persist because people want to believe them. In addition, the whole subject experienced a certain rejuvenation in 1965 when President Johnson, speaking at Howard University, drew attention to the breakdown of black family structure as one of the most important causes of black poverty. While he did not seem to mean that black poverty could be explained on simple racial grounds, his words sparked instant misunderstanding and anger. James Farmer of CORE, for example, saw President Johnson's statement as a "massive academic cop-out for the white conscience" that would provide fuel for a new racism. Martin Luther King, Jr., saw in the President's words a danger that the poverty of blacks would be attributed to innate black weaknesses, and therein he feared yet another basis for racial neglect and oppression.

Behind President Johnson's Howard University speech lay a theoretical paper written by Daniel P. Moynihan, then assistant secretary of labor. In what became known as the Moynihan Report, he had said:

> *At the heart of the deterioration of the fabric of Negro society is the deterioration of the Negro family.*
>
> *It is the fundamental source of the weakness of the Negro community at the present time.*
>
> *Once or twice removed, it will be found to be the principal source of most of the aberrant, inadequate, or antisocial behavior that did not establish, but now serves to perpetuate the cycle of poverty and deprivation.* [2]

[2]U.S. Department of Labor, *The Negro Family: The Case for National Action* (Washington, D.C.: Government Printing Office, 1965).

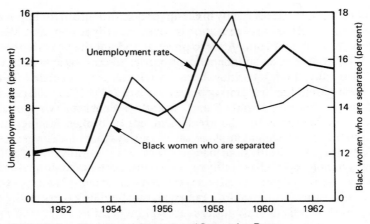

FIGURE 7.2   Black Unemployment and Separation Rates

Source: U.S. Department of Labor, *The Negro Family: The Case for National Action,* March 1965, p. 22.

Because the Moynihan Report sparked such a controversy, and because it deals explicitly with the relationship between family status and poverty, we will use it as a case study.

To recapitulate, the central issue is whether family breakup independently causes poverty, or vice versa. For most commentators, the Moynihan Report seemed to confirm black family structure as a cause of poverty. Moynihan himself, however, had in mind a more complex relationship. In the recesses of the report, Moynihan suggested, as had Frazier earlier, that family structure itself was shaped by prevailing social and economic forces. Hence, one could not argue that family breakup had caused poverty; at most, black family structures only reflected economic forces and made escape from poverty more difficult. Poverty and social injustice were more likely to cause family breakup, not the reverse.

One particularly interesting bit of evidence collected by Moynihan concerns the relationship between unemployment rates and family structure: looking at the trend of unemployment rates and family structures, Moynihan found that the rates of separation and divorce followed economic events very closely. Thus, the rate of separations among black women shot up shortly after the economy faltered, while it sank when the economy prospered (see Figure 7.2). Family stability was apparently the result, not the cause, of economic events. As a family faced increased unemployment and deprivation, the father's position as breadwinner and family head became untenable; divorce, separation, or desertion often followed.

Further support for this position was found in illegitimacy statistics: in poor black neighborhoods rates of illegitimacy were more than triple those of black neighborhoods with middle-class incomes. Again it appeared that family formation itself was significantly affected by economic circumstances. Those parents with little prospect for economic security foresaw little hope for family stability; they decided not to marry.

A. Philip Randolph, long a leader in labor and civil rights movements, found evidence similar to Moynihan's in World War II experience. During the exceptionally low unemployment years of the war, rates of divorce and illegitimacy among blacks took a sharp drop. Greater economic security thus manifested itself in greater family stability.

More recent information on families appears to further confirm Moynihan's observations and to extend his hypothesis to all families, black or white. Table 7.2 shows the pattern of marital status for men by income class. Among all men aged twenty-five to sixty-four who were ever married, 7 percent now have absent wives; they are divorced, separated, deserted, or widowed. The incidence of absent wives varies enormously by income class, however. Over one-fifth of married men in the lowest income class no longer live with their wives, while fewer than one out of twenty-five men in the highest income class are likely to be so positioned. This relationship conveys two important impressions: it appears to reconfirm the point that family stability is affected by economic conditions; and it suggests that economic impoverishment preceded family dissolution. Under these circumstances, restoration of the family would do little by itself to achieve economic security. A disproportionately high percentage of the departed fathers and husbands were, and are still, poor.

TABLE 7.2   ABSENCE OF THE WIFE, BY
INCOME CLASS, 1969

Income Class	Percentage of Married Men* with Wife No Longer Present
Under $3,000	21.0
$3,000–5,999	10.3
$6,000–9,999	5.6
$10,000 and over	3.5
All classes	7.4

*Aged twenty-five to sixty-four.
Source: U.S. Bureau of the Census.

The impact of economic insecurity on marital instability was also noted in a seven-year study of 5,000 families. The families were first interviewed in 1967, then reinterviewed in each of the following years, until 1973. These observations, by the University of Michigan Survey Research Center, show how divorce and separation are often linked to economic status. In general, average family income turned out to be the best predictor of family stability, for both whites and blacks. In addition, families that owned their own homes in 1967 or had significant savings were much more likely to be still intact in

1973. By contrast, families in which the husband was encountering employment problems in 1967 were more likely to have broken up by 1973.[3]

The essence of the Moynihan Report, then, is best described in a dynamic setting.[4] Continued economic deprivation is likely to undermine a family's stability. At some point, the family unit is ruptured, and the female-headed family is left to fend for itself. No loss of economic status is necessarily implied by the departure of the father, especially where he was unemployed and/or the female-headed unit turned to public assistance. In the University of Michigan study noted above, 20 percent of the families that broke up during the seven-year observation period did fall into poverty, and most of these turned to welfare. However, the average loss of income status amounted to only 6 percent of prior income status.

While at any point in time a high proportion of poor families will be female-headed, family breakup cannot be identified as a major cause of poverty. Family disunity may help sustain poverty, but in most cases it appears that poverty preceded, and itself helped to cause, family dissolution.[5]

This conclusion does not necessitate a purely economic-deterministic view of family relations. Clearly, not all divorces and separations are occasioned by financial stress. Family dissolutions will continue to take place even after all families are assured economic security. The point is that a disproportionately high percentage of family breakups occurs among the poor due to economic stress and that relatively few broken poor families were decidedly nonpoor before family dissolution occurred.

SUMMARY

Large families and broken families are among the most salient characteristics of the poor. Over 30 percent of all the poor are in families with at least five members, while one-fourth of the poor are in broken families; many of the latter are also from large families. Accordingly, there exists a strong presumption that family size and status are important causes of poverty. However, the

---

[3]Duncan, Greg. J., and James N. Morgan, eds., *Five Thousand American Families: Patterns of Economic Progress* (Ann Arbor, Mich.: Institute for Social Research, vol. IV, 1976). A parallel study of low-income and welfare families in Camden, New Jersey, found that the husband's economic performance was important for family attitudes and stability (see Samuel Klausner, "Six Years in the Lives of the Impoverished: An Examination of the WIN Thesis" (Philadelphia: Center for Research on the Acts of Man, 1978).

[4]Moynihan himself must bear much of the blame for not drawing attention to the dynamics of his thesis. He was too willing to let controversy and public attention focus on the passages quoted earlier.

[5]Evidence that economic stress contributes to mental illness and changes people's perception of self, family, and society is contained in D. D. and B. M. Braginsky, "Surplus People: Their Lost Faith in Self and System" and Berkeley Rice, "The Worry Epidemic," *Psychology Today,* August 1975.

presumed causal significance of family size and status does not fare well upon closer examination. For most of the families in question poverty prevailed before the family either grew larger or broke up. Moreover, economic insecurity itself may have contributed to the dissolution of the family or to excessive reproduction. Hence, stronger causality appears to flow from poverty to family size and status than in the opposite direction.

Some families do fall into poverty as a result of the burdens of additional children or an absent parent, but the number appears to be small. Family breakup and growth are more likely to extend and deepen a family's poverty than bring it about. Efforts to increase the economic opportunities of the poor should promote greater family stability and smaller family size. At the same time, direct efforts to make birth control available to the poor will do much to alleviate present poverty and retard its intergenerational transmission.

FURTHER READING

On Family Size

BOGUE, DONALD J., "A Long-Term Solution to the AFDC Problem: Prevention of Unwanted Pregnancy," *Social Science Review,* December 1975.

PODELL, LAWRENCE, *Families on Welfare in New York City.* New York: City University of New York Press, 1968.

SHEPPARD, HAROLD L. *Effects of Family Planning on Poverty in the United States.* Kalamazoo, Mich.: Upjohn Institute, 1967.

SHOSTAK, ARTHUR, "Birth Control and Poverty," in *New Perspectives on Poverty,* Arthur Shostak and William Gomberg, eds. Englewood Cliffs, N.J.: Prentice-Hall, Inc., 1965.

On Family Status

LIEBOW, ELLIOT, *Tally's Corner: A Study of Negro Streetcorner Men.* Boston: Little, Brown and Company, 1967.

RAINWATER, LEE, AND WILLIAM L. YANCEY, *The Moynihan Report and the Politics of Controversy.* Cambridge, Mass.: The MIT Press, 1967.

8 CULTURE AND RACE

Accusations that the poor bring about their own deprivation through excessive procreation or family instability are generally elements of a broader perspective. When people suggest, for example, that "welfare mothers would rather have another kid than a job," they are ascribing to the welfare poor a whole complex of attitudes, norms, and values. That is, the demographic forces we have reviewed tend to be mere details of the Flawed Character perspective. What makes theories of cultural and racial inferiority so interesting is that they are so much more explicit about Flawed Characters. Simply put, the cultural theory of poverty argues that the poor lack the aspirations, values, and motivation required to "get ahead." The poor just don't give a damn about improving their economic status. In this sense, poverty is self-imposed.

Racial theories of poverty build on the notion of cultural differences, but add another dimension as well. Racial theories assert that blacks (or Hispanics, Indians, etc.) not only have lower motivation, but that genetic deficiences inherently constrain their economic status. In terms of either the cultural or racial manifestations of the Flawed Character perspective, then, the poor bring little human capital to the labor market and are rewarded accordingly.

Although theories of racial inferiority have fallen into distinct disfavor in recent years, they are far from dead. On the contrary, they have enjoyed a certain renaissance in recent debates on IQ, and have persuaded at least one leading writer on the subjects of labor and poverty to conclude that the higher poverty rate among blacks is "the result of racial differences in endowment with genetic human capital."[1] But before examining the basis for such views we will consider the content of theories of cultural inferiority, theories that need not be restricted to one racial group among the poor.

THE "CULTURE OF POVERTY"

In colonial America poverty was regarded as the manifestation of vice and sin. Because everyone except Negro slaves was thought to enjoy the opportunity to acquire economic security by his own labor, those who did not attain such security were deemed to be morally flawed. Poverty thus became proof of moral bankruptcy, and the poor were treated accordingly. In Pennsylvania, paupers had the shoulders of their right sleeves adorned with the letter *P* to put unsuspecting strangers on notice. In other jurisdictions the poor were sent packing, sometimes having first been chastened with a public whipping. As the puritanical Humane Society summarized the situation in 1809," . . .by a just and inflexible law of Providence, misery is ordained to be the companion and punishment of vice."[2]

In more modern times the theoretical link of poverty to sin has not fared well. There now exists a general reluctance to ascribe the misery of the poor to the laws of Providence. Nevertheless, belief in the universality of economic opportunity remains firmly embedded in the American consciousness. Accordingly, there is need for a substitute explanation to account for the persistence of poverty in a land of abundance and opportunity. This, in part, explains the ascendency of cultural theories of poverty. To formulate a cultural theory of poverty is to assert that the poor lack sufficient desire and motivation to escape poverty. It is to allege that the goal of economic security is of lesser importance in the value matrix of the poor. By this hypothesis the poor are impoverished because their "culture" prevents them from taking advantage of opportunities to escape poverty.

If the poor are culturally bound to poverty, then the task of eliminating poverty becomes infinitely more difficult and time-consuming. Public efforts must be directed toward changing attitudes and environments, rather than simply toward changing opportunities. Communication between poor and nonpoor groups will also be more difficult, with interclass tension and anxiety the likely results. Hence, the culture of poverty thesis cannot be dismissed lightly.

[1]Lowell E. Gallaway, *Poverty in America* (Columbus, Ohio: Grid Publishing, Inc., 1973), p. 149.
[2]Cited by Paul Jacobs in Jeremy Larner and Irving Howe, eds., *Poverty: Views from the Left* (New York: William Morrow & Company, Inc., 1968), p. 40.

Norms vs. Traits

A completely satisfactory definition of *culture* is not easy to come by. Nevertheless, for the purposes of this inquiry, we may understand culture to refer to the norms, values, and aspirations of an individual or group. These components of culture are not observable, however. Only behavioral traits of individuals and groups are observable. We must *infer* underlying aspirations and values from observations of behavior. This means that the assertion of distinct cultural attributes among the poor is largely founded on observations of distinct behavioral patterns. The assertion, however, is vulnerable to criticism, as not all behavioral differences reflect cultural differences. Even persons with identical norms and aspirations may behave differently in different situations. Our task is to determine whether the inferential reasoning that underlies the cultural hypothesis is valid.

Consider the case of a welfare recipient who declines what appears to be a reasonable job offer. For many middle-class observers, such a rejection constitutes incontrovertible proof that the recipient lacks normal initiative, aspirations, and goals—clear evidence of a culture of poverty. Middle-class individuals, it is argued, would never reject an offer to improve their economic status, especially in the dire financial straits of the welfare recipient. The accusation can be challenged, however. It is possible that the rejection of employment opportunities reflects other circumstances not readily apparent to the nonpoor observer. The job offer itself may, of course, be inherently unattractive and provide no economic advancement. But the rejection may also be based on public welfare policy. If it is difficult and time-consuming to obtain public welfare assistance, then the individual who leaves the welfare roles for employment incurs a distinct risk. If the job proves to be unsatisfactory or temporary, then he and his family are left without any financial support while he awaits a new job or more welfare. For families at the margin of impoverishment and confronting largely transitory kinds of jobs, such a risk may be unwarranted. Thus, the job rejection may proceed not from different values and aspirations but from tangible behavioral constraints. Middle-class jobseekers, with savings accounts and better job prospects, are not subject to these same constraints.

The culture of poverty hypothesis requires rather stringent evidence. It must be shown that the norms and aspirations—not just the behavior—of the poor are different and that these differences impede escape from poverty. It should also be shown whether and to what degree such differences would disappear under changing socioeconomic circumstances.

Oscar Lewis is the most familiar and forceful proponent of the culture of poverty thesis. His observations of life-styles among the poor convinced him that the behavior patterns of the poor are different and that these differences reflect distinct values. Although his empirical research was confined largely to Mexico and Puerto Rico, he believed that these differences transcend national boundaries. He offered the following explanation for the perpetuation of poverty:

> *Once [the culture of poverty] comes into existence it tends to perpetuate itself from generation to generation because of its effect on the children. By the time slum children are age six or seven they have usually absorbed the basic values and attitudes of their subculture and are not psychologically geared to take full advantage of changing conditions or increased opportunities which may occur in their lifetime.* [3]

From Lewis's perspective, the poor are clearly prolonging their own impoverishment. As evidence, he identified no less than seventy behavioral traits that distinguish the poor, including little use of banks or museums and nonparticipation in labor unions. Although he acknowledges that the poor may be aware of, and even profess, middle-class values, he regards their aberrant behavior as proof that they do not share those values.

Other sociologists and anthropologists have been quick to follow Lewis's lead. Another popular diagnosis of the poor, for example, focuses on their alleged self-indulgence. Out of Lewis's more general depiction of lower-class culture, other observers claim to perceive a pattern of nondeferred gratification: whereas the middle-class person supposedly feels the need and desire to save, postpone, and renounce certain immediate pleasures, the poor person is alleged to experience no such motivations. This alleged impulse following is presumed to be embedded in the personality dynamics of the poor individual, thus obstructing his self-improvement.

This pattern of self-indulgence is additionally presumed to have strong intergenerational effects. Self-indulgent parents have little interest in their children's futures, thus contributing to further poverty. As one observer has asserted:

> *Where middle and upper class parents think in terms of a college education for their offspring, lower class parents' aspirations usually stop at a high school diploma, at the very best. Poor parents, with little education, are more likely to believe in luck than in education and to be contemptuous of "book learning".... Indeed, among low-income families, both the low educational attainments of the head of the household and the quality of family life create a social environment that leads the poor to believe that "education is not for them."* [4]

[3] Oscar Lewis, *La Vida* (New York: Random House, Inc., 1966), p. xiv.
[4] Oscar Ornati, *Poverty Amid Affluence* (New York: The Twentieth Century Fund, 1966), p. 66.

A Question of Opportunities

Not all sociologists, of course, share these views of lower-class culture. On the contrary, much recent sociological discussion has focused on some of the basic weaknesses in the culture of poverty thesis. It has been pointed out, for example, that the attribution of cultural differences based on the observation of behavioral differences incorporates many assumptions of questionable validity. Within the subject area of deferred gratification, the following conditions must be fulfilled before a valid inference about differential values can be made.

1. The satisfaction being deferred must be equally important to the poor and nonpoor.
2. There must exist equal opportunity to defer the satisfaction.
3. The poor and nonpoor must equally suffer from deferment.
4. The probability of obtaining gratification at the end of the deferment period must be equal for both groups.

If any or all of these conditions are violated, then behavioral differences may be explained by situational differences, by differences in opportunity; no reference to alleged cultural phenomena is necessary.

The case of educational attainment illustrates some of the foregoing conditions. The children of the poor undeniably drop out of school earlier than other children. But does this behavioral difference reflect cultural orientations? Schools in lower-income areas are notoriously ill-equipped to transmit interest, enjoyment, or ability in the learning process. Hence, the third and fourth conditions in our list are violated: middle-class school experience is both more pleasant and more profitable. Furthermore, the low-income family cannot afford to support a child's education for as long as a middle-class family: thus, the second condition is violated also. Given these inequalities in opportunity, it might be equally valid to conclude that the poor value education *more* highly than the nonpoor because of the greater sacrifices they make to get as far as they do.

A similar array of qualifications to the "impulse following" hypothesis is encountered when saving behavior is considered. The poor save less money less often than the nonpoor. Does this reflect a present-time orientation (as contrasted with a future-time orientation)? Perhaps not. The poor have very little to save in the first place. Whatever they do manage to put aside represents a real sacrifice in terms of present consumption. Hence, there is no foundation for inferring cultural inadequacies on the basis of observed differences in spending.

The central weakness of the culture of poverty proposition, then, is the assumption that behavioral differences between the poor and nonpoor reflect differences in goals and aspirations. In reality, the poor do not have an equal opportunity to fulfill, or even to pursue, their goals. Hence, there is a sharp divergence between the aspirations and the behavior of the poor that does not exist among middle-class groups. With more equal opportunities for achievement, there is a strong presumption that the entire foundation of the culture of poverty thesis would disintegrate. At the very least, we may say that the cultural thesis rests on a very uncertain foundation until that equality of opportunity is fully achieved.

If testimony of the poor themselves is valid, there is little reason to believe that behavioral patterns of the poor will remain the same under improved socioeconomic conditions. Welfare mothers, for example, express a strong desire to see their children attain better social and economic positions. Moreover, they perceive clearly—more so than many academic observers—the great divergence between their aspirations and their actual opportunities. One survey, for example, questioned welfare mothers about both their desires and their expectations for their children's employment. The responses, portrayed in Table 8.1, are illuminating. Seventy percent of the mothers have white-collar aspirations for their eldest child, yet only 46 percent have any expectation that their children will attain this status. (Even fewer actually do.) Hence, the lower occupational status of poor children apparently does not reflect their parents' aspirations so much as it reflects the opportunities of the poor.

TABLE 8.1   *WELFARE MOTHERS' DESIRES AND EXPECTATIONS FOR ELDEST CHILD'S OCCUPATIONAL STATUS (percent)*

Occupation	Desire	Expectation
Professional and managerial	48	27
Clerical	22	19
Craft	8	8
Police, army	2	6
Other paid work	6	14
Housewife	1	4
Don't know	13	23

Source: Lawrence Podell, *Families on Welfare in New York City* (New York: City University of New York Press, 1968), Tables 7-C and 7-D.

Other studies have come to similar conclusions regarding work orientations and other dimensions of "culture." When poor families are compared to nonpoor families of the same ethnic background (e.g., white, black, Hispanic), no significant cultural differences appear.[5] This conclusion also applies to

[5]See, for example, Barbara Coward, Joe Feagin, and J. Allen Williams, Jr., "The Culture of Poverty Debate: Some Additional Data," *Social Problems,* June 1974; Chandler Davidson and Charles Gaitz, "Are the Poor Different?: A Comparison of Work Behavior and Attitudes Among the Urban Poor and Nonpoor," *Social Problems,* December 1974; also Roberta H. Jackson, "Some Aspirations of Lower Class Black Mothers," Journal of Comparative Family Studies, Autumn 1975.

welfare recipients. After reviewing available studies of work attitudes and behavior of welfare mothers, Leonard Goodwin concluded that "welfare recipients do not differ markedly from other Americans with respect to general personality characteristics or with respect to the work ethic and basic life goals."[6]

If their aspirations and values were really as different as some observers claim, then the poor should be satisfied with their standard of living and resistant to new opportunity. Many modern cultural theorists argue, in fact, that the poor are content and unable to progress. (Similar arguments were once employed in defense of slavery.) Such views are not consistent with reality. Not only have organized groups of the poor repeatedly expressed their discontent, but the poor have demonstrated a marked ability to move out of poverty when economic opportunities improved (see Chapter 2).

Even the most adamant exponents of the culture of poverty do not argue, of course, that all persons in poverty are psychodynamically attached to impoverishment. Oscar Lewis himself estimated that only 20 percent of the poor in America are culturally bound to poverty. Walter Miller, another advocate of the culture of poverty position, does not specify what proportion of the poor are so afflicted but warns that the proportion is rising. Nevertheless, the basis for these propositions is no stronger than that for the rest of the theory.

Among the 25 million people who were poor in 1977, there were, no doubt, some individuals whose aspirations were extraordinarily low. Many (e.g., discouraged workers) may even have succumbed to a fatalistic attitude regarding their condition and future prospects, thus diminishing their ability to exploit new opportunities. It cannot be assumed, however, that this fatalism emerged from a cultural orientation or that it is totally impervious to changing circumstances. Yet it is on these assumptions that the culture of poverty theory rests. To the extent that some of the poor do believe their chances for advancement to be negligible, new opportunities will be grasped with hesitancy. The more the poor have experienced repeated failure and disappointment, the more skeptically they will respond to new policy initiatives. This does not necessarily imply cultural dissonance; it may very well be a rational response based on prior experience.

THE RACIAL INFERIORITY THEORY

Poor blacks are apt to appear particularly constrained by "cultural" patterns. They have been extended more new promises more often than any other group among the poor. Some promises of improved opportunity were well-

---

[6]Leonard Goodwin, "What Has Been Learned from the Work Incentive Program and Related Experiences: A Review of Research with Policy Implications." (Worchester, Mass.: Worcester Polytechnic Institute, 1977), p. 31.

intentioned, others were not; many remain unfulfilled. Many poor blacks respond accordingly—with cynicism and hesitancy—when still further promises and programs are offered. Unfortunately, whites tend to regard this absence of unbridled enthusiasm as additional evidence that blacks lack aspiration.

A distinctive cultural pattern is not the only explanation offered to explain black poverty by those who view previous policy initiatives and present opportunities to be ample, even generous. In addition to the culture allegation, many whites continue to regard the inferior socioeconomic position of blacks as a natural consequence of racial disabilities. In this section, the nature and basis of such racially based perspectives are examined.

In 1977 mean family income among black Americans was $12,000, while among white Americans the median was $19,000. As we have already seen, nearly one out of every three blacks was poor, while only one out of eleven whites was so disadvantaged. Hence, there is no question about whether a link exists between race and poverty; instead, we are concerned with the causal nature of the established link. Furthermore, in discussing the causal association between race and poverty, we need not worry about the circular kinds of relationships that attracted our attention earlier. Whereas poverty may lead to ill health, broken families, or more children, there is no prospect of poverty changing people's skin color. Accordingly, both the existence of a link and the direction of causality are known: being black does lead to poverty.

The causal path leading from race to poverty may be explained in two ways. It can be argued that inherent racial disabilities limit income-earning abilities. This, of course, is the racial argument that has arisen before. Another possible explanation for the established path emanates from the alleged existence of discrimination. By this argument, blacks are more apt to be poor, not because of differential physical, mental, or cultural capacities, but because they are treated differently by society. Whites have no difficulty in choosing between the alternative explanations of black status: the president's National Advisory Commission on Civil Disorders discovered that white Americans favor the racial explanation three to one. As recently as 1978, 1 out of 2 white Americans asserted that blacks have less ambition than whites. Fewer than 1 out of 6 whites saw racial discrimination as a serious problem.[7] Accordingly, we postpone a discussion of the discrimination argument until Chapters 10 and 11.

The thesis of racial inferiority is not new. Aristotle, for example, used it to explain Greek superiority over the European barbarians. Still later, the barbarians, who by then had produced Shakespeare, Kant, and Newton, used this argument to explain their superiority over the Greeks. Later still, English intellectuals were predicting that America would never achieve greatness

---

[7]Louis Harris and Associates, a study of attitudes toward racial and religious minorities and toward women. (New York: National Conference of Christians and Jews, 1978).

because its colonies were heavily populated by the rejected and inferior classes of Europe.

Despite the somewhat dismal record of racial theories, they remain popular. Among the most quoted proponents of a racial explanation of black socioeconomic status in America is Dr. William Shockley. Shockley is an inventor of the transistor and a recipient of the Nobel Prize in Physics. As he explained to the National Academy of Sciences in 1969: "The major deficit in Negro intellectual performance must be primarily of hereditary origin and thus relatively irremediable by practical improvements in the environment." In other words, blacks are poor because they are not smart enough, and they are not smart enough due to racial heredity.

Shockley is a rather extreme adherent of the racial inferiority thesis, but he is not alone in his beliefs about innate racial differences. Such beliefs are a common component of racial prejudice and linger on in the minds of many. They even acquire a certain plausibility for most people because of the demonstrated link between genetic characteristics and achievement: nearly everyone accepts the notion that smarter people do better and get further. Such a notion leads easily to the position that blacks fare poorly because they are not as smart as whites. The argument is easily extended to Puerto Ricans, Mexican Americans, American Indians, and other poor minorities.

Intelligence and Status

What keeps the racial inferiority debate going (aside from ingrained prejudices) is the fact that intelligence is an unobservable dimension of an individual's genetic endowment. Although we all give nodding agreement to the notion that mental capacities, like physical capacities, are inherited, we have no direct way of weighing or measuring that inheritance. Accordingly, we depend largely on inferential reasoning to provide us with clues about the relationship of intelligence to economic status. Unfortunately, such reasoning often turns out to be circular. We have all heard statements like "Wow! John made a fortune in the dry cleaning business; I never realized he was so smart." From this perspective, the true test of intelligence is a person's tax return. According to this test, poverty *must* be explained by a lack of intelligence. If blacks tend to be poorer than whites, their plight must be explained in the same way.

Fortunately, our knowledge of the relationship between intelligence and economic status does not depend exclusively on such superficial reasoning. We know, for example, that identical twins inherit identical genes, and thus identical intelligence (even if we cannot measure that intelligence). Accordingly, if genetic endowments are important for economic status, identical twins should end up with the same status. And they tend to. A study by English sociologists determined that even when they are separated and reared in different environments, identical twins attain very similar socio-economic statuses. Such observations confirm the significance of inherited abilities, at least for differences among *individuals.*

To demonstrate that genetic abilities are important for economic status does not deny the existence of environmental influences, however. In the studies of English twins, varying environments were shown to have *some* effect on achievement. Those effects would be still stronger where environmental differences were greater. The Osage Indians in America provide a dramatic illustration: not only achievements, but even measured IQ, increased substantially after the tribe discovered oil!

A broader understanding of human achievement recognizes that both genetic and environmental factors influence the attainments of individuals and puts the issue of racial differences in an entirely different setting. Because blacks and whites in America live in distinct areas and under different conditions, racial abilities alone cannot explain disparities in economic status. To the extent that differences in racial abilities exist at all, we are led to inquire what *proportion* of observed status disparities can be attributed to them. In logical order, then, we must focus on three separate questions:

1. Do genetic differences exist between whites and blacks?
2. If so, how large are any such differences?
3. What is the relative significance of any such differences for observed socio-economic status?

Very little interest attaches to the question of physical differences between whites and blacks, at least as far as socioeconomic status is involved. Instead, the issue of genetic differences focuses on the relative mental abilities of the two races. The first question, then, really asks whether whites are innately more intelligent than blacks.

IQ Scores

Because we have no way of directly measuring intelligence we cannot answer the foregoing questions directly. Instead, we must first find some independent indicator of intelligence, then test for differences among people on this basis. This is where IQ tests come in: an IQ score indicates how well an individual has performed on a standardized test relative to others of the same age. An IQ score of 100 indicates that one has performed up to average, while higher or lower scores indicate above- or below-average performance. There are a variety of such tests available, but all incorporate exercises of perceptual, verbal, arithmetical, and reasoning abilities.

Since the nineteenth century there have been literally hundreds of research studies directed toward measuring the relative IQs of blacks and whites. All of them have demonstrated that blacks, on average, score lower on intelligence tests than whites. The average difference between whites and blacks amounts to 15 to 20 IQ points, indicating that the typical black has an IQ of 80 to 85. These figures are now widely accepted; what is still debated is how they should be interpreted.

Basically, an IQ test measures various kinds of performance abilities, such as perception, memory, and verbal knowledge. Accordingly, it is subject to the influences of both genetic intelligence and environmental experience. A child who has never seen a giraffe or a waterfall, for example, has difficulty identifying them in an IQ examination, whatever his native intelligence may be. Because IQ scores incorporate both environmental and genetic experiences, there is no easy method for isolating genetic factors. All we can say with assurance is that IQ differences reflect genetic differences when administered to children who have shared very similar environmental experiences. Clearly, black and white children do not satisfy this condition.

The nature of IQ-score determinants suggests that black and white IQ scores could be brought into harmony by appropriate environmental changes. In fact, studies that have attempted to control for such differences by testing black and white children from similar backgrounds have narrowed the average IQ score difference to as little as five points. Black children adopted by white parents have also scored higher on IQ tests. Other research has demonstrated that the IQ test performances of blacks and whites move further apart the longer they are maintained in unequal situations—ghetto schools, for example. Accordingly, it appears that there is nothing natural or unchangeable in any observed racial pattern of IQ scores.

Further evidence of environmental impact on IQ scores is provided by the variation in these scores for individuals and groups. We have already noted the effect of oil discoveries for the Osage Indians. For the country as a whole, IQ scores have been rising consistently over the last fifty years. This suggests either that we are breeding selectively or that IQ scores are subject to environmental improvement (and perhaps even familiarity with testing procedures). More to our point, it has also been observed that black children moving from rural to urban areas raise their IQ scores significantly, reflecting an improved environment. Still other studies have shown that intensive teaching and supportive environments can materially improve the IQ scores of any group, even mentally retarded children! And finally, it has been demonstrated that improving the diets of poor expectant mothers results in higher IQ scores for their children.

Resolving the Issues

The relationship between intelligence, IQ scores, and economic status is summarized in Figure 8.1 Notice that IQ scores and economic status are directly affected by intelligence. But notice also that both IQ scores and

FIGURE 8.1   Intelligence, IQ, and Economic Status

economic status are influenced by environmental factors as well. Accordingly, any demonstrated link between IQ and status may be explained by environmental forces alone. At least we may be certain that differences in IQ scores and status are less likely to reflect intelligence differences the greater are the environmental differences between the two individuals or groups in question. And this turns out to be an important qualification when comparing blacks and whites in America.

With figure 8.1 and our previous discussion to guide us, we may proceed to answer the three questions we posed before. First, we may note that there is no basis for concluding that there exist genetic differences in intelligence between blacks and whites. This conclusion emerges from the fact that we do not really know what intelligence is and from the observation that the test scores we use to measure intelligence are themselves subject to environmental influence. We could just as easily assert that blacks are *more* intelligent than whites as the reverse. Indeed, many people argue that the entire search for an *explanation* of IQ differences is misplaced and racist. If IQ scores don't measure intelligence, then there is no white-black gap to explain.[8] In the absence of any evidence to the contrary, it seems most reasonable to conclude that there are no such genetic differences between the two racial groups.

Even if one were to adhere adamantly to the position that IQ scores accurately reflect intelligence, there would still be little basis for attributing the inferior economic status of blacks to genetic deficiencies. At most, such an argument would have to rely on the average IQ score difference of five to ten points obtained in controlled tests. It would be extremely difficult, if not outright comic, to suggest that this difference could account for an existing income disparity of nearly $4,000 a year. One would then be arguing that a 5 or 10 percent difference in intelligence could account for a 35 percent disparity in income. One would also be arguing that status differences were not at all affected by differences in opportunities. Hence, even the unfounded assertion that genetic differences do exist between blacks and whites leads to the conclusion that such differences are of relatively minor significance for observed socioeconomic status.

[8]See James Cronin et al, "Race, Class, and Intelligence: A Critical Look at the IQ Controversy," *International Journal of Mental Health,* Winter 1975; also Cedric X. (Clark), "The Shockley-Jensen Thesis: A Contextual Appraisal," *The Black Scholar,* July 1975.

Other Weaknesses of the Racial Doctrine

The foregoing observations demonstrate the essential weaknesses in the doctrine of racial inferiority. The evidence presented has been rather technical, but there are even simpler inconsistencies in the doctrine that discredit racial theories of black poverty. To begin with, blacks do not fare equally well or poorly in all regions of the country. For the nation as a whole, black incomes in 1977 were 68 percent as large as white incomes. In the South, however, they were only 60 percent as large, while in the West, 70 percent. Hence, to argue that genetic disabilities account for status disparities would require one to argue that western blacks are genetically better equipped than southern blacks.

A similar problem arises with the rise in black status over time. In the last ten years, black incomes have risen considerably relative to white incomes. A theory of racial determination would be compelled to explain this development on the basis of improving genetic abilities among blacks or declining genetic potential among whites.

Finally, and most damaging to the doctrine of racial superiority, is the concept of *race* itself. There is not, and never has been, a clear understanding of what the term race means, or for that matter, of how many races exist. As an English zoologist has noted, "geneticists believe anthropologists know what a race is, ethnologists assume their racial classifications are backed up by genetics, and politicians believe that their prejudices have the sanction of both genetics and anthropology."[9] In the resultant confusion, anywhere from three to thirty separate races have been identified at various times. In the American context, the term is used interchangeably to refer to religious, national, or ethnic groups. In the context of the immediate discussion, the term refers basically to skin color. Given the history of miscegenation in America, no one could conceivably argue that there exist distinctive pure white and black genetic characteristics: it is estimated that over 90 percent of American blacks have some white ancestry. Hence, American blacks hardly comprise a suitable test for racial theories of inherent differences.

Interestingly enough, adherents to the racial doctrine have attempted to employ this phenomenon of miscegenation to their advantage. They argue that the success of mulattos is due to the presence of "white" genes, which improve their intellectual endowments, and that such success proves the thesis of racial superiority. The argument is also used to explain rising black status over time. The evidence presented, however, is exceedingly weak. Mulattos apparently did fare relatively better than "pure" blacks during and shortly after the slave era, but children of mixed parentage were often favored by their white father-masters. Thus, they received greater opportunity and support. Other research has shown that more successful blacks today do not differ in

[9]Anthony Smith, *The Body* (New York: Walker and Company, 1968), p. 14.

112

patterns of white ancestry. Moreover, the highest black IQ score yet reported, 200, was attained by a child who had no traceable white heritage whatsoever. Hence, whatever the other virtues and liabilities of miscegenation may be, its effects on genetic abilities appear to be negligible.

SUMMARY

Theories of poverty causation based on cultural or racial phenomena have long commanded a certain acceptability. In part, they are based on prejudices of the nonpoor against the poor and, in part, on the confidence with which the nonpoor perceive economic opportunity to exist for all. Since the earliest days of colonization it has been asserted that anyone with enough stamina and initiative could succeed in America. Accordingly, those who did not succeed have been regarded variously as immoral, culturally apart, or racially inferior. This chapter has considered the latter two allegations and examined the direct evidence on which they are based.

The argument that the poor do not possess enough aspiration and initiative to raise themselves out of poverty rests on misconceptions rather than factual evidence. Divergent behavioral patterns, in themselves, do not prove the existence of divergent aspirations and goals; instead, they may well represent rational responses to continuing inopportune circumstances. Hence, the sometimes different behavior of the poor, in the areas of saving, education, and job acquisition, for example, may reflect great aspirations equally as well as it does small aspirations. Direct research on the goals and ambitions of the poor suggest that they share middle-class goals and await improved opportunities to pursue them.

Allegations about racial disabilities suffer equally from misconception and prejudice. There is no basis for concluding that differences in intelligence exist between whites and blacks. Not only do we not yet know what intelligence is, but the instruments we assume to measure it yield ambiguous results. Moreover, even the most extreme assumptions about the meaning and reliability of observed IQ scores would still lead to the conclusion that genetic factors are of negligible significance in explaining the existing economic disparities between whites and blacks.

FURTHER READING

On Culture

CAMERON, COLIN, *Attitudes of the Poor and Attitudes toward the Poor: An Annotated Bibliography.* Madison, Wis.: Institute for Research on Poverty, 1975.

DUNCAN, GREG, AND DANIEL HILL, "Attitudes, Behavior and Economic Outcomes: A Structural Equations Approach," in *Five Thousand American Families: Patterns of Economic Progress,* Greg Duncan and James Morgan, eds. Ann Arbor: Mich.: Institute for Social Research, vol. III, 1975.

GOODWIN, LEONARD, *Do the Poor Want to Work?* Washington, D.C.: The Brookings Institution, 1972.

LEWIS, OSCAR, *La Vida.* New York: Random House, Inc., 1966.

LIEBOW, ELLIOT, *Tally's Corner: A Study of Negro Streetcorner Men.* Boston: Little, Brown and Company, 1967.

WINTER, J. ALAN, ed., *The Poor: A Culture of Poverty or a Poverty of Culture.* Grand Rapids, Mich.: Wm. B. Eerdmans Publishing Co., 1971.

On Race

CARTWRIGHT, WALTER J., AND THOMAS R. BURTIS, "Race and Intelligence: Changing Opinions in Social Science," *Social Science Quarterly,* December 1968, pp. 603-18.

CLARK, CEDRIC X., "The Shockley-Jensen Thesis: A Contextual Appraisal," *The Black Scholar,* July 1975.

HARVARD EDUCATIONAL REVIEW, Winter, Spring, and Summer issues, 1969.

HERRNSTEIN, RICHARD, "I.Q.," *The Atlantic Monthly,* September 1971, pp. 43–64.

HUNT, MORTON, "The Intelligent Man's Guide to Intelligence," *Playboy.* November 1970, p. 94.

MYRDAL, GUNNAR, *An American Dilemma.* New York: Harper & Row, Publishers, 1962, Chs. 4–6.

RICHARDSON, KEN, AND DAVID SPEARS, eds., *Race and Intelligence.* New York: Penguin Books, 1972.

SOWELL, THOMAS, *Race and Economics.* New York: David McKay Co., Inc., 1975.

9 EDUCATION AND ABILITY

The empirical relationship between education and ability on the one hand and economic status on the other are essential components of American folklore. In fact, the observations that "to get ahead, get an education" and "you can't keep a good man down" have acquired the aura of ideological convictions. Everyone has heard of Horatio Alger, and no one doubts that doctors get rich. Conditioned by these examples and mindful of their own security, Americans react accordingly. Middle-class parents begin preparing their children for college soon after birth, and the children themselves learn to regard success as the reward to virtue, ability, and good grades in school. By the same token, those who do not succeed are regarded as less virtuous, less able, or less diligent in the pursuit of education. From this perspective, lack of ability or education emerges as an important cause of poverty. The distribution of poverty even acquires a democratic flavor, as it is also presumed that the development of abilities and education is largely a matter of individual choice.

The conviction that education and ability lead to material success is not easily challenged. Few persons even pause to reflect on the nature and reliability of the underlying associations. With educated people moving ahead all around them, how many individuals can take the time and effort to question the pace of events? Nevertheless, the implied importance of education for the existence of poverty demands that such an inquiry be made. Our discussion focuses on two issues: (1) whether educational achievement determines *who* is poor; and (2) whether the level of educational achievement determines *how many* people are poor. The same questions are asked of the relationship between ability and poverty.

EDUCATION AND INCOME

The conviction that more education leads to higher income finds extensive support in statistical data. The simple correlation between educational attainment and income is very strong and consistent: more years of education *do* lead to higher income. In 1977, for example, men with no more than eight years of schooling had an average income of only $8,505; high school dropouts commanded an average of $9,292; high school graduates had incomes of $12,092; and college graduates had average incomes above $20,223. Hence. there is an impressive foundation to the belief that education pays.

The relationship between education and income is equally effective in separating the poor from the nonpoor. The typical nonpoor family head has a high school diploma, while the average poor family head has completed fewer than nine years of school. This disparity in educational attainment is reflected in the incidence of poverty. As Table 9.1 confirms, the likelihood of impoverishment declines rapidly as a person scales the educational ladder. Only one out of thirty people who had attended college ended up in poverty in 1977, while more than one out of seven high school dropouts were so misfortunate.

TABLE 9.1   INCIDENCE OF POVERTY, BY EDUCATION OF HEAD OF FAMILY, 1977

Education	Number in Poverty	Incidence of Poverty (%)
Elementary school	1,860,000	18.0
High school dropout	1,209,000	14.7
High school graduate	1,334,000	6.9
College (1 year or more)	568,000	3.2

Source: U.S. Bureau of the Census.

Higher educational attainment contributes to income in several ways. It increases a person's productivity (his human capital) by expanding his knowledge and skills. Prospective employers also tend to regard educational degrees as proof of commendable diligence. Diplomas, regardless of their content, are likely to provide access to more jobs. Educational institutions may also serve as job placement services, providing employers and students with ready access to each other. The combination of these factors suggests that the person who stays in school longer will be treated and will perform differently in the labor market. Educational attainment affects every facet of labor market success. A person's participation in the labor force, his or her occupation, the frequency of his and her employment, the number of hours worked, and the wage rate received are all affected by the schooling the person has achieved. In conjunction, these factors determine an individual's income.

People with little education are least likely to get and hold a job. If they do obtain jobs, they are first to be laid off by employers as production schedules change. With fewer skills and credentials, their ability to acquire other jobs will be restricted. Consequently, they are apt to be unemployed far more often and for longer periods than those with greater educational attainments. In 1977, male high school dropouts experienced a 13.4 unemployment rate, while high school and college graduates confronted unemployment rates of 7.2 and 2.1, respectively (Table 9.2).

TABLE 9.2   EDUCATION AND THE LABOR MARKET, 1977*

	High School Dropouts	High School Graduates	College Graduates
Unemployment rates (%)	13.4%	7.2%	3.7%
Labor force participation (%)	67.6	85.4	85.9
Full-time workers (%)	74.9	89.7	90.6
Occupational status	Blue collar	Clerical	Professional
Average earnings	$9,291	$12,092	$20,223

* For full-time male workers aged sixteen and over.

Source: U.S. Department of Labor.

As was noted in Chapter 4, long and repeated spells of unemployment may induce people to leave the labor force altogether. Frustrated by lack of employment opportunities, they may give up the job search, relying instead on public or private financial assistance. Few men can, however, resign themselves to nonparticipation, in part because available social and financial supports are extremely limited. Nevertheless, the impact of educational attainment is discernible in the relevant statistics. Whereas 85 percent of all male high school and college graduates participate in the labor force, only 68 percent of high school dropouts do so.

Getting and holding a job does not guarantee financial success, of course. At least as important are the nature of the job one obtains, how many hours one works, and what wage one is paid. On all these fronts, the less educated individual fares poorly. High school dropouts are disproportionately concentrated in the blue-collar occupations as unskilled laborers, operatives, service workers, and craftsmen. By contrast, high school graduates are most heavily concentrated in the lower white-collar occupations, at the clerical and sales levels, for example, and in the higher blue-collar positions. College graduates crowd the professional and managerial classes and are virtually nonexistent in the lowest job categories.

The cumulative impact of these labor market phenomena is to differentiate sharply the incomes of the lesser- and greater-educated. As we have already noted, the income differences amount to thousands of dollars a year. Over a lifetime, this disparity reaches tremendous proportions. During their careers, high school graduates can anticipate earning $125,000 more than high school dropouts, while college graduates will earn $340,000 more than high school graduates before they retire.

Education and the Distribution
of Income

The weight of accumulated evidence on the association between income and education reinforces the belief that inadequate education is a major cause of poverty. It appears obvious, at this point, that the least educated will bring the least amount of human capital to the labor market and will therefore receive the least income. From this perspective poverty can be explained by a failure to stay in school, by underinvestment in one's own human capital.[1] Before fully accepting this interpretation, however, several additional issues must be considered.

Even if, on average, better-educated individuals can earn more money, it does not follow that all persons with more schooling will have higher incomes. No one has seriously suggested that education is the *only* determinant of income. Inherent ability, inherited wealth, geographical location, discrimination, economic conditions, and simple luck will all influence a person's income opportunities. Hence, we want to determine how consistent the relationship is between education and income and how much poverty can be explained by education alone.

The relationship between education and income is far from perfect. Indeed, the labor market rewards the educational attainments of some people much more handsomely than the attainments of others. Consider Figure 9.1, for example: each step up the educational ladder clearly improves the incomes of both blacks and whites. Even more striking, however, is the gross disparity shown on the graphs that exists between white and black males. A black college graduate, for example, earns on average little more ($12,649) than a white high school graduate ($12,633); while a white high school dropout earns more ($9,735) than a black high school graduate ($9,147). Whatever benefits education provides, they are clearly not equally accessible to all. Hence, if lack of education is regarded as an explanation for poverty, it must be recognized at the outset that that explanation is not complete.

The same kind of disparity can be observed between men and women (see Figure 9.2). Women college graduates earn significantly less on average ($8,160) than men who complete just eight years of school ($8,640). Moreover, the average male high school dropout commands an income ($12,309) that is higher than all groups of women, including those who have attended graduate school. Again, it is obvious that the rewards for educational achievement, while perhaps large, are not distributed evenly.

It is not difficult to find explanations for the income disparities that exist between races and sexes. Some of these are discussed more thoroughly in Chapters 10 and 11. For present purposes, we may confine ourselves to the

---

[1] The link of this perspective with cultural theories of poverty (Chapter 8) should be apparent.

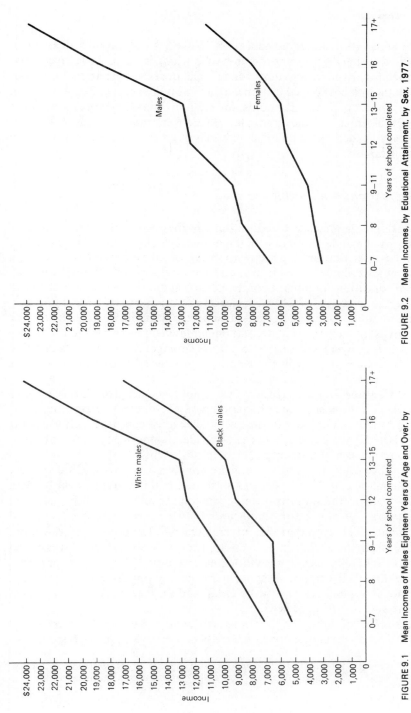

FIGURE 9.1   Mean Incomes of Males Eighteen Years of Age and Over, by Educational Attainment, by Race, 1977.

Source: U.S. Bureau of the Census.

FIGURE 9.2   Mean Incomes, by Eduational Attainment, by Sex, 1977.

Source: U.S. Bureau of the Census.

simple observation that more education, in itself, is no guarantee of escaping poverty. Keeping some poor persons in school longer may not effectively raise their incomes. Even in situations where racial or sexual discrimination is not present, the link between education and income is not perfect. There are over a million white high school dropouts, for example, who earn more money than one out of three college graduates. Moreover, there are more families in poverty headed by white male high school graduates than by white high school dropouts.

Education as a Sorting Device

The full significance of education for the distribution and extent of poverty can be understood only in the framework of the entire labor market. As we have seen, observing the relationship of average incomes to average educational attainments can lead to erroneous impressions about the importance of education. Within the context of any labor market situation there exists a certain quantity of job vacancies and so many prospective employees. When the number of vacancies falls far short of the number of job-seekers, the economy is in a depressed state, and unemployment rates are high. This implies that employers will be able to choose among many applicants in filling any job vacancy. How will the employer proceed? That is, on what basis should he or will he make his selection?

In Chapter 4, we suggested that employers will tend to select new employees on the basis of their human capital, their potential contribution to output. And in some cases, the process of selection is comparatively simple. If the job is highly technical, it may be easy to identify the most competent applicants on the basis of tests or prior accomplishments.

But differences in human capital are not always large or easily observed, compelling the employer to depend on some amount of guesswork. In these cases—probably the majority—employers come to rely on only a few selection criteria, one of the most important of which is usually educational attainment.[2] The employer has several reasons for separating the more educated from the less educated in the application process. First, it is assumed that more schooling usually results in greater ability. Then, too, the employer may feel that perseverance in school merits greater opportunity. And finally, educational minimums constitute a cheap and easy means for holding down the time and cost of interviewing.

The effect of these considerations is to transform educational credentials such as a high school diploma into admission tickets for job interviews, espe-

---

[2]Other important criteria are race and sex, implying that otherwise qualified blacks and women will gain access to jobs only after available white males have been hired (see Chapter 11).

cially in times of high unemployment. The recession of 1971 amply illustrated how selective employers can become; consider this help-wanted ad from the Austin, Texas, *American:*

> TOPLESS DANCERS. Must have two years college. Prefer English major, languages or humanities. [3]

From the standpoint of this employer, all prospective go-go girls are in competition for available jobs, and educational attainments separate the finalists from the rejects. Other employers are likely to react similarly when jobs are scarce. Hence, even though a high school dropout, for example, could easily perform the responsibilites of, say, a salesclerk, he is not given the opportunity if high school graduates are also available. As a consequence, he remains unemployed and poor.

The implications of this selection process for the relationship of education to poverty are profound. Quite obviously, the distribution of education will have a significant impact on the distribution of poverty. As a rule, those with the least education will end up in poverty. This will be especially true among otherwise similar labor market, racial, and sexual groups. But what about the extent of poverty? Will education have a similar influence in determining how many persons are poor?

Consider again the case of the high school dropout seeking the job of salesclerk. If he had a high school diploma, his competitive position would undoubtedly be stronger. But would his graduation, by itself, contribute to an increase in the number of such jobs available? Clearly not. His graduation may enable him to compete successfully for the available job, but his success will leave someone else unemployed. If there is only one job and four applicants, no amount of educational improvement or redistribution will succeed in leaving fewer than three persons unemployed. Education may influence who gets the available jobs, but the demand for labor will determine how many jobs there are (recall Figure 4.1, illustrating the interaction of market demand and supply).

Confusion about the causal significance of education comes from the failure to distinguish between individual and group needs, or, as an economist would say, between micro and macro phenomena. Observing that individual incomes are related to educational attainments leads easily to the supposition that raising the educational attainments of all the poor will eliminate poverty. Yet, bestowing a high school diploma, or even a Ph.D., on all the poor will do little to alter the number or kinds of jobs available. A few more vacancies might be filled, but the greatest impact would be to alter the composition of the poor and to raise their educational attainments. By itself, such an effort would do little to reduce the extent of poverty.

[3]Cited in *Playboy*, December 1971, p. 26.

The Content of Education

The foregoing discussion has said nothing about the content of education. Instead, the term has been used to refer to schooling in general. Accordingly, some of the most vital and controversial issues relevant to the education-income nexus have been neglected. Among the more salient of those issues are the questions of how much vocational content should be offered in school curricula and who should provide it. Training in specific skills might be especially valuable to those who are not going to pursue higher education. Greater earning potential could be generated by simply restructuring educational curricula rather than by extending them.

Of even greater importance for policy consideration is the question of access to education. Because educational attainments significantly determine who will be poor in any given economic situation, we must also determine who receives the necessary credentials and why. Some consideration of these issues is taken up in Chapters 10 and 11. For the present, we may note that neither the issue of educational content nor of access materially alters the conclusions cited above. Regardless of what is taught or who it is taught to, education, of itself, can do very little to alter the number of jobs available at any given moment.[4]

ABILITY AND INCOME

Ability, like education, is presumed to be an important determinant of income. In fact, it is generally deemed desirable for the distribution of incomes to reflect the distribution of productive abilities. We are accustomed to thinking that greater ability merits richer rewards and, indeed, that material success manifests ability. It is, of course, possible to question the idea that income *should* reflect ability. Why, for example, should a man who inherits the capacity to learn to steer rockets through space command a higher income than the man who is born with the capacity to learn to drive buses? Are justice and equity any better served when rewards are distributed according to inherited genes rather than according to inherited dollars?

In Chapter 8, we encountered some of the difficulties that engulf discussions of individual ability. The term *ability*, as it is commonly employed, incorporates elements of both innate capacity and developed performance. Accordingly, there is a certain vagueness in the question whether the income distribution reflects the ability distribution. If we mean to refer to innate abilities, then we really have no means for answering the question because we

---

[4]Over a longer period of time rising educational attainments may increase national productivity and employment, however, even if there is little immediate impact on the level of poverty.

do not know precisely what innate abilities are or how to measure them. However, if we look only at developed performance, we must recognize that we are departing from the pattern of innate abilities, as all individuals do not share equal opportunity to develop their capacities. Hence, an income distribution based on performance abilities may not meet our standards of equity.

Another problem with the measurement of performance ability is the fact that no single, all-inclusive performance criterion exists. The ability to sing or to run is distributed differently from the ability to solve complex mathematical problems. There are literally hundreds, if not thousands, of varied abilities, all distributed uniquely among the population. It is an impossible task to determine whether incomes accurately reflect even performance ability. At most, one could assert that the distribution of incomes reflects the distribution of abilities valued highly in the marketplace. But even that cautious assertion masks a tautology. One could assert that *any* income distribution reflects the same thing. There is no means for determining whether a given income distribution departs from the distribution of abilities. In the face of this impasse, we are accustomed to proceed in reverse. That is, we gauge the distribution of abilities by inference from the distribution of incomes: people with more money are *assumed* to be more able. In this way the income distribution becomes a justification unto itself.

In view of these considerations, it is apparent that we have little basis for assessing objectively the fairness or appropriateness of any existing income distribution. At most, we may simply observe how well the distribution reflects certain specific kinds of attainments or characteristics. We must then resort to our own values to determine how appropriate these criteria are and how equitably they are reflected in incomes. The inherent subjectivity of this approach does not render it impracticable, but it does make consensus difficult.

Two kinds of abilities continue to attract the most attention in discussions of income distribution—measured IQ and educational attainment. IQ is of interest both because it gauges highly valued performance abilities, such as perception and problem solving, and because, despite admonitions to the contrary, it is assumed to reflect innate capacities. Educational attainment is of interest for much the same reasons. Accordingly, we may ask how well the existing income distribution reflects these criteria. Figure 9.3 provides the answer to this question.

The educational, IQ, and income distributions are all depicted in Figure 9.3. One can see, for example, that slightly less than 30 percent of the male population completed just twelve years of school; that somewhat under 10 percent had an income of about $2,000; and that approximately 15 percent had exactly average IQ. One striking impression obtained from the graphs in Figure 9.3 is that the shape of the income distribution is very different from those of the education and IQ distributions. There is a relatively high concentration of

FIGURE 9.3   Distribution of Income, Education, and IQ for Males, Twenty-five Years of Age and Over, 1965.

Source: Lester C. Thurow, *Poverty and Discrimination* (Washington, D.C.: The Brookings Institution, 1969), p. 68.

persons in the lower end of the income scale, say under $5,000, while relatively few people are in the lower educational or IQ categories. One way of expressing this disparity is to say that incomes are distributed much less equally than are IQs or educational attainments. Or, one could say that the distribution of poverty is not well explained by the distributions of either IQ or educational achievement.

Some interesting implications follow from Figure 9.3 and our previous discussions of ability and education. We have already suggested that high IQ scores are not equally accessible to all individuals of similar genetic capacity (see Chapter 8). Black children, for example, have less of an opportunity to develop their capacities into performing abilities. This implies that the income distribution is even less representative of innate capacities than is suggested by its observed relationship to IQ. In the same vein, it may be noted that educational attainments depart considerably from the IQ distribution, suggesting that access to, and the quality of, education are not uniform. These observations are considered further in Chapter 10.

SUMMARY

Individuals with greater educational attainments unquestionably earn more money, on average, than persons with less education. Persons with highly-valued abilities also tend to earn larger incomes. Accordingly, it is hardly surprising to discover that the poor tend to have less education and fewer marketable skills than the nonpoor. While the evidence reviewed in this chapter demonstrates that these relationships are not perfect, they do have a general validity. More important than the question of association, however, is that of causality. What we really seek to discover is not whether the poor are undereducated or underskilled, but whether a lack of education or skills is responsible for their poverty.

Education does operate as a powerful mechanism in determining the distribution of poverty. Where only a limited number of income opportunities are available, they will be reserved on a "least-educated last" basis. That is, the person with educational credentials will have a competitive edge in the labor market, at least within racial or sexual population groups. Hence, there is some basis for attributing the poverty of individuals to educational deficiency.

The relationship between education and poverty is not so simple on an aggregate basis, however. The competitive position of all workers cannot be raised simultaneously; if one individual's relative educational position rises, someone else's falls. Hence, education cannot be a cause of aggregate poverty unless direct links from educational attainments to social productivity to wages can be demonstrated. Such links are plausible, especially in the long run. In the short run, however, the link between education and the extent of total poverty is not so apparent.

The relationship of ability to poverty is also more complex than commonly assumed. Because we lack standard definitions and measurements of ability, there is no firm basis for declaring that the poor are less able. At most, such an observation means only that the poor make less money. Even when confined to measures of performance, such as IQ, we find that the relationship of ability to income is oblique. The distribution of incomes diverges considerably from educational or IQ distributions and even further from the distribution of innate talents.

FURTHER READING

BERG, IVAR, *Education and Jobs: The Great Training Robbery*. New York: Frederick A. Praeger, Inc., 1970.

BRITTAIN, JOHN A., *The Inheritance of Economic Status*. Washington, D.C.: The Brookings Institution, 1977.

HAUSER, ROBERT M. AND THOMAS N. DAYMONT, "Schooling, Ability, and Earnings: Cross-sectional Findings 8 to 14 years After High School Graduation," *Sociology of Education*, July 1977.

HERRNSTEIN, RICHARD, "I.Q.," *The Atlantic Monthly,* September 1971, pp. 43–64.

JENCKS, CHRISTOPHER et al., *Inequality*. New York: Basic Books, Inc., 1972. *Who Gets Ahead? The Economic Determinants of Success in America.* (New York: Basic Books, 1979).

SCHILLER, BRADLEY R., "Equality, Opportunity, and the 'Good Job'," *The Public Interest,* Spring 1976.

THUROW, LESTER, AND ROBERT LUCAS, "The American Distribution of Income: A Structural Problem," a study prepared for the Joint Economic Committee, U.S. Congress. Washington, D.C.: Government Printing Office, 1972.

10 DISCRIMINATION IN EDUCATION

Education appears to have a major impact on the distribution, if not necessarily the extent, of poverty. Accordingly, anyone denied an equal opportunity to acquire an education has an increased probability of being poor. In other words, discrimination in education helps determine who will be poor.

Discrimination in labor markets has similar effects. To achieve non-poverty status, an individual must be able to employ his abilities in the labor market. Acquisition of acceptable characteristics alone is no guarantee of escape from poverty. If there exist forces that prevent or limit access to the labor market, the rewards to demographic achievements are never realized.

Barriers to either the acquisition or utilization of one's demographic characteristics, or, in economic terms, one's human capital, are the subject of this and the following chapter. The discussion in this chapter begins with a consideration of the meaning and nature of "discrimination" and ends with an examination of discriminatory barriers in the educational system. Chapter 11 focuses on discrimination in the labor market.

DISCRIMINATION

The terms *discrimination, prejudice,* and *racism* are widely used in American society today. Seldom do they fail to evoke emotional, often heated responses. While most people do not always understand what is meant by these concepts, they stand forever ready to deny or proclaim the significance of each. A striking illustration of just how volatile these words can be was provided by the report of the National Advisory Commission on Civil Disorders (the "Riot Commission") in early 1968. In searching for an explanation of the urban strife that was becoming characteristic of American cities, the commission concluded that white racism was a principal source of injustice and unrest. In the reaction that followed, heated exchange took precedence over reasoned debate. Very few white Americans, the President included, were ready to accept the commission's sweeping indictment. White Americans generally felt neither significantly prejudiced nor sufficiently involved in the ghetto to be responsible for the conditions therein.

Much of the misunderstanding revolving around the commission's report is traceable to the oftentimes vague meaning of the term *racism*. For many people, it conveys an impression of aggressively hostile attitudes and behavior, exemplified by burning school buses, racial taunts, or the mob scenes and protests that have accompanied crosstown school busing, both in the North and South. Relatively few Americans identify easily with such characterizations. Racism, however, may have other meanings. In fact, as used by the commission, the concept transcends the attitudes and behavior of individuals. Instead, the commission's indictment refers to entire patterns of racial interaction and the institutional character of much discrimination.

To approach an understanding of the nature of racism, we may begin by distinguishing between attitudes and actions. People often think differently than they act. As a result, they may adopt patterns of behavior that are injurious to others without consciously wishing to inflict injury. Or, conversely, they may harbor hostile feelings toward particular individuals or groups but refrain from acting them out due to personal, moral, or legal inhibitions. The term *prejudice* refers to the unfavorable feelings and attitudes that people harbor against others, especially other population groups. These are to be distinguished from unfavorable actions or behavior, which fall under the heading of discrimination. Hence, prejudiced individuals may or may not discriminate, and discrimination does not necessarily imply the existence of prejudice.

While the prejudices of people are often the origin of discriminatory behavior and may be appropriate targets for public policy, they are relevant to our discussion only in so far as they find expression in behavior. Accordingly, we focus on the nature of discrimination. We may note here, however, that the broader term, racism, encompasses the concepts of both prejudice and discrimination.

The concept of discrimination need not convey notions of injustice or injury. In general, it refers only to the differential treatment of persons. Thus, we discriminate when we assign the tallest boys to the basketball team or when we cheer for the local football team. Yet we hardly think of these phenomena as being related in any meaningful way to, say, the exclusion of blacks from higher status jobs or classrooms. Clearly, a concept of discrimination that is so general as to encompass both kinds of situations is too anemic to be of practical use. But how, then, are we to identify the kind of discriminatory treatment that we regard as the proper concern of public policy?

We can move closer to a relevant concept of discrimination by recognizing the criteria on which differential treatment is based. Assigning taller boys to a basketball team, for example, serves a very specific and productive function. Hence, the criterion of selection is directly relevant to the task at hand. The same cannot be said for the selection of a less qualified white competing with a more qualified black. Here the basis of selection, color, is irrelevant to the task at hand, and the resultant choice is actually counterproductive. Hence, we could refine our concept of discrimination by incorporating the relevancy of selection criteria. The kind of discrimination that is based on irrelevant or nonproductive criteria must be considered as injurious to the public welfare.

The U.S. Supreme Court employed this "relevancy" concept of discrimination when it restricted the use of aptitude tests for job-seekers. The Court observed that intelligence tests and other hiring criteria used by the Duke Power Company were not related to job performance. That is, the tests performed no useful economic function. Yet they were effective in screening out black job-seekers. In *Griggs* v. *Duke Power Company* (1971), the Court ruled that such practices were unfairly discriminatory.

Unfortunately, even this refinement of the concept of discrimination does not provide a completely workable definition. There remain many choices we would consider socially injurious that are still not identifiable by the criterion of relevancy. The choice of one's neighbors is an example: the only obviously relevant criterion in choosing neighbors is one's own desires and satisfaction. Thus, the choice of a white neighbor over a black one conforms to the standard of relevancy. Nevertheless, we have come to regard racial discrimination in housing as a socially pernicious practice. On what grounds do we distinguish this kind of individual choice from others? Are there fundamental differences between the situation where a homeowner chooses a white neighbor and, say, the situation where you choose to listen to a rock singer rather than an opera singer? Both situations reflect the free expression of individual choice.

There are few objective grounds for distinguishing between the choice of neighbors and the choice of singers. In both situations, someone is harmed by the selection decision: the opera singer loses potential income and the black home-seeker loses a potential residence. Our distinction between the two situations rests instead on more subjective grounds. Racial discrimination in housing is singled out for special attention because it violates our subjective notions of social justice. Against a combined background of religious, moral, legal, and historical considerations, we have collectively determined that racial discrimination is a particularly deleterious form of individual choice. It is on the basis of this subjective determination that racial discrimination has become a pressing public concern.

An important factor in our subjective judgment about the nature of racial discrimination is our perception of its effects. Where all whites discriminate against all blacks, the expression of free choice becomes especially pernicious. The black home-seeker is denied not one potential home, but all potential homes in white areas. Free choice for whites thus implies restricted choice for blacks and, hence, violates a basic dimension of freedom. Other choices that are less uniform or pervasive are not equally worthy of public concern. Racial discrimination itself would cease to be a public concern were it the practice of only a relatively few, scattered whites.

Costs and Benefits
of Discrimination

While it is obvious that blacks suffer real and intangible losses from the practice of racial discrimination, it is not so apparent whether or how the white community gains. Psychologically, of course, many whites will feel better off for having subordinated someone else. And if white individuals actually feel uncomfortable around blacks, on the job, in school, or at home, we may conclude that they are even happier as a result of discrimination.[1] But our immediate concern here is with the economic costs and benefits that may accrue to the white community.

Many whites do reap tangible benefit from the practice of discrimination. Where blacks are discriminated against in the labor market, for example, black workers will receive lower wages than white workers who possess equal qualifications. As a result, two groups of whites gain: white workers who are immunized against competition from blacks obtain higher wages than otherwise; and those employers (laundries and hotels, for example) who actually hire black workers benefit by getting higher quality labor than they are, in fact, paying for. In the educational field, white children gain from discrimination by monopolizing better facilities and teachers. White children of lesser ability are also released from the necessity of competing with more able black children in the quest for admissions, as long as racial discrimination is practiced.

Not all whites gain directly, however, from racial discrimination; some, in fact, actually lose. White workers who cannot escape menial occupations suffer from increased competition from blacks. The wages of white laundry and hotel workers, for example, will be held down by the large number of blacks excluded from other occupations, as illustrated in Figure 10.1. Some

[1]The perception of psychological benefits may, of course, rest on prejudices, in which case the nature of benefits could be altered by illuminating and reducing racial stereotypes.

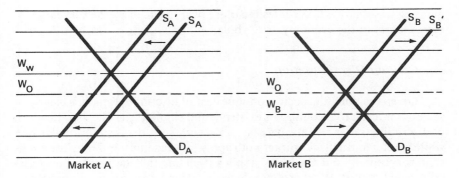

FIGURE 10.1

Suppose there are only two kinds of jobs, those in Market A and those in Market B. If everyone is allowed to move freely from one market to another, the equilibrium wage will end up at W_O in both markets. Why? Because if wages were higher in A than B, people would move out of B and into A, thus lowering the marginal revenue productivity in A while raising it in B. Hence, freedom of movement between Markets A and B assures an equality of average wage rates.

But now suppose black workers in A are kicked out and sent to Market B, making A a "whites only" preserve. This has the effect of shifting the labor supply curve in A to the left (to S_A') and the labor supply curve in B to the right (to S_B'). The net result indicated by the new supply and demand intersections is to raise wages in A (to W_W) and to lower wages in B (to W_B). Thus, black workers and any white workers trapped in Market B suffer lower wages, while the white workers in Market A end up with higher wages.

employers, too, will suffer losses. In a segregated community employers will often incur higher labor costs through the use of lesser-qualified whites. In the field of education, many whites will suffer from racial discrimination. Not all whites can flee the inner city. Those left behind, primarily the poorest, will be trapped in increasingly inferior educational systems, unable to enjoy the fruits of suburban white monopolies. They, like their black neighbors, will find their human capital potential underdeveloped.[2]

On an individual basis, then, some whites gain and some lose as a direct result of discrimination, making it difficult to calculate the net microeconomic gain or loss to the white community. No such ambiguity attaches to the indirect losses that are incurred on an aggregate, or macroeconomic level, however. Where discrimination against blacks is pervasive, society as a whole loses potential human capital. Black abilities and creativity remain underdeveloped and underemployed. Hence, total output of goods and services is less than it would be in the absence of discrimination. Estimates of the size of this loss run into tens of billions of dollars a year. In addition, much of the output we do produce is directed to relatively unattractive uses such as the surveillance of homes, streets, jails, and welfare case loads. Thus, whatever direct

[2]As we shall note later, some whites may also suffer from policies designed to eliminate vestiges of discrimination against blacks; where blacks are given *preferential* (not just equal) access to schools or jobs some whites suffer reverse discrimination.

gains or losses individual whites incur are overwhelmed by the very large in-direct losses to the economy as a whole.[3]

Proving Discrimination

Given the potential socioeconomic cost of discrimination, it is clearly in society's interest to recognize its existence and eliminate it. The identification of discrimination is not always easy, however. Consider a situation where a white worker and a black worker both apply for the same job. The white applicant is accepted, and the black applicant claims that he was unfairly discriminated against. What grounds do we have for accepting the charge of discrimination, as opposed to, say, the charge that the black applicant is simply a poor loser?

The easiest cases of discrimination to prove are those that involve blatant discrepancies in treatment. In our example, if the black applicant was required to take special tests or possessed identifiably superior qualifications, the issue is readily resolved. The same simplicity exists where black children are confined to dilapidated schools or a prospective black home buyer is turned down after offering to pay the full retail value of a house.

But the practice of discrimination is not always so apparent. Indeed, with the public eye focused on discrimination, those who engage in discriminatory practices are likely to develop great subtlety. Accordingly, evidence of discriminatory treatment may have to rest on the observation of end results. If a metropolitan area company has four thousand employees, none of whom is black, there exists a strong presumption that its hiring procedures are not impartial. So it is with the schools: if blacks and whites go into the educational system comparatively equal but come out with gross disparities in ability, we may conclude that they were treated differently somewhere along the line. Evidence of discriminatory treatment may be gathered by direct observation of treatment or by inference from results. Both types of evidence will be considered in our discussion of the educational and labor market systems.

RACIAL DISCRIMINATION IN EDUCATION

Discrimination in the American educational system was once both blatant and pervasive. In the eighteenth and early nineteenth centuries, the teaching of slaves was barred in most southern states. In 1885, California adopted a school segregation law allowing the exclusion of Chinese and Mongolian children

---

[3]White workers as a class may also lose if racial discrimination weakens worker solidarity, reducing labor's share of total income. See Michael Reich, "Who Benefits From Racism? The Distribution Among Whites of Gains and Losses From Racial Inequality," *Journal of Human Resources,* Fall 1978.

from white public schools. A county school superintendent in Texas proclaimed that "our Mexicans" were better off transplanting onions than going to school. In 1876, a black student admitted to the University of Pennsylvania Medical School was asked to sit behind a screen in the classroom, so as not to offend the white students. White students at Harvard University simply ejected the black entrants.[4]

The U.S. Supreme Court effectively condoned all this behavior by declaring in 1896 that "separate, but equal" education was constitutional (*Plessy* v. *Ferguson*). Even separate but *un*equal was tolerable, as long as the inequalities were not motivated by racial hostility (*Cumming* v. *Richmond County Board of Education, 1899*).

Discrimination still exists in American schools, even though it is much less pervasive or blatant than in the past. While this assertion will suprise very few readers, it is worthwhile to review the evidence on which it is based. Blacks and whites go into the educational system comparatively equal but come out of the system very different. In fact, the longer whites and blacks remain in the system, the further their respective abilities diverge. Nine-year old black students, for example, are 12 percent behind white students in math performance and 11 percent behind in reading. By the time they graduate from high school, black students are 20 percent behind in math and 16 percent behind in reading. The same kind of slippage occurs among Hispanic students.[5]

Strong as these grounds are for believing that the education provided whites and blacks is not equal, they tend to *understate* disparities in black and white educations. The ability comparisons of black and white high school seniors, for example, necessarily exclude those students who dropped out of school before reaching the twelfth grade. Yet, the decision to quit school may itself reflect inferior educational opportunities and recognition of widening achievement disparities. Seen in this light, black dropout rates are especially disturbing. While nearly 90 percent of white students now graduate from high school, less than 80 percent of black students graduate.

Perhaps the most complete statement of black educational deficiencies is the rate of functional illiteracy among black youth. In 1975, the U.S. Office of Education sponsored a survey of the nation's seventeen-year olds still in school. Students were asked to respond to eighty-six questions on reading items encountered in everyday life (e.g., street signs, telephone directories, store coupons). Ninety-two percent of all white seventeen-year-olds were rated as functionally literate, having answered correctly at least three-fourths of all the questions. By contrast, only fifty-eight percent of the black seventeen-year-olds were considered functionally literate.[6]

[4]These and other historical examples are cited in U.S. Commission on Civil Rights, *Toward Equal Educational Opportunity: Affirmative Admissions Programs at Law and Medical Schools* (Washington, D.C.: Government Printing Office, 1978).

[5]National Center For Education Statistics, *The Condition Of Education, 1978* (Washington, D.C.: Government Printing Office, 1979) p. 94.

[6]Congressional Budget Office, *Inequalities in the Educational Experiences of Black and White Americans* (Washington, D.C.: Government Printing Office, 1977), pp. 8–9.

TABLE 10.1   COLLEGE COMPLETION RATES, BY ETHNIC BACKGROUND, 1975

Racial/Ethnic Group	Percent of Persons 25 to 29 Years Old Who Have Completed at Least 4 Years of College
Males	
Majority whites	34
American Indian/Alaskan natives	8
Blacks	11
Mexican Americans	11
Puerto Ricans	6
Females	
Majority whites	22
American Indian/Alaskan natives	4
Blacks	11
Mexican Americans	5
Puerto Ricans	4

Source: U.S. Commission on Civil Rights.

Table 10.1 offers one final perspective on the outcomes of the educational process. This table shows the percentage of different groups that complete at least four years of college. One-third of all majority-white (Anglo) males graduates from college. Only eleven percent of black or Mexican-American males attain that much education; Puerto Ricans, American Indians, and Alaskan natives have even lower rates of college completion. Among females, the same kind of differences are apparent. If minorities and whites really do enter the educational system with equal potential, these differences in educational outcomes require further explanation.

Segregation in the Schools

The indirect evidence indicating discriminatory treatment in the educational system is highly suggestive. In fact, the observed disparities in achievement between white and black students are so great that direct evidence of discrepancies in educational opportunity should be easy to find. Segregation of facilities provides one such example: where separate schools are maintained for whites and blacks, the documentation of inequalities is simple.

Before looking at the extent of continuing racial segregation in American schools, we need to establish some perspective on the meaning of segregation. When most people refer to *integrated schools,* they are encompassing all schools serving both whites and blacks. Such a definition is deceptive, however. Consider the case of a city with only two high schools: School A has 2,000 students, only one of whom is black; School B's 1,000 students, on the other hand, are all black. By the usual criterion of biracial enrollment, School A would be regarded as integrated, yet the racial isolation common in both schools is surely of greater significance than School A's dubious claim to biracial enrollment.

A more meaningful concept of integration must refer to the proportion of students that attend school with children of another race. From this perspective, we are able to identify the completeness of integration. Complete integration, of course, would be a situation where all black students attended school with white children, and vice versa. By this stricter definition of integration, the distinction between School A and School B disappears. For the city as a whole, we may say that only 0.1 percent of the black population attends school with whites. This is far more descriptive than saying that 50 percent of the city schools are integrated.

This broader concept of integration has tremendous significance for our perceptions of educational desegregation. Ten years after the Supreme Court's historic order to desegregate, the state of Florida boasted that nearly a third of its schools were integrated. Closer scrutiny revealed, however, that only 2.65 percent of Florida's black pupils were attending school with whites. Progress was even slower in other southern states.

Table 10.2 summarizes the extent of school integration across the country in 1976. This table reflects segregation not only of black students, but other minority students as well. The table indicates, for example, the percentage of minority students who attend schools that are comprised almost exclusively (80 to 100 percent) of minority students. Such extreme segregation was experienced by 44 percent of all minority students in 1976. Another 23 percent of all minority students attended schools that were predominantly (50 to 79 percent) minority. While there were significant regional variations, the basic segregation of educational facilities prevailed everywhere. Whether he lives in the North or the South, in the city or on a farm, a black, Hispanic or other minority child is very unlikely to attend a truly integrated school. Racial isolation in the schools is still the hallmark of the American educational system.

TABLE 10.2   SCHOOL INTEGRATION, 1976

Regional	Percent of Minority Students in Schools Where Enrollment Is:		
	80–100% Minority	*50–79% Minority*	*Less Than 50% Minority*
U.S. total	44	23	33
Northeast	65	18	17
Midwest	59	16	25
West	35	30	35
South	33	26	41
Border States	51	16	33

Source: U.S. Department of Health, Education, and Welfare.

One additional note of caution about the concept of integration is necessary. The concept of integration we have offered goes no further than the outer walls of the school, but even an ostensibly integrated school may be severely segregated within. Students may be assigned rooms, teachers, and facilities within the school on an explicitly racial basis. An extreme illustration of such internal segregation was encountered in Milwaukee. Like most other cities, Milwaukee was prodded by the courts to integrate its schools. In part, integration was achieved by busing black pupils to previously white schools. The substance of educational opportunity was little changed, however. The bused-in black pupils were maintained in separate classrooms and bused back and forth to their old schools for lunch. Black students who lived close to the white schools were even required to proceed to the more distant black schools for bus transportation to the receiving schools!

Not all internal school segregation is as explicit and extreme as the case in Milwaukee. A more popular and subtle form of segregation is embodied in the so-called *tracking systems,* under which the more able students are separated from the rest and provided special opportunities to advance, while the least able students are held back for intensive remedial work. What makes the system so racially discriminatory is the fact that black pupils have received inferior education prior to integration, so that using IQ tests or other achievement examinations to allocate pupils serves to perpetuate racial separation. A still subtler form of segregation within the classroom may prevail where teachers regard black pupils as innately or culturally incapable of attaining success.

Equality of Facilities

The statistics of Table 10.2, together with our observations on the nature of integration, provide a sobering view of our efforts to provide equal opportunity "with all deliberate speed." In light of that background, we may argue that blacks and other minorities still attend school separately from majority whites. How equal, then, are their separate opportunities?

A comparison of educational opportunities at the local level is easily made: visit any black (or Mexican-American) school and any (Anglo) white school in the same city. You can readily detect enough qualitative differences in their educational environments to make a judgment about the relative attractiveness of the minority school. These local observations of school quality cannot be expanded across the country, however. It would be too expensive and time-consuming to visit all the school districts across the nation in order to assess the average quality of black and white schools. Even if we had enough time and money, our judgments would depend on the perspectives and standards of many different observers. And, finally, any conclusions we reached would be limited to such statements as "white schools are better (or very much better)," with no clear indication of how great existing inequalities are. Accordingly, we are compelled to seek more objective, easily quantified measures of school quality.

In the most comprehensive survey of educational facilities ever undertaken, the U.S.Office of Education employed sixty-seven separate measures of school quality. These measures ranged from the number of books in the school library to the education of the teacher's mother. They represented a concerted effort to capture and measure every dimension of the educational environment that might distinguish white schools from black schools. What the Office of Education discovered is that black and white schools differ on a multitude of separate measures but that such individual differences were relatively small. The only clear pattern to emerge from their mountain of statistics was that black schools tended to be most deficient in primarily academic facilities such as science labs, textbooks, and debate clubs.

In assessing these results, the Office of Education recognized many limitations in their approach. They reported that:

> *The school environment of a child consists of many things, ranging from the desk he sits at to the child who sits next to him, and including the teacher who stands in front of his class. Any statistical survey gives only the most meager evidence of these environments, for two reasons. First, the reduction of the various aspects of the environment to quantitative measures must inherently miss many elements, tangible and more subtle, that are relevant to the child. The measures must be comparable from school to school; yet the elements which are experienced as most important by the child will likely differ from one school to another, and may well differ among children in the same school.*
>
> *Second, the child experiences his environment as a whole, while the statistical measures necessarily fragment it. Having a teacher without a college degree may indicate an element of disadvantage; but in the concrete situation, a schoolchild may be taught by a teacher who is not only without a college degree, but who has grown up and received his schooling in the local community, who has never been out of the State, who has a 10th-grade vocabulary, and who shares the local community's attitudes.*
>
> *For both these reasons, the statistical examination of difference in school environments for minority and majority children will give an impression of lesser differences than actually exist.*[7]

We are left, then, with a very incomplete assessment of the school facilities available to whites and blacks. All we can say with certainty is that both everyday observation and the survey of the Office of Education lead one

[7]U.S. Office of Education, *Equality of Educational Opportunity* (The Coleman Report) (Washington, D.C.: Government Printing Office, 1966), p. 37.

to conclude that there exist tangible (and intangible) differences in black and white educational facilities. We have no summary measure, however, of how large those differences are or how important they may be.[8]

Inherent Inequalities

The Supreme Court provided a way out of this statistical ambiguity when it determined in 1954 that segregated facilities were *inherently* unequal. The Court declared that "to separate them [black children] from others of similar age and qualifications solely because of their race generates a feeling of inferiority as to their status in the community that may affect their hearts and minds in a way unlikely ever to be undone."[9] The Court thus relegated the issue of tangible facilities to one of distinctly secondary importance. Even ostensibly "equal" schools for blacks and whites could never generate equal educational opportunity.

There were several specific considerations that led the Supreme Court justices to their landmark decision. They recognized that black pupils in segregated schools would have low self-esteem, knowing they were surrounded by failures and in schools regarded as inferior. Moreover, they would acquire a personal sense of futility knowing that, regardless of their individual attainments, they would always be identified by the community as members of a group viewed as less able, less successful, and less acceptable. Hence, the individual black child would see little reason to develop his individual talents. Community views would also affect the attitudes of teachers. Aware of, and probably sharing, the white community's low regard for blacks, teachers attached to black schools would tend to accept and transmit low expectations. They would not teach as much, or as well, to children deemed less teachable.

Impressive evidence in support of the Court's judgment was assembled by the U.S. Commission on Civil Rights in 1967. The commission discovered that black pupils of similar backgrounds performed quite differently in varying racial situations. In particular, it found that black educational achievements increased substantially where schools were more thoroughly integrated. In addition to the fact that white schools were generally better, it was observed that black pupils benefited from integration by believing that their opportunities had improved and by seeing others succeeding around them. Discrimination, then, and more especially school segregation, were seen to be major determinants of black achievements and status.[10]

---

[8]For differing views on the importance of school inputs for educational achievement, see Christopher Jencks, et al., *Inequality* (New York: Basic Books, Inc.), 1972, and Anita A. Summers and Barbara L. Wolfe, "Do Schools Make a Difference?" *American Eonomic Review,* September 1977.

[9]*Brown* v. *Board of Education*, 347 U.S. 483 (1954).

[10]More recent evidence confirms the Court's view. See Congressional Budget Office, op. cit., pp. 10–11.

CLASS DISCRIMINATION
IN EDUCATION

While blacks do suffer from serious and pervasive discrimination in the educational system, there is no reason to believe that they alone are singled out for substandard treatment. On the contrary, it is clear that other minority groups, among them Mexican Americans, Puerto Ricans, and American Indians, confront barriers at least as formidable as do blacks. Accordingly, nearly everything we have said about racial discrimination against blacks applies with equal force to all minority group members. But including other minority groups in our discussion does not completely cover the subject of discrimination. As we are just beginning to perceive, racism has its counterpart in what has become known as *classism*. Poor individuals as a group, irrespective of their ethnic origin, are provided substandard facilities and opportunities in America.

We have already noted that many whites lose out as a result of racial discrimination in education, namely those who are not able to escape predominantly black neighborhoods and schools. But even where blacks are not present, poor whites may be confined to separate and substandard schools. Neighborhoods are even more likely to be homogeneous by income classes than by race; that is, poor families will be located in distinct areas of any city. Moreover, because school expenditures and decisions are determined by administrative bodies composed largely of the nonpoor, schools in low-income neighborhoods are likely to receive less than equal facilities.

Inequality of educational opportunities across income classes tends to be reinforced by the way schools are financed. Slightly over half of all elementary and secondary school expenditures are financed by local property taxes, with most of the remainder financed out of state revenues (only 10 percent of elementary and secondary school expenditures are financed out of federal revenues). What this implies is that children in poorer states and poorer school districts will be provided with fewer resources. And so they are: in 1975-76, for example, average annual revenue per pupil varied across states by nearly $1,600 (from a low of $1,094 in Mississippi to $2,699 in New York). Within states, disparities across school districts are often just as large. In Georgia, Connecticut, Massachusetts, and California, high-spending school districts spend more than twice as much per pupil as do the school districts with lowest per pupil expenditure.[11] When, on top of all this, we recall that expenditures within a school district may be distributed unequally, it is apparent that educational opportunities are not the same for all income classes.

[11]Several state courts have ruled this pattern of school financing to be an unconstitutional denial of Fourteenth Amendment rights, but the U.S. Supreme Court failed to uphold such decisions (March 21, 1973).

The analogy of class discrimination to racial discrimination goes beyond differences in school facilities. Like blacks, poor white children tend to be surrounded by families that have failed to achieve material success. Poor white children see few demonstrations of personal aspiration and talent leading to higher socioeconomic status. Furthermore, they are aware that society regards material success as a mark of personal worth and thus see themselves and their families as stigmatized by the larger community. They know, too, that their schools are inferior and that completion of their studies will leave them ill-prepared to compete in the labor market. As a consequence, they are likely to internalize a sense of futility and inferiority.

The cumulative impact of class discrimination is apparent in the educational attainments of lower-class children. Poor children drop out of high school at over twice the rate of nonpoor children. Even more startling is the fact that a substantial number of poor children leave the educational system even before they enter high school. And those relatively few lower-income children who do manage to make it through until high school graduation cannot depend on their abilities to get them into college. College admissions are still reserved for those who can support themselves or forego several years of employment income.

Table 10.3 provides some perspective on the barriers to higher education imposed by low incomes. This table includes all families with at least one child eighteen to twenty-four years old. Within this group of families, the table indicates the percentage of families within each income class who have at least one child attending college full time. For example, 58 percent of all high-income ($25,000 plus) families have at least one child in college. Among the lowest-income families (under $5,000), only 16 percent have a child in college. As the first row of Table 10.3 reveals, the likelihood of attending college increases markedly with family income.

Another notable feature of Table 10.3 is the absence of significant racial differences *within* income classes. Look at the group of families with incomes

TABLE 10.3   PERCENT OF YOUTH ATTENDING COLLEGE FULL TIME, BY FAMILY INCOME AND RACE

Group	Under $5,000	$5,000–9,999	$10,000–14,999	$15,000–19,999	$20,000–24,999	$25,000 and over	Total
All youth	16	23	32	36	45	58	36
White	15	21	31	35	46	58	39
Black	15	27	34	35	—	—	22
Spanish-speaking	13	23	35	—	—	—	—

Source: U.S. Bureau of the Census, "School Enrollment—Social and Economic Characteristics of Students: October 1977," February 1979, Table 12.

of $5,000–9,999, for example. Within this income class, black and Spanish–speaking youth are actually *more* likely to attend full-time college than (Anglo) white youth. Within other income classes, racial differences are negligible. This suggests that *racial* differences in educational opportunity may, in fact, reflect *class* differences. From this perspective, blacks and other minorities do worse than whites in the educational system because their families' incomes are generally lower.

The Question of Ability

It is generally assumed by the nonpoor that poor children do not attain higher educational status because they are uniformly less able, but there are some very obvious weaknesses in this assumption. For example, a very talented poor youngster has no control over his family's finances. Hence, if the family cannot afford either to forego his earnings or even to supply him with school clothes and lunches, he will not be able to take advantage of even a "free" high school education. Furthermore, there are no scholarship or loan programs for high school students. Hence, we may anticipate that many talented poor children will never complete high school. Even for those who do attain high school diplomas, college admission will be barred by similar financial obstacles and by a legacy of inferior schooling.

It is not easy to determine how many bright, poor children are denied higher education because of their poverty. IQ tests remain our only standardized measure of ability, and those tests create problems for poor whites similar to those for blacks. Because their schools are substandard, poor whites fall increasingly far behind the nonpoor in educational performance. Hence, they demonstrate decreasing IQs over time, and it is difficult to discern how many originally bright children existed among the poor. And yet, even on the restrictive criterion of IQ tests, we can identify a large number of poor and able high school graduates who never attained a college degree.

As Table 10.4 reveals, the socioeconomic status of one's family has tremendous impact on a child's chances for college education. For any

TABLE 10.4   COLLEGE GRADUATION RATES, BY SOCIOECONOMIC
STATUS AND IQ (PERCENT)

| Socioeconomic | | IQ Score | |
Status	Low	Middle	High
Low	0.3	8.9	20.1
Middle	3.0	11.8	40.0
High	10.5	29.9	64.0

Source: Adapted from William Sewell and V. Shah, "Status, Intelligence and the Attainment of High Education," *Sociology of Education*, Winter 1967, Table 4.

demonstrated level of twelfth-grade IQ, children from higher status families are far more likely to reach college graduation. What is especially noteworthy here is the comparatively small proportion (20 percent) of very able poor students who graduate from college. Children of lesser ability but more prosperous families take the places of the more gifted among the poor. Educational opportunity is distributed neither equally nor even on the basis of demonstrated ability.

Class discrimination in education, then, is a strong force in the educational system and helps to determine the distribution of poverty. Whatever aggregate level of poverty exists, we may confidently predict that the children of the poor will be heavily overrepresented in the poverty statistics. It is also possible that class discrimination has become a stronger force in American society than racial discrimination. The U.S. Commission on Civil Rights, for example, found that schools were severely segregated by socioeconomic class and that the social class composition of schools is a stronger determinant of achievement than race. Moreover, there is mounting evidence that middle-class whites, if forced to choose, would prefer as neighbors middle-class blacks to poor whites. Poor persons, of whatever color, are least accepted by the larger society. All this will be of little comfort to poor blacks and other minorities, of course, who are likely to be the subject of both racial and class discrimination.

SEX DISCRIMINATION IN EDUCATION

The educational handicaps of minority and lower-class groups are reasonably easy to document, but the disadvantages that women confront in the educational system are more subtle, at least in the early grades. For the most part, the sex barriers that characterize primary and secondary educational systems consist of sex-typing certain kinds of curricula. Girls are encouraged to take home economics, foreign languages, and typing, but gently discouraged from taking manual crafts, business courses, and science. The barriers emanate both from school counselors—who want to be "realistic" about occupational goals—and, perhaps even more important, from parents and peers who are attuned to certain kinds of expectations with respect to male and female roles in society. As the Carnegie Commission on Higher Education has noted:

> Almost from the moment of birth, boys and girls are subject to a wide variety of cultural influences that tend to prepare them for differentiated roles in life. Little girls are typically given dolls or miniature cooking utensils for toys; boys are generally given trucks and electric trains and mechanical toys. School readers show pictures of father going off to

work and mother waving good-bye at the window, or of father playing baseball with his sons while mother bakes cookies. Girls play jump rope or tag on the school playground, while boys play ball. At about the seventh or eighth grade, boys take a course in manual training, while girls are taught cooking and sewing.

We are not suggesting that matters ought to be reversed, or that little girls should be forbidden to play with dolls, but rather that there ought to be more freedom of choice. Girls who show signs of a mechanical bent should be given an opportunity to play with mechanical toys and to enter the course on manual training. Boys should not be barred from courses on cooking and sewing if they are interested.[12]

This kind of acculturation tends to restrict the educational aspirations of female students and to frustrate them when they challenge those restrictions.

More explicit manifestations of sex discrimination in education have been apparent at the postcollege level. As suggested earlier, female college graduates have had a difficult time gaining access to the professional schools that confer the necessary credentials for many desirable jobs. Secretarial schools have always been easy to get into, but law schools, medical schools, and business schools have often been a different story. Figure 10.2 depicts the proportion of different educational degrees awarded to women in the 1975–1976 period. As is evident, women accounted for a very substantial percentage of graduate enrollments in education schools, but were poorly represented in law or medicine, and virtually nonexistent in engineering schools.

To a large extent, this pattern of graduate education is the consequence of sex-differentiated roles and expectations nurtured from the crib to the campus. But these forces are reinforced at the graduate–admissions level by a tendency to reject female applicants with superior qualifications in favor of male applicants with lesser qualifications. Together these forces result in the fact that as recently as 1976 only 23 percent of female college graduates went on to graduate school, as compared with 28 percent of male graduates.

The same kind of observation has been made by the Council of Economic Advisers. In a special 1973 study on the economic role of women, the council noted that although fewer women receive college and postcollege degrees:

Even more striking are the differences in the courses taken. At both the undergraduate and advanced levels, women are heavily represented in English, languages, and fine arts—the more general cultural fields. They are poorly represented in disciplines having a strong vocational emphasis and promising a high pecuniary return. In 1970, 9.3 percent of the baccalaureates in business and 3.9 percent of the masters in busi-

[12]Carnegie Commission on Higher Education, "Opportunities for Women in Higher Education" (New York: McGraw-Hill Book Company, 1973), pp. 42-43.

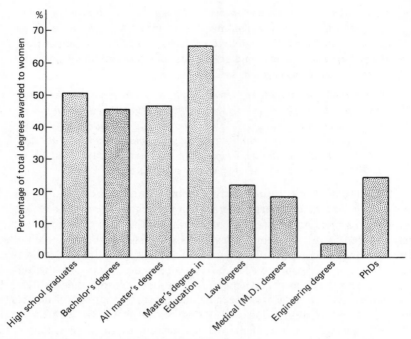

FIGURE 10.2   Women in Education, 1975–76

Source: National Center for Education Statistics

ness went to women. In the biological sciences, women had a larger share, taking about 30 percent of the bachelor's and master's degrees and 16 percent of the doctorates. But only 8.5 percent of the M.D.'s and 5.6 percent of the law degrees went to women. Most of these percentages, low as they are, represent large gains from the preceding year.

The situation is quite different in the so-called women's occupations. In 1971, women received 74 percent of the B.A.'s and 56 percent of the M.A.'s given in education. In library science, which is even more firmly dominated by women, they received 82 percent of all degrees in 1971. And in nursing 98 percent of all the degrees went to women.[13]

The implication of this pattern of sex discrimination is that women will enter the labor market with less valuable human capital than men.[14] As

[13]Economic Report of the President (Washington, D.C.: Government Printing Office, 1973), pp, 101–2.

[14]This point was underscored by a 1975 report of the Carnegie Council on Policy Studies in Higher Education that identified under-recruitment of women to appropriate graduate programs as the major obstacle to greater equality of jobs in higher education.

a consequence, we anticipate that a disproportionate number of women, especially those who try to raise families on their own, will end up in poverty.

SUMMARY

Discrimination on the basis of race, income class, or sex violates commonly accepted standards of social justice. Where discrimination is pervasive, the freedom of minority groups is severely restricted, as are their opportunities for achievement. Such limitations harm not only those discriminated against, but also the larger community. Talents go undeveloped, potential output is irrevocably lost, and markets are unnecessarily restricted.

In the American educational system, racial discrimination has resulted in a pattern of segregated and inferior schools for blacks and other minorities. Nearly half of all minority students continue to attend virtually all-minority elementary and secondary schools. The inferiority of the education these children receive derives not only from disparities in school facilities but, more importantly, from a sense of isolation and subjugation imposed by the white community. The consequences of this discrimination are manifest in the low educational attainments of minority youth.

As serious and pervasive as discrimination against minorities is, it is not the only kind of discrimination practiced in the educational system. Poor children, in particular, are maintained in schools segregated largely by socioeconomic class and provided with substandard facilities. They and their families are also stigmatized by the larger community for failure to attain material success. As a result, children of poor families drop out of school at alarming rates and generally lag behind nonpoor children in demonstrated achievement. Even those relatively few poor children who do demonstrate high levels of achievement are denied higher levels of education. Class discrimination, then, is directly analogous to discrimination against racial or minority groups.

Finally, we must recognize that women are discriminated against in the educational system as well, even if such discrimination is more subtle. To the extent that such discrimination restricts later job opportunities, particularly for those women who end up as heads-of-households, it too contributes to the level and distribution of poverty.

Because educational attainments are a prime determinant of the distribution of poverty, those discriminated against in the schools are most likely to be among the poor. For whatever level of aggregate poverty exists, the children of yesterday's poor, blacks, and female-headed families will be grossly overrepresented in the poverty statistics. Children of poor black families headed by women will be the most disadvantaged, as they may be subjected to all forms of discrimination.

FURTHER READING

On the Nature of Discrimination

DOLLARD, JOHN, *Caste and Class in a Southern Town*. Garden City, N.Y.: Doubleday & Company, Inc., 1957.

FRANKLIN, RAYMOND S., AND SOLOMON RESNIK, *The Political Economy of Racism*. New York: Holt, Rinehart and Winston, 1973.

FRIEDMAN, MILTON, *Capitalism and Freedom*. Chicago: University of Chicago Press, 1962, Ch. 7.

MASTERS, STANLEY H., *Black-White Income Differentials*. New York: Academic Press, Inc., 1975, Ch. 1.

On Discrimination in Education

CONGRESSIONAL BUDGET OFFICE, *Inequalities in the Educational Experiences of Black and White Americans*. Washington, D.C.: Government Printing Office, 1977.

HAUSER, ROBERT M., AND DAVID L. FEATHERMAN, "Equality of Schooling: Trends and Prospects," *Sociology of Education,* April 1976.

JENCKS, CHRISTOPHER, et al., *Inequality*. New York: Basic Books, Inc., 1972, Ch. 2.

MOSTELLER, FREDERICK, AND DANIEL P. MOYNIHAN, eds., *On Equality of Educational Opportunity*. New York: Random House, Inc., 1972.

SUMMERS, ANITA A., AND BARBARA L. WOLFE, "Do Schools Make a Difference?" *American Economic Review,* September 1977.

U.S. COMMISSION ON CIVIL RIGHTS, *Toward Equal Educational Opportunity: Affirmative Admissions Programs at Law and Medical Schools*. Washington, D.C.: Government Printing Office, 1978.

11 DISCRIMINATION IN THE LABOR MARKET

In 1927, a clothing manufacturer in New York City advertised for help with the following wage offer: "White Workers $24; Colored Workers $20."[1] His offer embodied one of the most flagrant forms of racial discrimination in the labor market; namely, the payment of unequal wages for equal work. Few employers are so blatant today, and certainly no one advertises his discriminatory practices in print anymore. Nevertheless, it is still believed that blacks and other minority workers do not receive equal treatment in the labor markets.

If minority workers are discriminated against in the labor market, they are being denied full use of their productive abilities. As a consequence, their incomes will be depressed, and they will be heavily represented in the ranks of the poor. Hence, racial discrimination in the labor market tends to affect both the distribution and extent of poverty. In this chapter, we examine the consequences, forms, and practices of discrimination in the labor market. As in Chapter 10, we begin with a discussion of racial discrimination and then consider the phenomena of class and sex discrimination.

RACIAL DISCRIMINATION IN THE LABOR MARKET

We know that there are tremendous disparities between the incomes of blacks and whites. In Chapter 2 we noted that nearly one out of three blacks is poor compared to only one out of ten whites, and in Chapter 8, we observed that

---

[1]Cited by Orley Ashenfelter, "Changes in Labor Market Discrimination Over Time," *Journal of Human Resources*, Fall 1970, pp. 403–30.

average black family incomes are nearly $7,000 less than white incomes. Moreover, we have observed that racial or cultural theories cannot explain these inequalities. Thus, there are strong grounds for assuming that blacks continue to be the subject of discrimination, despite the lack of advertising to that effect.

It would be mistaken, however, to conclude that all existing income inequalities can be explained by discriminatory practices in the labor market. We know, for instance, that blacks enter the labor market with much less human capital than whites as a result of racial discrimination in the schools. Accordingly, a labor market that rewarded all individuals only on the basis of demonstrated achievement would still provide less income for blacks than whites. A very high proportion of blacks also continue to live in the South, where employment levels and wages are generally lower. Hence, income disparities alone do not prove the existence of racial discrimination in the labor market; they simply create a presumption that discrimination will be discovered if sought.

Even if we find that income disparities continue to exist after we have accounted for educational and geographical differences, we cannot conclusively assert that discriminatory practices are rampant in the labor market. If discrimination against blacks ceased altogether, black workers would still be handicapped by past labor market discrimination. They would be less skilled and experienced and lower on seniority ladders, for example. As in the area of education, blacks would remain disadvantaged by past discrimination, even if present discrimination were eliminated.

The observed income disparities between whites and blacks, then, are primarily the result of three forces: nonmarket discrimination, past labor market discrimination, and present labor market discrimination. What we seek to identify in this section is that portion of existing income disparities attributable solely to continuing racial discrimination in the labor market.

Disparities in Earnings

White families have accumulated vast amounts of wealth over time in the form of property, savings accounts, bond holdings, and stock ownership. Stockholders' equity alone now amounts to over $800 billion, while another $1,700 billion is tied up in savings, cash, and government bonds. Black families have comparatively little access to this store of wealth, as they have been denied equal opportunity to earn and accumulate money in the past. Thus, the average white family has six times as much wealth as the average black family.[2]

[2]Data on wealth are not very reliable. Estimates of black-white differences in wealth are contained in Henry S. Terrell, "Wealth Accumulation of Black and White Families: The Empirical Evidence," *Journal of Finance, May 1971; and James D. Smith, ed., The Personal Distribution of Income and Wealth* (New York: Columbia University Press, 1975).

Such disparities in wealth between blacks and whites tend to overwhelm differences in income.

For the most part, these differences in wealth do not reflect current labor market discrimination. They do, however, tend to distort comparisons of current white and black incomes. Current income includes money derived from accumulated wealth, especially money received in the form of dividends, interest, and capital gains. Accordingly, *total* income differences between blacks and whites are much larger than differences in *earnings*, that is, income derived from labor market activity. To assess the impact of racial discrimination in the labor market, then, we need to focus on racial disparities in earnings alone.

In 1977, the average earnings of white male workers aged 25-44 was $15,152. For black workers, the average was only $11,540, a mere 76 percent of white earnings. The earnings of Hispanic (Mexican American, Cuban, or Puerto Rican) workers were just slightly lower than those of black workers. In absolute terms, the earnings gap between (Anglo) white and minority workers was approximately $3,600 per year.

How much of this difference was due to discrimination in the labor market? To isolate the impact of racial discrimination on this disparity, we need to identify the influence of other earnings determinants. Education, skills, age, and geographic location are all significant in impact. Only as we control for these other factors can we perceive the independent influence of racial discrimination in the labor market.

We have already noted the tremendous importance of educational attainments for income. Therefore, we must control for the influence on earnings of the nonmarket discrimination suffered in schools. This may be done by observing the comparative earnings of workers with equal educations. If there were no racial discrimination in the labor market, blacks, Hispanics, and whites with equal education should command approximately equal incomes. When this adjustment is actually made, however, the gap in earnings between white and minority workers is only partially closed. Table 11.1 shows that black and Hispanic workers earn less than white workers with equal

TABLE 11.1   MEAN EARNINGS, BY RACE AND EDUCATION FOR MEN AGED TWENTY-FOUR TO FORTY-FOUR, 1977

	Mean Earnings of:		
Education	*White Workers*	*Black Workers*	*Hispanic Workers*
High school dropout	$11,935	$ 9,227	$ 9,785
High school graduate	15,176	11,149	12,367
Some college	15,499	13,384	14,104
College graduate	17,887	15,348	17,037

Source: U.S. Bureau of Labor Statistics.

educational credentials. Although the "adjusted" earnings gap closes somewhat, especially for college-educated workers, a substantial and unexplained earnings differential remains.

To some exent, the earnings gaps remaining between white and minority workers of equal years of schooling might be explained by differences in the *quality* of schooling. Years of schooling do not have the same educational significance for blacks and whites (see Chapter 10). Hence, a complete adjustment for nonmarket discrimination would have to control for the significant differences in the *quality* of education received by each group. We must recognize that a typical black worker with twelve years of schooling comes to the job with as little educational preparation as the typical white worker with only nine years of schooling. When this additional control for nonmarket discrimination is imposed, observed labor market disparities shrink further. Black workers of equivalent educational backgrounds, including both quantity and quality of schooling, earn incomes approximately 90 percent as large as their white counterparts.

It appears, then, that most of the earnings disparity between whites and blacks can be attributed to prior (nonmarket) discrimination in the schools. This means that no more than half the observable earnings disparity can be attributed to present labor market discrimination. Indeed, the combined influence of other factors, including skills, age, and region, reduce the disparity further. Recent studies of discrimination have estimated that only about one-fourth of existing earnings disparities are directly attributable to discriminatory labor market practices.[3] We may say, then, that roughly one-half of the $3,600 earnings disparity is due to nonmarket discrimination (education, residence); one-fourth due to past market discrimination (work skills and experience); and one-fourth to current labor market discrimination.

While nonmarket discrimination appears to overwhelm other types of discrimination, some caution is necessary in interpreting these conclusions. First, an annual earnings loss of $900 is a substantial setback to black workers. Racial discrimination in the labor market is, thus, a large and important racial barrier, even if outsized by discrimination in education. Furthermore, it cannot be assumed that these proportions are fixed. If, in fact, the quality and quantity of schooling for blacks increases—as they have been in recent years— we have no assurance that black educational attainments will continue to be rewarded at the same rate. As more educated black workers emerge, racial discrimination in the labor market may intensify. Much potential discrimination in the labor market is now averted due to the fact that so few blacks are able to

[3]See James Gwartney, "Changes in the Nonwhite/White Income Ratio, 1939–67," *American Economic Review*, December 1970; Leonard Weiss and Jeffrey G. Williamson, "Black Education, Earnings and Interregional Migration: Even Newer Evidence," *American Economic Review*, March 1975; James P. Smith and Finis Welch, "Race Differences in Earnings: A Survey and New Evidence" (Santa Monica, Calif.: Rand Corporation, 1978); and Stanley H. Masters, *Black-White Income Differentials* (New York: Academic Press, Inc., 1975).

compete directly with whites. As black educational attainments—and thus labor market competition—increase, the situation may be altered dramatically. Accordingly, we have no firm basis for predicting a linear reduction of earnings disparities as educational opportunities become more equal. These calculations illustrate where the locus of discrimination is now; they cannot predict where it will be in the future.

Components of Earnings Disparities

While the image is provocative, it is mistaken to picture a thief called Discrimination openly robbing minority workers of $3,600 each year, even though the effect may be the same. Instead, we must realize that the consequent income loss emerges from several dimensions of the labor market process. Minority workers are not robbed of their earnings outright. Very little of the discrimination that takes place in the labor market is of the sort exemplified by the New York garment manufacturer who paid different wages to white and black workers. Aside from being illegal, the visibility of such practices makes them especially vulnerable to public scrutiny and civil rights action. In addition, such overtly inequitable treatment violates the consciences of most employers. Rather, minority workers are hired less often, for fewer hours, for less desirable jobs, and at lower wages (see Figure 11.1). It is the sum total of these different forces that leaves the minority worker poorer. A more thorough understanding of discrimination is attained by considering the relative importance of each of these forces.

Because minority workers are less educated, less experienced, and less attractive to most employers than available white workers, they are least likely to be hired. In any given job situation white workers will be hired first and laid off last. Hence, the frequency of employment and the number of hours worked will differ for minority and white workers as the combined result of nonmarket and market racial discrimination. Indeed, a significant part of the observed

FIGURE 11.1   Components of Earnings Disparities

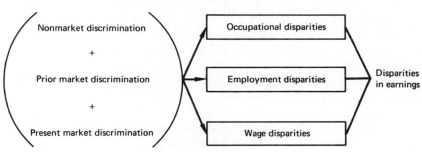

earnings disparity derives not from the decision to pay minority workers lower wages but from the decision to employ them less often. Table 11.2 shows that black workers are more than twice as likely to be unemployed as are white workers. Moreover, black workers tend to remain unemployed for a longer time. Hispanic workers also have experienced unemployment more frequently, although for shorter periods of time.

TABLE 11.2   UNEMPLOYMENT OF MALE WORKERS BY RACE, 1979

	Whites	*Blacks*	*Hispanics*
Unemployment rate (%)	5.2	12.7	7.4
Average duration of unemployment (weeks)	10.9	13.7	10.0

Source: First quarter, 1979, U.S. Bureau of Labor Statistics.

Of still greater significance to the observed earnings disparity is the decision to employ black and Hispanic workers at different kinds of jobs. Once again, all forms of discrimination take their toll. Minority workers are denied entrance to many occupations because they lack necessary educational attainments or credentials. They also often lack required work skills and experience. And finally, there are many jobs that whites regard as inappropriate for blacks and from which they are, therefore, excluded. Garbage collection and bus driving are regarded as acceptable black or Hispanic occupations; retail sales, management, or even teaching are not regarded by whites as equally appropriate. And only in the most dire of circumstances could most whites imagine trusting themselves to the services of a black doctor or lawyer (not to mention a female one of any race). Accordingly, most minority workers are largely excluded from full participation in the more pleasant and remunerative occupations. Table 11.3 indicates the general nature of existing occupational patterns.

White workers of either sex are much more likely to hold white-collar jobs than are minority workers. Especially noteworthy is the very small percentage of black and Hispanic workers in managerial and administrative jobs. Apparently, minority workers seldom have the opportunity to be the boss.

Occupational disparities are further aggravated by the fact that minority workers who do gain access to the better occupations end up in the lowest and least desirable jobs *within* each occupational group. Within the professional, technical, and managerial class, for example, white workers tend to be lawyers, doctors, engineers, and social scientists. Black workers, on the other hand, are more likely to be funeral directors, welfare workers, and teachers in segregated schools. The same situation exists in the other occupational categories, sometimes in even more extreme form. For example, among clerical workers are grouped both white insurance adjusters and black postal

TABLE 11.3 OCCUPATIONAL STATUS, BY RACE AND SEX, 1979 (percent)

Occupational Status	Male Workers		Female Workers	
	White	Minority	White	Minority
White collar	43.7	27.4	65.5	47.1
Professional and technical	16.3	11.0	15.9	13.8
Managers and administrators	15.1	6.8	6.5	2.9
Sales workers	6.5	2.1	7.4	3.1
Clerical workers	5.9	7.5	35.7	27.2
Blue collar	44.8	52.8	14.3	18.6
Craftsmen	21.6	17.0	1.9	1.3
Operatives	11.5	15.6	10.5	15.3
Transport drivers	5.6	8.1	0.7	0.5
Nonfarm laborers	6.1	12.1	1.2	1.4
Service workers	7.6	16.3	18.8	33.4
Farm workers	3.8	3.6	1.4	0.9

Source: U.S. Bureau of Labor Statistics.

clerks, among salesworkers both white stockbrokers and Puerto Rican sales clerks. In other words, the tremendous disparities evident in occupational distributions reveal only a relatively small proportion of the job barriers that actually confront minority workers.

At the bottom of the occupational ladder, the respective concentrations of blacks and whites are, of course, reversed. As Table 11.3 reveals, two-thirds of all black workers are concentrated in the lower occupational categories, and, again, the disparities in actual jobs are great. Black women are maids in private homes or maids in hotels and office buildings. Black men are bootblacks, elevator operators, porters, and janitors. The better service and blue-collar jobs, including firemen, police, bartenders, and teamsters, are largely reserved for whites. The fact that minority workers are employed less often and for fewer hours is of relatively little significance in comparison with this uneven distribution of occupational opportunities.

Who Discriminates?

It is not easy to visualize so much discrimination taking place in the labor market. It is even more difficult to picture those persons or groups who actually engage in discrimination. Very few of us can readily identify anyone as an outright racist. The whole notion of purposeful maltreatment simply runs counter to the way we are accustomed to viewing ourselves or the marketplace. Nevertheless, a list of discriminators would encompass a catalogue of all labor market participants. Employers, unions, employees, employment agencies, and training programs are all implicated in the charge of labor market discrimination. To understand how so many individuals and groups are implicated, we must return to the nature of discrimination.

Much discrimination in the market is not intended. As we saw previously, even persons free of prejudice or animosity may engage in discriminatory patterns of behavior. While such unintentional practices make fewer headlines, their impact on minority employment opportunities is no less important. Traditional company recruitment practices provide a simple illustration. Most companies, large or small, rely heavily on existing employees for new recruits. If new jobs open up, present employees usually are able to locate friends or relatives who want the new positions, and a word-of-mouth recruitment system is remarkably efficient. Present employees know the company, the jobs, and the applicants; therefore, they are in a position to match jobs and people accurately. Word-of-mouth recruitment is also inexpensive; no outside agencies need be contacted, and advertisement costs are kept to a minimum. Large companies are so impressed with this recruitment system that they offer bonuses to employees who bring in new workers.

Although efficient, word-of-mouth recruitment practices tend to exclude minority workers from better jobs. Would-be minority applicants do not have a network of friends already in better employment positions. Accordingly, they are seldom aware of developing opportunities and are rarely brought to the attention of recruitment personnel. Even in the absence of willful discrimination, they are effectively cut off from new jobs.

Recruitment outside the firm does not always yield much better results. Companies are generally unfamiliar with the people and skills available in minority residential areas, especially ghetto areas. They do not know who, how, or where to recruit. As a result, they tend to rely on traditional sources and agencies of recruitment more readily accessible to whites. Would-be minority applicants also experience a certain hesitancy in approaching unfamiliar companies or employment agencies. Knowing that prejudice exists and having possibly confronted explicit discrimination themselves, minority job-seekers are often reluctant to risk embarassment or harassment. They rely, instead, on familiar sources and companies that have established reputations in the community for fair treatment. Recent converts to equal employment opportunity thus have difficulty in communicating their new intentions.

While these institutionalized patterns of behavior constitute a barrier to truly equal employment opportunity, we cannot ignore the impact of overt discrimination. Not all discriminatory practices are innocent. Some persons and groups willfully exclude minority workers from employment opportunities. Here we can only review the most obvious and widespread examples.

The Unions

Labor unions are a popular target for attack from many fronts, and the subject of racial discrimination provides no exception. It is widely believed that unions constitute the greatest barrier between minority workers and improving employment opportunities. Labor unions are large, highly visible, and often contain outspoken racist members. They also tend to control access to the better-paid jobs for which minority job-seekers are presently most qualified. High-status employment areas of lesser union strength, among them clerical, technical, and professional work, tend to require higher educational credentials. Hence, unions are in a position to provide the fastest route to improved economic status.

The past history of labor unions is not very encouraging. While the American Federation of Labor (AFL) was founded on the principles of racial and worker solidarity, its practices quickly departed from that philosophy. As early as 1895, nine years after its inception, the AFL compromised on the issue of racial equality by admitting deliberately discriminatory unions. By 1899 the AFL was even admitting unions whose constitutions explicitly forbade black membership, thereby forsaking even the pretense of racial equality. This development was particularly damaging to black workers, because the AFL was strongest in those areas where black employment skills were concentrated, namely the crafts, such as carpentry, blacksmithing, and mechanical arts. Indeed, at the time of the Civil War black workers dominated craft employment in the South, outnumbering white craftsmen five to one. As the craft union movement grew, however, blacks lost their foothold in the job market. Black craftsmen were forced out of their jobs and denied access to new ones. Apprenticeship programs were also closed, thereby eliminating future opportunities for employment.

While racial prejudices were clearly at the root of much union discrimination, there is abundant evidence that economic motivations were dominant. The nascent unions knew that their strength and welfare depended on their ability to control job entry. Any potential craftsman was viewed as a direct economic threat. The AFL unions not only sought to eliminate existing and potential competition from blacks but also worked vigorously to restrain all immigration from abroad. The Chinese were viewed as "people of vice and sexual immorality who were incompatible with our moral concepts."[4] Japanese and Koreans were no less undesirable. Even European immigrants were viewed as a threat to economic security and organizational strength. Hence, it is probably fair to conclude that the AFL was egalitarian in its discriminatory practices; that is, it discriminated against all potential competition with little regard to race, creed, or color! Where racial arguments were employed, their primary purpose was to camouflage narrower economic interests. Nevertheless, black workers were most abused, since they were the largest and closest competition.

The Congress of Industrial Organizations (CIO) emerged in 1935 in a changed economic climate and with a different constituency. Whereas the

---

[4]Cited by Herbert Hill in Arthur M. Ross and Herbert Hill, eds., *Employment, Race, and Poverty* (New York: Harcourt Brace Jovanovich, Inc. 1967), p. 389.

AFL had focused on craft labor, the CIO directed its attentions to the mass of workers on assembly lines and in less skilled jobs. These jobs generally required less training and experience and were concentrated more in the North. Not only were blacks significantly represented in these jobs, but they furthermore constituted an enormous threat to future union strength. If excluded from the industrial unions, black workers could be used by employers as strikebreakers to undercut union power. The same possibility did not exist in craft unions because specific skills were required for available jobs. Hence, the CIO had a powerful economic incentive to lower racial barriers to union entry. This, combined with the egalitarian outlook of its leaders, especially John L. Lewis, led the CIO to establish nondiscriminatory membership policies.[5]

The AFL–CIO merger in 1955 did not revolutionize union practices. While the new union was founded on stronger antidiscrimination principles, it did little to alter the actual practices of local affiliates, especially the older AFL locals. Local unions retain a broad range of autonomy, and the national leadership has little power or incentive to discipline them on the subject of racial equality. Consequently, black workers continue to be excluded from many unions and relegated to inferior jobs or separate seniority lines when admitted. Experienced black workers are oftentimes required to undergo long and low-paid apprenticeship courses as a condition for union entry; inexperienced black workers find that they cannot enter apprenticeship programs at all.

Employers

Like unions, business management tends to reflect the interests and attitudes of its members: some employers harbor racial prejudices and stereotyped views of minority workers. Even more prevalent, however, is a general reluctance to engage in actions that are controversial or merely tangential to primary business pursuits. Employers are hesitant to challenge traditional practices in hiring or to confront what they regard as the community's racial attitudes. Hence, employers will often ignore potential minority workers, not as a result of their own prejudice, but because they fear that such hiring will trigger the prejudices of white employees or existing customers. Employers have very little incentive to stir up racial troubles or even to bother determining whether such troubles would actually emerge. Profits, politics, recreation, and even the community chest command more attention and commitment. As a result, only the most cautious antidiscriminatory actions are undertaken,

[5]The tendency of craft unions to be more discriminatory continues today. See Orley Ashenfelter, "Racial Discrimination and Trade Unionism," *Journal of Political Economy,* May 1972, and Duane E. Leigh, "Racial Discrimination and Labor Unions," *Journal of Human Resources,* Fall 1978.

and then usually only as a result of economic or social pressures, such as boycotts or legal action.

Another barrier to more affirmative action on the part of business management arises from the nature of collective bargaining. Where management does, in fact, decide to hire minority workers on a more equal basis, the unions are likely to demand reciprocal concessions. Unions tend to view management's initiatives as an encroachment on their own prerogatives. Changed hiring practices are interpreted as a concession to the desires of management, so the union seeks compensation in other areas, chiefly in wages or working conditions. Thus, the cost of affirmative action escalates, and management is even less likely to press for the elimination of discriminatory employment patterns.[6]

Just how cautiously management may proceed in the area of race relations was amply demonstrated in Birmingham, Alabama, during the early 1960s. While managers in several steel companies there did make some progress in formal hiring and promotion practices, they were reluctant to tamper with the vestiges of Jim Crow. White and Colored signs were removed from drinking fountains and bathhouses, but twin facilities were maintained. Naturally, no workers took it upon themselves to integrate the newly desegregated facilities.

Finally, even "objective" hiring practices of employers may have discriminatory effects. We have already observed how word-of-mouth recruitment and traditional advertising may tend to exclude minority workers. Another obstacle emerges from the use of employment tests and other credentials as hiring criteria. All too often, test and educational credentials used to screen out prospective employees exclude a disproportionate number of minority workers. Moreover, such tests may have no direct relationship to job performance. Under such circumstances, the tests simply reduce an employers' hiring costs by reducing the number of extended interviews. In the process, however, many minority workers lose potential job opportunities. Such nonfunctional tests were outlawed by the U.S. Supreme Court in 1972 (*Griggs* v. *Duke Power Company*), but have not been eliminated completely.

Even if all such tests were eliminated, minority workers would still suffer from "statistical discrimination." In reality, employers do not know for sure which job-seekers will turn out to be the best employees. Tests and educational credentials are used to help reduce such uncertainty. If all such screening criteria are eliminated, employers may rely more on racial characteristics. Because white workers have, on average, more education, skill, and experience than do minority workers, an employer is statistically "safer" in hiring white workers. In other words, screening out minority workers on the basis of

[6]Large, highly unionized firms in concentrated industries apparently do discriminate more than other firms. See Walter Haessel and John Palmer, "Market Power and Employment Discrimination," *Journal of Human Resources,* Fall 1978.

their lower *average* qualifications may be an efficient recruitment technique, particularly if no surer screening mechanisms are available. In this case, minority workers are excluded from equal consideration on statistical grounds, not because of employer prejudice.[7] To the minority job-seeker, the end result is the same, of course.

CLASS DISCRIMINATION IN THE LABOR MARKET

Minority racial groups are not the only workers who suffer discrimination in labor markets. Racial discrimination has a counterpart in class discrimination. In this case, individuals from low-income backgrounds are consistently denied equal access to better jobs and pay.

Poor whites do not suffer the indignities of Jim Crow facilities or even explicitly separate hiring and promotion lines, but they are, nevertheless, at a disadvantage in the employment process. Employers, like the larger society, tend to have low estimates of the capabilities of job applicants who are poorly dressed or from "bad" neighborhoods. There is an underlying conviction that poverty reflects personal inadequacy (Flawed Characters), and, as a result, poor applicants are viewed differently than others and must exhibit exceptional talents to obtain competitive jobs. If their talents are only equal to, say, middle-class applicants, then prejudice is likely to deny employment to the poor. Prejudices are reinforced, of course, by the use of academic achievement tests that often have little or no relation to the content of the available job.

These discriminatory practices are often institutionalized in the recruitment procedures of companies. As we noted earlier, corporations tend not to recruit in poverty areas. They know virtually nothing about available talent in poor neighborhoods and expend little effort to increase their knowledge. As a consequence, poor job-seekers and company recruiters seldom make contact. The same kind of isolation results from the word-of-mouth recruitment practices previously mentioned. Like blacks generally, poor whites tend to have comparatively few friends or acquaintances employed at higher-status jobs. They thus have little knowledge of or access to good jobs that are opening up. What jobs they hear of are those they have always encountered: dirty, low-paid, and menial.

Class discrimination in the labor market, then, means that poor job-seekers have less chance to obtain employment than nonpoor job-seekers of

[7]The concept of "statistical" discrimination is discussed in Edmund S. Phelps, "The Statistical Theory of Racism and Sexism," *American Economic Review,* September 1972, and Dennis J. Aigner and Glen G. Cain, "Statistical Theories of Discrimination in Labor Markets," *Industrial and Labor Relations Review,* January 1977.

equal ability. Racial discrimination has the same effect for blacks and other minority groups, sex discrimination the same effect for women. In all cases, discrimination takes place as a result of individual prejudices and institutionalized practices. The poor, like blacks, have many personal characteristics and backgrounds unfamiliar to middle-class employers, employment agencies, and even unions. Conduct, speech, and dress are among those factors that create communication barriers. Employers tend to see these differences as indicators of ability rather than as the result of socioeconomic environment. It is assumed that the poor will not be as able or dependable on the job. Hence, workers are not sought from poorer areas and, when they come forth, are unfavorably considered.[8]

SEX DISCRIMINATION IN THE LABOR MARKET

The same forces that tend to constrain the earnings of minorities and the lower-income classes also operate to limit the employment and income opportunities of women. Here, again, of course, we must take into account the fact that women enter the labor market with less human capital than men do, especially when measured in terms of advanced degrees. And they tend to be trained for different kinds of work, as a result of both societal pressures and overt discrimination in the educational system. These handicaps help explain why women exhibit less labor force participation, inferior occupations, and lower pay. But such handicaps do not provide a complete explanation, as female workers additionally suffer from discrimination in the labor market, from limited access to jobs for which they are otherwise qualified.

As we noted in our discussion of racial discrimination (see Table 11.3), occupational segregation is a major source of earnings disparities. This tendency is especially important for women as well, as they tend to be relegated to a limited number of occupations and an even more limited number of jobs within each occupation. The statistics in Table 11.4 provide a clue as to how high the sex barriers are when one begins to examine the labor market in some detail. Within the "professional and technical" occupational category, for example, we discover that there are clearly "female jobs" and "male jobs": 97 percent of all registered nurses are women, while only 2 percent of our engineers are women. The same kind of imbalance is evident throughout the list.

Nor is this the end of the story. Even within the more detailed occupations of Table 11.4, men and women tend to be employed at different kinds of jobs, in different industries, or in different work settings. Consider just one example,

---

[8]Some of the intergenerational effects of inequality are explored in John A. Brittain, *The Inheritance of Economic Status* (Washington, D.C.: The Brookings Institution, 1977).

TABLE 11.4   A NONLIBERATED LABOR FORCE (percent)

	The Jobs That Women Hold	Proportion of Jobs Held by Women	The Jobs That Women Don't Hold	Proportion of Jobs Held by Women
Professional and technical	Librarians	82	Engineers	2
	Registered nurses	97	Lawyers and judges	5
	Elementary teachers	84	Doctors	9
	Dieticians	92	Clergy	3
Managers and administrators	Restaurants, cafeterias, and bars	34	Public agencies	6
Salesworkers	Demonstrators	91	Sales representatives	7
Clerical and kindred workers	Secretaries	97	Mail carriers	8
	Bank tellers	86	Shipping clerks	15
	Telephone operators	95	Dispatchers	17
Craftsmen	Bookbinders	58	Electricians	2
	Decorators	58	Telephone linemen and service	3
Operatives	Dressmakers	95	Taxicab drivers	6
	Laundry and dry cleaning	70	Truckdrivers	2
Service	Practical nurses	96	Police officers	4
	Waiters and waitresses	89	Bartenders	21

Source: Council of Economic Advisers, Economic Report of the President, (Washington, D.C.: Government Printing Office, 1973), Table 33.

that of waiters and waitresses. Women comprise a whopping 89 percent of that category, but how many of them are employed in the best restaurants (where prices and tips are highest, incidentally)? Very few. Is it because they don't speak French as well?

The Baby Question

Perhaps it is because they have babies. Not on the job, of course, but for 84 percent of all women, at some time in their lives. The job interruption that typically accompanies childbirth translates into lost job experience and thus less human capital development, at least from a labor market point of view. Can't this "natural" barrier to female productivity explain occupational and income differentials?

Partially, but only partially. As the President's Council of Economic Advisers has observed:

> *One important factor influencing the (earnings) differential is experience. The lack of continuity in women's attachment to the labor force means that they will not have accumulated as much experience as men at a given age. The relatively steeper rise of men's income with age has been attributed to their greater accumulation of experience, of "human capital" acquired on the job.*

> *(But) a differential, perhaps on the order of 20 percent, between the earnings of men and women remains after adjusting for factors such as education, work experience during the year, and even lifelong work experience.* [9]

Accordingly, we cannot dismiss occupational and earnings differentials between men and women on the basis of "natural" responsibilities of childbirth. Discrimination is clearly at work here: the pay and job status of women workers are being constrained by exclusionary employment practices. Moreover, we must take care to note that the same kind of negative feedbacks that constrain the human capital development of blacks affect women, too. Why should a woman postpone childbirth or pursue a lengthy and difficult course of study if it appears that she will not receive commensurate rewards in the labor market? Role differentiation and labor market discrimination tend to reinforce each other. [10]

SUMMARY

Minority racial groups, women, and the poor generally start out in the labor market at a distinct competitive disadvantage, largely as a result of discrimination in the educational system. Their handicaps do not end there, however. In the labor market itself, these groups do not even have an equal opportunity to make the best of their disadvantaged beginnings. Prejudice and institutional employment practices combine to handicap them still further.

Racial and class discrimination in the labor market takes many forms. Some employers and unions willfully exclude blacks. Others, perhaps less

[9]*Economic Report of the President* (Washington, D.C.: Government Printing Office, 1973), pp. 104–6.

[10]This point and additional criticism of the *Economic Report*, cited above, are contained in Barbara Bergmann and Irma Adelman, "The Economic Role of Women: A Review," *American Economic Review*, September 1973.

prejudiced, rely on recruitment procedures that have the same effect on minority racial groups, women, and the poor. Doubts about the capabilities of individuals who fall into any of these categories also limit employment and promotional possibilities. Notions of what kind of work is "proper" for blacks and fear of employee or community disapproval restrains even unprejudiced, but profit-maximizing, employers from providing equal opportunity. The cumulative impact of these practices is evident: members of minority or poor populations end up working less often, for fewer hours, at less attractive jobs—and, ultimately, for less income.

FURTHER READING

BERGMANN, BARBARA R., "The Effect on White Incomes of Discrimination in Employment," *Journal of Political Economy,* March 1971.

CONGRESSIONAL BUDGET OFFICE, *Income Disparities Between Black and White Americans.* Washington, D.C.: Government Printing Office, 1977.

FREEMAN, RICHARD, "Black Economic Progress Since 1964," *The Public Interest,* Summer 1978.

MARSHALL, RAY, "The Economics of Racial Discrimination: A Survey," *Journal of Economic Literature,* September 1974.

MASTERS, STANLEY H., *Black-White Income Differences.* New York: Academic Press, Inc., 1975.

U.S. COMMISSION ON CIVIL RIGHTS, *Social Indicators of Equality for Minorities and Women.* Washington, D.C.: Government Printing Office, 1978.

Part 3

PUBLIC PROGRAMS AND POLICIES

Introduction

The preceding nine chapters have focused on the potential causes of poverty in America. A variety of factors has been examined to determine what causal significance each might possess. The purpose of these detailed inquiries was twofold: to increase our understanding of poverty; and to establish a substantive basis for meaningful discussion of poverty policies. Part 3 focuses attention on those policies. References to our findings on causation are made throughout Part 3, while Chapter 15 provides a summary of causal links and policy directions.

There are three basic approaches to reducing poverty: (1) provision of income; (2) provision of jobs; and (3) elimination of barriers between existing jobs and individuals. All three approaches are followed in current antipoverty efforts to some extent. Each approach does not command equal attention or support, however, nor do they have equal impact on the distribution and extent of poverty. What we seek to determine in Part III is how much emphasis is currently accorded each approach, what kinds of programs are implemented, and the potential effectiveness of each.

There are, of course, literally hundreds of distinct programs and policies that impinge in some way on the poor. Rarely does a session of Congress go by when less than a dozen new programs or amendments to existing ones are proposed. To discuss all of these programs would consume thousands of pages. Fortunately, such an exhaustive review is not necessary. Many antipoverty programs are very similar in structure and scope and need not be examined individually. Instead, we may review the major features of some representative programs to acquire a perspective on the direction and magnitude of public efforts.

12 INCOME MAINTENANCE POLICIES

Income transfer payments are amounts of money transferred from one person to another through the medium of government taxes and payments. Given their apparent simplicity, they are often proposed as the most compelling and obvious solution to poverty. Simply give the poor enough money, it is argued, and poverty will disappear. Among others, economist Milton Friedman and urbanologist Irving Kristol have wondered aloud whether our public commitment to end poverty is sincere in light of our failure to provide the obvious remedy.[1]

The apparent simplicity of income transfer solutions to poverty is deceptive, however. We could, of course, provide enough money to close the poverty gap, the difference between what the poor now have (including existing income transfers) and what they need to maintain minimum standards of living. In 1977 that gap was only $18 billion, less than 1 percent of the nation's total output.

The transfer of another $18 billion to the poor—were it politically feasible—could create significant problems, however. First, exclusive reliance on income transfers as a "solution" to poverty serves to perpetuate the poverty problem. If an expansion of income transfers is adopted as an alternative to expansionary aggregate demand policies and increased efforts to expand and equalize educational opportunities, then there will be as many people in need of public assistance next year as there were this year. Simply transferring income to the needy does little to improve their opportunities for employment and upward mobility. The added income makes life easier for the poor, of

---

[1]Recall that other observers argue that we *have* eliminated poverty with income transfers; see Chapter 2.

course, but otherwise leaves their circumstances unchanged. Thus, income transfers are best viewed as an interim form of support, especially for those who are in a position to benefit from increased education or employment opportunities.[2]

Even on an interim basis, however, income transfers give rise to problems. Suppose that we guaranteed everyone an income equal to the 1979 poverty standard. This would amount to approximately $7,400 for a family of four (or approximately $8,100 in 1980 dollars). Any family earning less than this amount would receive an income transfer payment to make up the difference, thus bringing everybody up to the established minimum standard. We would clearly eliminate the existing poverty problem if we followed this approach, but we would create a few new problems in the process. Persons just above the poverty line—for example, those working at dead-end, low-paying jobs—would have strong incentive to abandon employment and join the ranks of the nonworking poor. The decision to work is largely a response to the financial and psychological rewards associated with employment. People in dull, dirty, low-paying jobs get little of either. Hence, by quitting their jobs, declaring themselves poor, and accepting a guaranteed transfer payment income, they would gain much more leisure at minimal financial or psychological cost. Similarly, people already counted as poor would have an incentive to substitute public transfers for whatever employment income they already possessed. This is the kind of behavior former Treasury Secretary William Simon had in mind in 1975 when he characterized our transfer programs as a "haven for the chiselers and rip-off artists."[3] Accordingly, we must recognize that the provision of income transfers may conflict with established work incentives, and consequently that both the observed size of the poverty population and the need for income transfers may be sensitive to the particular form our income transfer policies take.

These basic problems of income transfer have led to a proliferation of income maintenance programs. Some programs provide income for persons on the basis of need alone, while others provide transfers on the basis of previous contributions. When you pay social security taxes, for example, you are providing income transfers for the elderly while establishing your right to receive such transfers in old age. Other programs demand no such contributions. To receive benefits from state general assistance programs, you need only be poor and unable to obtain employment or other support. In this case, money is transferred from the taxpaying public directly to those in need.

---

[2] If the education and employment opportunities are slow in coming, however, the "interim" support may have to continue for a long time. In the interim the children of the poor will at least benefit from improved nutrition and shelter.

[3] August 12, 1975, address to the Junior Achievement conference in Bloomington, Indiana. Simon's characterization was strongly challenged by many, including Senator George McGovern (*Washington Post,* August 13 and 14, 1975).

Those income maintenance programs that provide assistance on the basis of need alone are usually referred to collectively as "the welfare system." Although many people tend to think of welfare as one big, centrally administered program, the realities of welfare are very different. First, the welfare system is composed of two distinctly different kinds of assistance. Some programs provide *cash assistance* to the poor, while others provide *in-kind assistance*—things like housing, food, and medical services. Furthermore, within each classification there are a variety of programs, each with its own characteristics, regulations, and objectives. We begin our analysis of income maintenance policies by examining welfare programs and conclude with a look at Social Security.

WELFARE: THE CASH ASSISTANCE PROGRAMS

Table 12.1 provides a summary view of the major programs that provide cash assistance to the poor. The three programs listed in the table are directed to very different population groups. The federal Supplemental Security Income (SSI) program was established for the aged, the blind, and the permanently disabled. It was introduced in July 1973, and took the place of three previous programs.[4] As of 1979 it was providing cash assistance to about 4 million people at an estimated annual cost of approximately $7 billion. By contrast, the federal-state Aid to Families with Dependent Children (AFDC) program was serving more than 10 million people in the spring of 1979, at an annual cost of

TABLE 12.1   CASH ASSISTANCE PROGRAMS, 1979

Program	Number of Current Recipients	Average Benefit per Recipient (per month)	Total Annual Payments (billions)
Supplemental Security Income (SSI)	4,200,000	$132	$ 6.7
Aid to Families with Dependent Children (AFDC)	10,300,000	$ 87	10.7
General Assistance (GA)	750,000	$131	1.2
Total	15,250,000		$18.6

Source: U.S. Department of Health, Education, and Welfare.

[4]The SSI program was enacted as part of the 1972 Social Security Act Amendments and consolidated the Old Age Assistance (OAA), Aid to the Blind (AB), and Aid to the Permanently and Totally Disabled (APTD) programs.

roughly $11 billion. The third program, General Assistance (GA), is operated solely under state and local auspices to provide help to those who are poor but do not fit one of the other two categories.

Inadequacies

The statistics provided in Table 12.1 suggest that we are giving a lot of money to a lot of people. Hence, it is not too surprising that in the minds of most hard-working taxpayers welfare conjures up visions of the easy life—a can of beer on a hot afternoon, color television at night. As we noted earlier, former Treasury Secretary Simon characterized welfare programs as a "haven for the chiselers and rip-off artists," while former President Nixon referred to welfare as a "free ride." But it is clear from actual welfare experience that very few welfare families are even tolerably comfortable, much less riding high. The typical AFDC family (mother and two or three children), for example, received only $3,200 of cash assistance in 1979, approximately half the amount the government has determined such families need. A budget that small simply does not go far, no matter how thinly it is spread. Just recall how little food, shelter, and clothing is provided by the much larger poverty budget. It would be a strange individual who forsook any but the poorest paying and most loathsome job for such a "free ride."

Table 12.2 shows a recent monthly budget for an AFDC family of four in California, one of the more generous states. In computing the needs of an AFDC family, the state legislature scrutinized each individual potential expense, using a procedure identical to the one we used earlier to construct

TABLE 12.2   MAXIMUM MONTHLY BUDGET FOR
AFDC FAMILY IN CALIFORNIA, 1978

Consumption Items	Amount Allowed
Food	$144
Clothing	50
Personal and incidental	9
Recreation and education	13
Community participation	—
Telephone service	—
Transportation	4
Household operations	22
Intermittent needs	7
Rent (maximum)	120
Utilities (maximum)	21
Total	$390

Source: California Department of Human Resources; updated.

hypothetical poverty lines. These figures, however, are real; they represent the maximum standard of living for a California AFDC family in 1978. Note that they were allowed no more than $120 for rent, no telephone, and only $13 per month for recreation and education! In less generous states, of course, the situation was far worse.

In light of the pittance available to AFDC recipients, it seems most unlikely that wage earners, even low paid ones, would rush to the welfare rolls. To guard against this remote possibility, however, stringent property limitations have been established for those who seek public assistance. You cannot turn to welfare, at least not for long, just because you run out of money. To enter and remain on the welfare rolls, you must also dispose of nearly all property. In most states a welfare family may possess no more than $1,000 in personal property, although there is sometimes an additional asset allowance if the family owns a house. Very few Cadillacs are maintained at that price. In the state of Maryland a family may own only $300 of property. A sampling of other states' asset limitations is contained in Table 12.3.

A discussion of welfare programs must begin, then, from the observation that financial dependence on public assistance is not comfortable. Families turn to public assistance only after they are impoverished and no other support is available. When on welfare, families will be maintained below levels society otherwise deems to be minimally adequate.

TABLE 12.3 AFDC PAYMENTS AND ASSET LIMITATIONS IN SELECTED STATES, 1978

State	Average Monthly Payments per Family	Asset Limitation
California	$332	$1,000 except value of boats, cars and snowmobiles and home
Colorado	222	$2,000 maximum, excluding prepaid burial contract, books, 1 cow, 10 sheep, and feed for 6 months; 1 wagon, plow, and harrow, and personal effects and house
Indiana	188	$750 and house
Mississippi	80	house up to $3,500 assessed value and $1,500 in property
Tennessee	114	house up to $9,000 equity value plus $1,000 of personal property, excluding one car and burial insurance

Source: U.S. Department of Health, Education, and Welfare.

Inequities

In addition to providing inadequate levels of income maintenance, the welfare system is also beset with inequities. Notice first that fewer than 16 million people received cash assistance in 1979, even though more than 24 million people were counted as poor. Clearly, the welfare system provides some help to many, but none at all to others. The question is: who is not helped and for what reasons?

Conspicuously missing from the welfare rolls in nearly every state are male-headed poor families. As we noted above, the SSI program aids the aged, the blind, and the disabled, while the AFDC program is supposed to provide help to families with children. But of the nearly 17 million poor people in families with children (see Figure 2.3), only 10 million were receiving AFDC assistance (Table 12.1). Thus, being poor in a family with children is not sufficient qualification for receiving AFDC support; a further distinction is made between the deserving and the undeserving poor. In this case, the deserving are those whose fathers or husbands are dead, deserted, or otherwise absent from the home. The presence of a male adult in the home is taken as prima facie evidence that the family is capable of its own support. AFDC payments are reserved for fatherless homes, regardless of whatever needs poor male-headed families may have.[5]

Even among those poor families fortunate enough to receive welfare payments, there are tremendous disparities in the amount of support provided. Notice in Table 12.1, for instance, how differently recipients of SSI and AFDC are treated: SSI recipients receive on average 50 percent more aid as do AFDC recipients. This disparity arises in part from taxpayers' sympathy for the aged and disabled, combined with their distrust of younger poor families. The distrust of AFDC families stems largely from the assumption that they could support themselves if they so chose. Not only are the adults who benefit from AFDC relatively young but their marital status—which the program itself constrains—is suspect. Public distrust of the program is heightened by the fact that large numbers of blacks, Hispanics, families headed by women, and illegitimate children participate in the program. Even more distressing to taxpayers is the observation that the program's growth appears to be impervious to advances in the economy. Thus, provision of AFDC benefits usually begins against a background of public mistrust and resentment.

[5]An exception to this rule is the AFDC-UF program, which provides benefits to poor families with unemployed fathers, but the program is too small and restrictive to merit attention here. At the spring of 1979, only 473,000 persons were receiving AFDC-UF benefits. For a summary of who receives various transfer benefits, see Sheldon Danziger, Robert Haveman and Robert Plotnick, "Income Transfer Programs in the United States: An Analysis of Their Structure and Impact," A study for the Joint Economic Committee of the U.S. Congress, May 1979.

Further inequities in the cash assistance programs arise from the different levels of benefits received by families in identical situations. Although the "average" AFDC family received $3,200 in cash assistance in 1979, actual benefits varied widely across states: AFDC families in New York and Michigan received $4,400 in welfare payments, while identical families in Mississippi received only $690 a year. Table 12.3 indicates how benefits varied in other states.

Disparities in support reflect far more than differences in the cost of living. In essence, they reflect the ability and willingness of taxpayers in each state to provide for the needy. At present, federal, state, and local governments must contribute to the financing of AFDC. If the county or state cannot or will not provide adequate "matching" funds, the federal contribution is proportionately diminished. Welfare payments in Mississippi, for example, are low, both because there is little public or private money in the state and because white Mississippians do not want to spend what little there is in providing for the poor, many of whom are black.[6]

Work Disincentives

In view of the inadequacies and inequities of our cash assistance programs, it is not surprising to learn that welfare recipients are upset with "the system." Not surprisingly, no one else is particularly happy with it either. Liberal critics of the program are dissatisfied with AFDC's coverage, its benefits, and the "red tape" and humiliation associated with the receipt of public assistance. Taxpayers generally are unhappy with the spiraling costs of the program and continue to view recipients with disfavor and suspicion. And finally, all critics unite in pointing out that the welfare system tends to undermine the motivation to work.

The work incentive problem arises from the way in which a family's welfare benefits are calculated. When a family applies for welfare, it is obliged to report any income at its disposal. A woman with small children, for example, might earn $50 a month by babysitting for neighbors. Up until 1967 welfare authorities subtracted any such income from the family's needs—as determined by those same authorities—and provided the difference. Suppose the welfare authorities concluded that Ms. Jones and her three children needed $300 a month: they paid her only $250, knowing that she could provide the rest.

[6]See Larry Orr, "Income Transfers as a Public Good," *American Economic Review,* June 1976, and Bradley R. Schiller, "Income Transfers as a Public Good: Comment," *American Economic Review,* December 1978.

Although the foregoing procedure for calculating welfare benefits might appear to be reasonable, it had the effect of destroying all monetary incentives for going to work. To appreciate the dynamics of this situation, imagine that Ms. Jones was offered regular part-time employment—as a nurse's aid, for example—at $3.50 an hour for ten hours a week. Ms. Jones may be reluctant to leave her small children in the care of others, but she could certainly use the money. Consequently, she is inclined to accept the new job rather than continue babysitting, especially if transportation problems (she has no car) and child-care arrangements can be worked out. But what will happen to her actual income if she takes this step toward self-improvement? Absolutely nothing. The welfare authorities simply noted that she is earning $140 a month rather than $50, reckoned that she is better providing for her own needs, and reduced her welfare payment to $100. Her family's income remained at $300 whether or not the family head found employment and regardless of how hard she strove for self-improvement. From Ms. Jones' perspective, work clearly did not pay.

The reduction in welfare benefits that took place when Ms. Jones accepted the nurse's aid job amounted to an implicit tax on her earnings. Indeed, the *marginal tax rate* turns out to be 100 percent in this case, as Ms. Jones loses one dollar in welfare benefits for every additional dollar she earns. Faced with such a high tax rate, how many people would seek additional employment? Very few; which is the heart of the work incentive problem.

The Social Security Amendments of 1967 alleviated the work incentive problem somewhat by reducing the marginal tax rate. The significance of this change is illustrated in Figure 12.1. Consider the case of Ms. Jones again. If she does not work at all, she will receive $3,600 a year ($300 a month) from welfare, a situation designated by point A. Now suppose she is offered the nurse's aid job, for 500 hours a year (ten hours a week). If she accepted the job under the old AFDC system, she would move to point E, working more but with no change in total income. Under current regulations, however, she moves to point D and increases her well-being by working. D is obviously a more desirable place to be than E, as it represents more income for the same amount of effort. Hence, whatever Ms. Jones' feelings about work, she is more likely to take a job under the new system than the old one. In this sense, the new system provides a greater incentive to work.

How does Ms. Jones get to point D under the new system? First, the welfare authorities now recognize that there are certain costs associated with working, things like transportation expenses, additional clothes, and added meal costs, which may amount to as much as $60 a month (or $720 a year). To assure that Ms. Jones takes home at least enough income from her new job to cover these costs—and thus to eliminate the possibility of her incurring a net loss from working—the welfare department "disregards" that much income

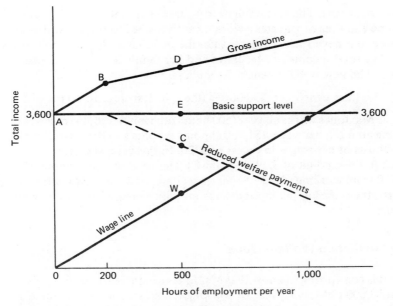

FIGURE 12.1   Work Incentive Provisions under AFDC

in calculating her welfare benefits. Whereas they would have deducted $720 from her welfare checks under the old system, they now deduct nothing, thus enabling her to receive both the $3,600 in welfare benefits and the first $720 she earns.[7] In effect, the marginal tax rate, the rate at which welfare benefits are reduced as earnings increase, on the first $720 of earnings has dropped from 100 percent to 0 percent. As a result, Ms. Jones can move to point B without welfare department interference.

Only as Ms. Jones' earnings exceed $720 a year does the welfare department begin to take notice of her added income and start reducing her welfare check. Accordingly, beyond point B, Ms. Jones' total income rises more slowly than her increased earnings. But it does rise, because the welfare department no longer reduces her benefits by a dollar for every additional dollar she earns. That is, they no longer impose a 100 percent marginal tax on earnings beyond point B, but instead allow her to keep something for herself. Under the new AFDC system the marginal tax rate is 67 percent, so that the welfare department reduces her benefit check by only sixty-seven cents for every additional

---

[7]Federal welfare regulations require individual states to "disregard" $30 a month, one-third of the remainder, and all reasonable "work-related expenses" and child-care costs. Thus, the amount of the disregarded (exempted) income varies from state to state and among individuals within a state. The figure of $720 used here is an approximation to the typical AFDC case.

dollar she earns. The remaining thirty-three cents enhances Ms. Jones' total income and thus constitutes a work incentive. The incentive is still modest, to be sure, but nevertheless greater than the one that earlier existed (nothing).

The total income of Ms. Jones and her family at point D is easily computed. The new welfare benefit formula is:

Welfare benefit = $3,600 − (0.67 × Earnings in excess of $720)

If Ms. Jones works all year (500 hours) at her new job, she receives the following amount: her wages ($1,750 at point W) plus a welfare check reduced by two-thirds of her wages in excess of $720. In this case, she receives a welfare check in the amount of $2,913 (point C). Her total income at point D is thus $1,750 from working plus $2,913 from welfare, or $4,663. By her own modest efforts, then, she has managed to substantially increase her family's economic status.

Conflicting Welfare Goals

It is comforting to know that Ms. Jones can increase her family's income from $3,600 to $4,663 a year by working ten hours a week as a nurse's aid. It might, however, be nicer still if the welfare department would let her keep a little more of the money she earns from making beds, emptying bedpans, and sterilizing bandages. After all, the life of a nurse's aid is not exactly glamorous and Ms. Jones obviously needs the money. So why not lower the marginal tax rate from 67 percent to, say, 25 percent, or even zero? That would clearly solve the work incentive problem while giving Ms. Jones a real chance to make a few bucks.

The difficulty with this solution to the work incentive problem is that it compromises other goals. Three distinct goals are commonly associated with welfare systems: income provision, work incentives, and cost minimization. To the extent that we want to protect people from the indignities of poverty, we should provide a high income floor (or guarantee). If we also desire to encourage employment and self-improvement, we must impose low marginal tax rates (allow a recipient to keep a substantial share of her earnings above the minimum). And if we desire to hold program costs down to some reasonable level, we must limit the coverage of the program to those in need. All these objectives are worthwhile, just as the means for achieving them are clear. Nevertheless, they are mutually exclusive. We cannot move in all three directions at once.

Suppose that we actually eliminate the marginal tax rate on Ms. Jones' earnings, thus allowing her to keep everything she earns. In that case, her total income would rise to $5,350 ($3,600 in benefits plus $1,750 in wages). Still no life of luxury, but improving. Now suppose that the hospital technicians form a union and pay scales are increased. Ms. Jones is offered a raise to $4 an hour, provided that she works 1,500 hours a year (thirty hours a week). Because we no longer reduce her welfare benefits as her earnings increase, this stroke of good fortune will give Ms. Jones the opportunity to take home a total income of $9,600. Terrific. But should we still be providing $3,600 in welfare payments to someone who earns $6,000 on her own? How about someone earning $8,000? $10,000? Or, to make a long story short, where should we draw the line? Clearly, if we do not impose a marginal tax rate at some point, everyone will be eligible for full welfare benefits and we will preclude our third goal, that of cost minimization.

The conflict between the goals of income provision, work incentives, and cost minimization can be summarized in a neat little equation:

$$\text{Break-even income level} = \frac{\text{Income floor}}{\text{Marginal tax rate}}$$

The break-even income level refers to the amount of money a person can earn before losing all welfare benefits. In Ms. Jones' case, excluding the $720 disregard, the break-even point under the current AFDC system would amount to $5,373 ($3,600/.67); beyond that level of earnings, she would be on her own.[8] If the marginal tax rate were 100 percent as under the old system, the break-even point would be $3,600 ($3,600/1.00), meaning that people who earned $3,600 on their own would get no assistance from welfare. Under our aborted proposal to lower marginal tax rates to zero, the break-even point would rise to infinity ($3,600/0), and we would all be on welfare.

As is apparent from the arithmetic above, a lower break-even income level can be achieved only by sacrificing a high income floor or low marginal tax rates. Hence, cost minimization can be fulfilled only by sacrificing income provision or work incentives. More generally, we may observe that fulfillment of any two objectives necessitates sacrificing the third. The choice of how far to pursue each objective will ultimately have to be made in the political arena. As a rule, we have voted to sacrifice a little income provision and work incentive in order to hold down the size and costs of welfare.

The Goal Compromise

Obviously, the compromise we strike between the goals of income provision, work incentives, and cost minimization is not going to please everyone. More important, however, we should note that the same compromise is not necessarily appropriate for all population groups. For those people who are really not capable of working, a sacrifice of income provision for the sake of

---

[8]If we complicate the break-even formula with a disregard (earnings exemption), then Ms. Jones could earn $5,373 plus $720. for a total of $6,093.

enhancing work incentives would be ridiculous. On the other hand, high-income guarantees for those who are capable of working might seem unnecessary. Hence, it would make sense to strike a different compromise of welfare goals for two distinct groups, those who can work and those who cannot.

Unfortunately, it is not always possible to draw such a neat distinction. A ninety-two-year-old woman confined to a wheelchair would seem to have very few employment opportunities; for her, income provision would be more appropriate than work incentives. But what about the father of four children who loses his job? Or the mother who is left with a five-year-old child when her husband skips town with the next-door neighbor? Or what about the coed who got pregnant and is now trying to raise a child on her own? Are work incentives irrelevant in these cases? Our collective response, as reflected in welfare regulations, has been "no."

Although it is often difficult to distinguish the potentially employable from the rest of the poor, we attempt to approach this distinction by segregating needy families into different welfare classifications. This is why we have a separate welfare program (SSI) for the aged, the blind, and the handicapped, a program that provides higher income guarantees and smaller work incentives. In the process, of course, many younger families who are temporarily unable to find or accept employment end up at the margins of deprivation. This is especially true for those impoverished families headed by unemployed or underemployed males that we exclude from cash assistance because of their assumed employability.

WELFARE: THE IN-KIND PROGRAMS

The variety of cash assistance programs available to the poor does not constitute society's entire income transfer response to poverty. As we noted earlier, the welfare system really incorporates two kinds of programs, those that provide cash income and those that provide income in kind. In recent years, the in-kind programs have been growing much more quickly than the cash-assistance programs. In the following paragraphs, we review a few of the major in-kind programs.

Food Stamps

Food stamps are the most familiar of in-kind welfare benefits. Food stamps are simply coupons ("stamps") that allow a person to buy food. The stamps may be "spent" at the grocery store, where they are accepted at face value. The grocer, in turn, cashes the stamps in at a local bank, which itself redeems them at face value from the government. In effect, then, food stamps are a direct substitute for cash. Food stamps are not fully equivalent to cash, however, since they may be used only for food purchases.

Food stamps are distributed to poor families on the basis of need. The value of stamps given to a family depends on its income and family size. The average food-stamp allotment in 1979 was $35 per month per person (about thirty cents per meal), or $140 per month for a family of four. The value of food-stamp transfers is automatically increased each year to account for higher food prices.

Medicaid

Even larger than the food-stamp program is Medicaid, the program that provides medical services to the poor. Under Medicaid an eligible person can use the services of a doctor or hospital just like anyone else. The difference is that the Medicaid patient simply passes the bill on to the government, rather than paying for it himself or submitting it to a private insurance company. Obviously, the amount of benefit a poor family gets from Medicaid depends on how often it requires medical treatment. In 1979 nearly all public welfare recipients made some use of Medicaid, as did many others who had incomes just above the poverty standard. The average value of the services received exceeded $1,000 per year for a family of four.

Housing Assistance

In addition to food and medical services a poor family can also receive housing assistance. For the most part, such assistance is provided in the form of public housing, usually large housing projects owned and operated by the government. In a public housing project the tenants enjoy cheap (subsidized) rents, although not a great deal more in terms of quality of environment. Nevertheless, the fact that they are paying less than the market value of their apartments means that they are effectively receiving an income transfer, which on average works out to approximately $1,000 a year. Fewer than a million families receive such transfers every year.

In addition to the public housing projects. there are also housing assistance programs for low-income people who are renting or even buying their apartments and homes in the private market. In these programs, the rent or mortgage payment is reduced, with the government (the Department of Housing and Urban Development, or HUD) making up the difference.

Just on the basis of these three in-kind welfare programs, we may conclude that the noncash benefits available to poor (and near-poor) families are substantial. Were a family of four eligible for the average benefits available from food stamps, Medicaid, and housing assistance, it could receive an in-kind subsidy valued as high as $3,700 a year. This would be in addition to the average *cash* benefit of $3,600 a year available from AFDC. Hence, the combination of both cash and in-kind assistance is capable of lifting a family out of poverty. Table 12.4 depicts the total costs and average benefits associated with the major in-kind programs.

TABLE 12.4   IN-KIND WELFARE PROGRAMS, 1979

Program	Number of Recipients (millions)	Average Benefit per Recipient per Month	Total Annual Cost (billions)
Food stamps	15	$35	$ 6.3
Medicaid	25	58	17.4
Housing assistance	2.5	40	1.2
School lunch program	15	7	2.2
Total			$27.1

Source: U.S. Departments of Health, Education, and Welfare, Housing and Urban Development, and Agriculture.

The Goal Conflict

It is clear that in-kind programs substantially raise the standard of living for the poor; but of course, they do so at the expense of certain identifiable costs. In the first place and most obviously they involve a substantial amount of public expenditure, over $27 billion in 1979. More important, however, the provision of substantial in-kind benefits materially alters the goal compromise we observed earlier. As we noted, the cash assistance programs, particularly AFDC, sacrifice more of the income-provision goal in order to better fulfill the work-incentive and cost-minimization goals. Now we observe that that compromise has been tampered with by the introduction of food stamps, Medicaid and housing assistance.

Although it might seem that the in-kind programs are a way of meeting all three of our welfare goals simultaneously—of filling in the gaps left in our earlier compromise—such an assumption is merely whistling in the dark. The three goals remain irreconcilable, and the provision of in-kind assistance serves only to strike a new compromise, not to render our separate goals more compatible.

The impact of in-kind programs on our policy compromise can be seen in Figure 12.2. In this figure we reconstruct the opportunities available to Ms.

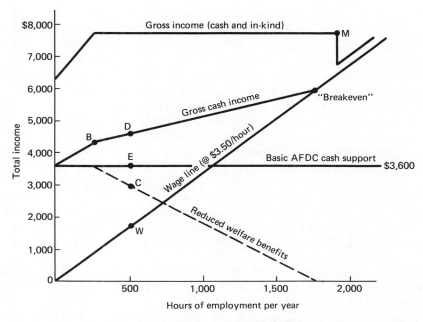

FIGURE 12.2   Effect of In-Kind Benefits on Income and Work Incentives

Jones under the AFDC program ("AFDC only" line). As we noted earlier, Ms. Jones has an incentive (albeit limited) to take a job under AFDC, as she can increase her standard of living (move to points B and D) by so doing.

The new and higher line in Figure 12.2 represents the opportunities available to Ms. Jones and her family from the *combined* provisions of AFDC, food stamps, Medicaid, and housing assistance. As is evident, Ms. Jones' family enjoys a much higher standard of living when it gets not only welfare checks, but lives in subsidized housing, gets free medical services, and buys food stamps as well. There is something else noteworthy about the new opportunity curve confronting Ms. Jones, however. Notice what happens to her total gross income as she works more hours. Her gross income rises slowly at first, then not at all for most of her employment experience (the gross income curve is flat). Ultimately (at point M), her gross income actually *falls* as her work effort increases! Not only does Ms. Jones now feel less *need* to work as a result of her greater public subsidy, but she now confronts less *incentive* to work, Thus, the attainment of greater income provision has been achieved at the sacrifice (opportunity cost) of work incentives. That is not to say that the new compromise is any better or worse than the old one, but simply to point up the fact that the old goal conflict still exists.

The reduction in work incentives comes about from an increase in the marginal tax rate, of course. As Ms. Jones works more, her welfare benefits now decline at an increased rate. But this is not due to any change in AFDC benefit calculations: AFDC still allows her to keep 100 percent of the first $720 she earns and 33 percent of everything above that. Rather, the sad truth is that she now loses some of her in-kind benefits as her income rises.

Recall that the value of a family's food-stamp allotment depends on a family's income. Families with higher incomes get fewer stamps. Hence, part of what Ms. Jones earns is effectively taken away in the form of food-stamp losses; this acts as an additional tax on earnings. The same is true of housing assistance: As Ms. Jones' earnings increase, she will have to pay a larger share of the market value of her rent. All these provisions are perfectly compatible with the equity concept of reserving welfare assistance for the neediest. However, they also diminish the net rewards associated with employment. In this case, the *combined* marginal tax rates from AFDC, food stamps, and housing assistance are assumed to equal 100 percent. In other words, there is no monetary incentive for working.

The greatest blow to work incentives occurs at point M, the point at which Ms. Jones' earnings rise above Medicaid eleigibility ceilings. Only those who have an income less than 133 percent of the relevant poverty standard are eligible for Medicaid assistance. If Ms. Jones' income rises above that limit, she will have to pay her family's medical bills herself, thereby losing $1,000 (on average) in Medicaid benefits. Accordingly, her total income (including the value of in-kind assistance) drops by $1,000 at point M. How many people would work an extra hour or day if they were going to be rewarded with that kind of income loss? Clearly, the higher standard of living that in-kind welfare benefits make possible also diminishes the incentives to seek employment.

WELFARE REFORM SUGGESTIONS

In view of the inadequacies, inequities and work disincentives associated with the current mix of cash and in-kind welfare programs, it should not be surprising that suggestions for welfare reform abound. In 1977 President Carter observed that "the welfare system is neither rational nor is it fair; it is antiwork and antifamily. It is unfair to the poor and wasteful of taxpayers' dollars." To remedy this situation, Carter proposed "a complete and clean break with the past."[9] He proposed to replace the existing welfare system with a sweeping reform plan, entitled the Program of Better Jobs and Income (PBJI).

[9]Presidential statement, Plains, Georgia, August 6, 1977.

The cornerstone of PBJI was its classification of poor people into two groups, depending on their employment potential. Each group would be provided with a different mix of income support, as follows:

Tier 1:

> *Families not expected to work* (i.e., the aged, blind, disabled, and single-parent families with children under seven years)

Tier 1 families would be provided with a basic income guarantee of $4,200 per year (for a family of four), and a marginal tax rate of 50 percent. Thus, the break-even level of income would be $8,400.

Tier 2:

> *Families expected to work* (i.e., two-parent families, single-parent families with older children, single individuals, childless couples)

Tier 2 families would be provided with a basic guarantee of only $2,300. But the marginal tax rate would be zero on the first $3,800 of earnings, thereby permitting a family to attain a poverty standard of living ($6,100) by working. Thereafter, a marginal tax rate of 50 percent would be imposed, creating a break-even of $8,400 for these families also.

The basic objective of the PBJI proposal was to minimize work-incentive problems while assuring all families an adequate level of income support. The potential success of President Carter's proposal depended on two critical assumptions: (1) that the employable poor can be distinguished from the non-employable poor (PBJI's two tiers), and (2) that the people in Tier 2 will be able to find jobs. We have already observed that the first assumption is doubtful in many cases. Poor families move in and out of the labor force repeatedly, and for a variety of reasons (see Chapters 4 and 5). "Employability" is not a permanent characteristic of a family or its members. Hence, the separation of poor families into two "employable" and "unemployable" groups requires high administrative costs and invites subterfuge.

The assumption that all "employable" families will find work—and thus survive with their minimal welfare support—is potentially even more troublesome. We have already observed (Chapter 4) that millions of individuals are poor because too few jobs are available. To meet this criticism, President Carter proposed to create 1.4 million jobs in public service employment. These jobs would be temporary and pay the minimum wage.

Congress began to debate the PBJI in late 1977. Among the criticisms leveled at the Carter proposal were that it was too expensive; that its work requirements were not strong enough, especially for single-parent families; that it did not provide enough jobs; and that its benefit levels were too low. The debate was not resolved by the 95th Congress: energy legislation and the 1978 congressional elections sidetracked welfare reform.

In 1979 the Carter Administration developed a scaled-down welfare reform plan. A major objective of the revisions was to reduce the size and cost of the public-jobs component of the program. Unfortunately, any reductions in the number of guaranteed jobs threatened the financial capability of Tier 2 families. In other words, the two-tier system could not be maintained without assured full employment.[10]

Negative Income Taxes

A common objective of most welfare-reform proposals is to provide a more coherent and equitable welfare system. In terms of their mechanics they appear much like the negative income tax plans that have been suggested for many years. A negative income tax (NIT) is a tax system wherein people automatically receive transfers ("negative taxes") from the government if their incomes fall below established levels. Thus, they consist of (1) a guaranteed income floor, and (2) a marginal tax rate, which together determine who will receive income transfers and how much. What distinguishes such systems from our current welfare programs are two features: universality and simplicity.

The universality of NIT plans arises from the fact that their benefits would be available to everyone on the same basis, that is, the basis of need; their simplicity derives from the consolidation of all welfare programs. As we have noted, the current patchwork of public assistance programs necessitates a case-by-case determination of eligibility, need, and grant levels. Not only is such a determination expensive and frustratingly slow; it often leads to administrative abuse. Welfare authorities have demonstrated a special concern for the morals of recipients and have even conducted midnight raids on the homes of AFDC mothers. Moral fitness requirements have been established by state legislatures and welfare authorities to supplement more objective income criteria of eligibility. Under a negative income tax program, case-by-case determinations would be unnecessary and administrative abuse unlikely.

Another consequence of present administrative arrangements is that welfare regulations are confusing and vary by state. Recipients have little access to information regarding the rules that govern them or the benefits to which they are entitled. Generally, they are compelled to rely on program personnel, in the usual situation, caseworkers, for this information. In some jurisdictions the information is freely available; in others it is systematically

---

[10]This same conflict between the welfare goals of income adequacy and work incentives helped defeat President Nixon's earlier (1969) welfare reform proposal (the "Family Assistance Plan"). For a detailed analysis of President Carter's plan, see Sheldon Danziger, Robert Haveman, and Eugene Smolensky, "The Program for Better Jobs and Income—A Guide and Critique," A study prepared for the Joint Economic Committee of the U.S. Congress, October 1977.

withheld. The net result is to render the recipient totally dependent on the capability and benevolence of local authorities.

NIT programs would overcome most of these deficiencies by standardizing eligibility criteria and by making assistance available as a matter of right. Every poor family would receive identical aid based on the number of family members. Access to financial assistance would be as simple and direct as income taxes now are, and similar verification procedures would be utilized to certify eligibility. Local authorities would have no discretionary control over the behavior of recipients, whose identity would be confidential.

Although NIT-type proposals are attractive, they are no panacea for our welfare problems. We still have to struggle with the conflict between the goals of adequacy, work incentives, and cost minimization. There is simply no way to achieve all three goals within the context of any single program. Thus, the continuing debate on welfare reform will largely reflect differing views on the appropriate goal compromise.

One of the impediments to a goal compromise is a continuing lack of information about the effects of a NIT on work behavior, family stability, and welfare costs. The U.S. Department of Health, Education, and Welfare has funded large, multiyear experiments with various NIT programs. Each experimental program has been distinguished by a particular combination of income guarantee and marginal tax rate, and has been offered a particular NIT program, while another group is left to fend for itself or to rely on the regular AFDC system. The behavior of the experimental families is then compared with that of the nonexperimental families to determine the effects of the NIT program.

Although NIT experiments have been under way since 1968, their findings have not been conclusive. Early results from experiments in New Jersey and North Carolina did not deter work effort. In other words, greater income adequacy could be achieved without significant loss of work incentives. Later experiments in Seattle and Denver, however, indicate that labor-supply reductions might be substantial, particularly for secondary workers (e.g., wives of employed husbands). On average, the labor supply of husbands declined by 5 percent as a result of the experimental NIT, while the labor supply of wives fell by 22 percent. The work effort of female heads of families was reduced by 11 percent.[11] In addition, the guarantee of income support appears to induce family breakup.[12]

The results from the Seattle-Denver experiments again underscore the potential conflict between the goals of income adequacy and work incentive.

[11]Michael C. Keeley et al., "The Estimation of Labor Supply Models Using Experimental Data," *American Economic Review,* December 1978.

[12]Robert G. Spiegelman, testimony before the Senate Finance Committee, U.S. Senate, May 1, 1978; see also Bradley R. Schiller, "When Welfare Families Know Their Rights," *Wall Street Journal,* July 11, 1978.

Although the estimates themselves, as well as their policy implications, have been challenged, they highlight a basic policy dilemma.[13]

Another problem that NIT-type programs must confront is the immediacy and variability of families' income-maintenance needs. Families who we count as "poor" aren't necessarily in need of income maintenance all year round: their low income for the year may reflect adequate income part of the year and no income for the rest. By the same token, families whose *annual* income ranks them among the nonpoor may have experienced short-term deprivation and needed assistance. One of the reasons our present welfare system is so complex and costly is that it is responsive to such variation; thousands of families move on and off welfare every month. By contrast, NIT-type systems, modeled after our regular tax system, envision longer accounting periods and less responsiveness. Unfortunately, families who experience sudden income losses can neither eat last year's income nor afford to wait until assistance comes later, on a retroactive basis. Hence, NIT-type proposals are likely to be amended in practice and end up with more administrative complexities than their authors envision.

SOCIAL SECURITY

The Old Age, Survivors, Disability and Health Insurance Program—or Social Security—is a very different kind of income maintenance program. Social security benefits are not reserved for those in need. Instead, they are distributed primarily to those who have made prior contributions to the program's funds. Thus, the program is neither intended nor operated as an antipoverty mechanism. The majority of the 35 million individuals who receive social security payments have never experienced poverty. Yet, they receive more than $130 billion in annual payments, triple the size of annual public assistance payments (cash and in-kind).

The financing of social security is carried out by the imposition of special taxes on employment income. In 1980, social security taxes were 6.13 percent on the first $25,000 of wages.[14] Thus, a person earning $25,000 or more

---

[13]For a discussion of the NIT experiments and their significance, see Joseph Pechman and P. Michael Timpane, eds., *Work Incentives and Income Guarantee* (Washington, D.C.: The Brookings Institution, 1975) or the symposium published in the *Journal of Human Resources,* Spring and Fall issues, 1974, and John L. Palmer and Joseph Pechman, eds., *Welfare in Rural Areas* (Washington, D.C.: The Brookings Institution, 1978). For alternative models, also see Mark Killingsworth, "Must a Negative Income Tax Reduce Labor Supply? A Study of the Family's Allocation of Time," *Journal of Human Resources,* Summer 1976, and Ronald Hoffman and Bradley R. Schiller, "Work Incentives of the Poor: A Reconsideration," *Review of Economics and Statistics,* August 1970, or Frank Levy, "The Labor Supply of Female Household Heads," *Journal of Human Resources,* Winter 1979.

[14]Both the amount of earnings subject to social security taxation ("the tax ceiling") and the level of retirement benefits increase automatically each year according to the rate of inflation in wages and prices; only the tax *rate* is set by Congress.

contributed $1,532 to the social security program. His employer contributed an identical amount. These contributions are not reserved for those who currently pay taxes. Rather, they are used to provide benefits to those individuals over sixty-two who no longer work but once made contributions to the program. Disabled workers and survivors of deceased retirees also receive monthly benefits from social security. Later generations are expected to provide the funds for present workers when they retire or become disabled.

Social security finances are a unique combination of insurance and income redistribution principles. To some extent, the amount of any person's eventual benefit is conditioned by the size of his earlier payments. A person who earned $25,000 or more in 1980 paid more social security taxes, that is, higher premiums, than people earning less. Accordingly, he or she is entitled to greater benefits when he or she retires. In 1980, the maximum monthly social security benefit was nearly $600 per person, while the minimum payment was only $150.

Were social security benefits distributed solely according to previous contributions, the program's ability to alleviate poverty would be negligible. People who received high benefits after retirement would be those who had higher income while working. Those who are poor while in the labor force are unable to pay high premiums and would receive only meager benefits in old age. Thus, conditioning retirement benefits on the basis of previous ability to pay would have the effect of perpetuating impoverishment.

The social security program does not operate exclusively on insurance principles, however. Some redistribution of income is built into social security financing. Persons who earn little and thus pay very low social security taxes receive proportionately larger benefits than individuals who pay high premiums. Thus, workers near the bottom of the income distribution receive more retirement benefits for every dollar of taxes they pay than workers near the top of the income distribution. Nevertheless, minimum benefits for a retired couple remain below the poverty line, and many aged individuals must rely substantially on public assistance (SSI) or do without. Still others receive no retirement benefits because they or their spouses were never employed in occupations subject to social security taxation.

Even people who managed to avert poverty while working are subject to impoverishment after retirement. This contingency applies especially to those who were at the margins of poverty while young and lose their primary source of income when old. For them, social security payments may represent the difference between poverty and nonpoverty in old age. In 1978, over 6 million aged persons fell into this category. They would have been poor were it not for the fact that social security benefits supplemented their modest pensions and savings.

The impact of the social security program testifies to its potential effectiveness as an antipoverty mechanism. The program has done a remarkable job of reducing the number of aged poor and of alleviating the condition of those who remain poor. Nevertheless, there are many observers who argue that we could further reduce poverty by increasing social security benefits. Across-the-board increases in benefits would extend to the poor and nonpoor alike, of course. Thus, if we wanted to aid the aged poor while holding down program costs (and payroll taxes!), minimum benefit levels would have to be raised faster than average benefit levels.

There are strong objections however, to raising minimum benefit levels faster than average benefit levels or, for that matter, raising any benefit levels at all. The first objection is that the Social Security system should retain as much of its insurance character as possible, and not become a straightforward welfare program. What is feared is that the further substitution of welfare (income redistribution) objectives for insurance objectives will undermine the popular support that the Social Security system enjoys. Thus, Congress walks a thin line when it seeks to aid the aged poor while maintaining broad public support.

A second objection to increased benefits arises from fears about the system's financial viability. As we have noted, current benefit payments depend on current payroll taxes. Hence, the system will no longer function in its present form if benefit amounts outstrip payroll tax receipts. This became a source of increasing concern in the 1974–75 recession when employment, payrolls, and thus payroll tax receipts all suffered a setback. In the longer run, there is also concern that our reduced rate of population growth implies that a smaller number of workers will be supporting a larger number of retirees. Such a situation could work, but only with inordinately high payroll tax rates, reduced benefit levels, or alternative sources of financing. Conservative critics argue for lower benefit levels, while liberal critics urge Congress to dip into general revenues (the regular federal budget) to help finance social security.

INCOME MAINTENANCE AND POVERTY

Together, our welfare and social security programs transfer substantial sums of money and alleviate much poverty. Table 12.5 shows just how much poverty has been reduced by these income transfer programs. In the absence of social security and welfare programs, 27 percent of all U.S. families would be poor (column 1 of Table 12.5). Social security alone, however, cuts the poverty rate to 15.7 percent. Most of this antipoverty effect is concentrated among older families, of course. The cash and in-kind welfare programs cut the poverty rate even further. After all nonmedical welfare benefits are distributed, only 11.3 percent of all families remain poor by official standards. If medical benefits (e.g., Medicaid) are also included, the poverty rate drops even further. Thus, the income transfer system is very effective in reducing the incidence of poverty.

TABLE 12.5 THE IMPACT OF INCOME TRANSFERS ON POVERTY, 1976
(Percent)

Group	(1) Pre-tax, Pre-transfer Income	(2) Pre-tax, Post-social Security Income	(3) Pre-tax Post-welfare Income
All families	27.0%	15.7%	11.3%
Aged families	59.9	21.5	14.1
Nonaged families	18.6	14.2	10.6

Note: Welfare transfers include food stamps and housing assistance, but exclude medical assistance.

Source: Congressional Budget Office, *Welfare Reform: Issues, Objectives, and Approaches* (Washington, D.C.: Government Printing Office, July 1977), p. xxii.

The income transfer system would eliminate still more poverty if benefits were increased further and distributed more widely. Higher welfare benefits are not, however, what society has in mind when it talks of eliminating poverty. Public-opinion polls consistently record the view that too many people are already on welfare, and receiving too much money. Taxpayers seek not only to alleviate the plight of the poor but to eliminate the *need* for welfare. If the elimination of poverty is achieved only by greater transfer payments, there is no prospect of diminishing welfare rolls and costs; income transfers will have to be continued into perpetuity. Meaningful reduction of both poverty and welfare costs necessitates that welfare families be given greater opportunity to provide for themselves. To what extent does the welfare system yield this kind of long-run benefits?

The greater financial resources provided to families under our income transfer programs most certainly do have some long-term effect. At the extreme, the payments at least enable families to avert starvation and function normally. In some cases, they even provide enough money for children to stay in school, properly fed and clothed, and for parents to seek a job. Adequate financial assistance may even help hold a family together. All this doubtlessly contributed to personal and economic development. Higher standards of living also raise morale, aspirations, and initiative. As former Senator Fred Harris of Oklahoma pointed out during congressional deliberations on welfare reform: "If you provide an adequate level of income, people are in fact encouraged to work, and initiative and incentive are increased, while incomes below what is necessary for decent health, housing, and living standards destroy initiative and make it difficult for succeeding generations to break the welfare cycle."[15]

[15]Senate Committee on Finance, *Hearings* on H.R. 16311 (Washington, D.C.: Government Printing Office, 1970), p. 158.

As important as these many contributions to personal and economic well-being are, however, they must still be evaluated within a more general economic context. Greater nutrition, stability, and initiative are necessary but not sufficient conditions for economic independence. To achieve independence, one must also have access to a meaningful job. Yet, welfare systems themselves do nothing to alter the number or types of jobs available. They were neither intended nor designed to expand employment opportunities. In essence, welfare programs strive only to provide income maintenance for families until and unless other economic opportunities emerge.

The inherent limitations to welfare programs render them relatively ineffective as long-term solutions to poverty. They cannot be abolished because to do so would be to totally ignore the plight of the poor. And even in the best of economic and racial situations, many individuals will be temporarily or permanently incapable of self-support. Yet we must not confuse welfare reform with expansion of opportunity, Nor should we indulge in the fiction that more generous assistance today will eliminate the need for assistance tomorrow. We must expand and improve the welfare system to provide for those in need. But to reduce the number of people who need assistance, we must expand opportunities for financial independence.

SUMMARY

There is no coherent *system* of income maintenance in the United States. Instead, we rely on a variety of diverse income transfer programs, designed and implemented independently of each other. Despite these patchwork origins, however, current public assistance and social security programs do provide much aid for the poor. Social security eliminates poverty for millions of individuals, while social security and public assistance together relieve the hardships of impoverishment for still more persons.

Analysis of income maintenance programs may proceed from two distinct perspectives. We may inquire first how efficiently and equitably current programs now perform their intended transfer functions. However, it is also necessary to ask how appropriate *any* kind of income maintenance system is as a long-run solution to poverty.

While current income maintenance programs do provide much assistance, they do so with much inequity and little efficiency. Public assistance programs are particularly inequitable in their disregard of the needs of poor families with working fathers. These *working poor* are excluded from assistance due to a misplaced concern for work motivation and a general desire to contain public expenditures. Also maltreated are those who are eligible for categorical assistance programs but reside in impoverished or unsympathetic states. Even after receiving assistance, they remain pitifully below acceptable standards of living.

To a large extent, proposed reforms of public assistance promise to correct some of these deficiencies. A negative income tax plan would move slightly further in the same direction with more universality and less implied control over behavior. Even these programs, however, would have to contend with the competing objectives of income provision, work encouragement, and cost minimization.

The social security program is the largest and most popular income transfer program. Yet, its ability to eliminate, rather than perpetuate, poverty depends on its ability to depart from insurance principles. The small departures that have been made in the past have yielded significant benefits for the aged poor. Still further increases in minimum social security benefits could virtually eliminate poverty among the aged, but are resisted in order to retain the insurance character of the program and to assure continued financial viability.

Existing and foreseen income maintenance programs do have the potential of alleviating poverty. They are not a solution to the poverty problem, however, as they fail to provide more than a marginal impetus to financial independence. They can meet the need for income support, but they cannot eliminate the need itself. If relied on exclusively, public assistance programs would perpetuate poverty and the need for extensive public assistance expenditures. This is not consistent with the needs of the poor, the objectives of the taxpaying public, or the requirements of a viable economy. Income maintenance policies must be complemented by the policies that provide opportunities for economic independence.

FURTHER READING

AARON, HENRY J., *Why Is Welfare So Hard to Reform?* Washington, D.C.: The Brookings Institution, 1973.

ANDERSON, MARTIN, *Welfare.* Palo Alto, Calif.: Hoover Institute, 1978.

CONGRESSIONAL BUDGET OFFICE, *Welfare Reform: Issues, Objectives, and Approaches.* Washington, D.C.: Government Printing Office, 1977.

DANZIGER, SHELDON, and ROBERT PLOTNICK, *Has the War on Poverty Been Won?* New York: Academic Press, 1980.

JOINT ECONOMIC COMMITTEE, U.S. Congress, *Income Security for Americans: Recommendations of the Public Welfare Study.* Washington, D.C.: Government Printing Office, 1974.

MUNNELL, ALICIA H., *The Future of Social Security.* Washington, D.C.: The Brookings Institution, 1977.

PAGLIN, MORTON, *Poverty and Transfers in Kind.* Palo Alto, Calif.: Hoover Institute, 1979.

PALMER, JOHN L., and JOSEPH A. PECHMAN, *Welfare in Rural Areas.* Washington, D.C.: The Brookings Institution, 1978.

PECHMAN, JOSEPH, and P. MICHAEL TIMPANE, eds., *Work Incentives and Income Guarantees.* Washington, D.C.: The Brookings Institution, 1975.

13 EMPLOYMENT POLICIES

If meaningful and long-term solutions to the problem of poverty are to be implemented, public policy will have to venture beyond income maintenance. Simply providing money to the poor, particularly in meager amounts, has little potential for stimulating financial independence. The only possible lasting solution to the problem of poverty is to assure that decent jobs are available to all who seek them. Under such circumstances, the occurrence of poverty and the need for income maintenance will be at a minimum.

The government has several alternatives at its disposal when it seeks to expand employment opportunities. At the most general level, it may seek to increase the demand for labor by stimulating aggregate demand. A variety of fiscal and monetary measures are available to implement such a decision. On the other hand, government policy may concentrate on the supply of labor. Rather than stimulate new demand, government policy may focus on training unemployed workers for jobs already available. Or the government might take still more direct action by creating jobs itself. Public employment programs might even combine the features of labor demand and worker training through a judicious selection of employment opportunities.

To some extent, each of these policy alternatives has been implemented, but they have received markedly different degrees of attention. In the 1930s a heavy emphasis was put on public employment. After World War II the government placed primary reliance on aggregate economic policies to provide the necessary job opportunities. Only in the late 1950s and early 1960s did an awareness emerge that other approaches were also necessary to provide a requisite number of jobs; at that time, a variety of training programs was introduced. In the early 1970s we rediscovered that public employment programs may also have a place in our job provision efforts. This chapter deals with the nature, history, and potential of each of these alternatives for eliminating poverty.

AGGREGATE DEMAND POLICIES

It is comforting to believe that the United States could have averted the Great Depression were we as knowledgeable in 1930 as we are now about the workings of the economy. In fact, some recent economic advisors to the president have suggested as much. The implication is that economists can now manage the economy to a degree formerly unheard of. Present-day arguments between economists concentrate, not on the issue of whether the level of demand can be affected, but on how much exactitude can be achieved by such policies.

The claims of modern economists inspire hope for the plight of the poor. If we really can manage aggregate demand we can provide enough jobs for the unemployed, the underemployed, and the discouraged poor. Anyone who has even skimmed through an introductory economics textbook can provide an outline for action. Fiscal policies can expand demand through increased government expenditures, consumer tax cuts, or enlarged investment and depreciation allowances. Monetary policy may provide a stimulus to demand by making access to credit easier and cheaper. Together, such policies could move millions of persons out of poverty.

The question remains as to why this has not yet been done. Either our claims to precision are exaggerated or we lack the necessary resolve. Both of these factors are evident.

Our resolve to expand aggregate employment opportunities visibly weakens when other objectives appear to conflict. As discussed in the appendix to Chapter 4, the goal of full employment is readily sacrificed whenever inflation threatens. Our abandonment of full employment stems in part from a lack of total commitment to the elimination of poverty. It also stems from an incomplete understanding of the relationship between price stability and employment expansion. We simply do not take our claims to economic prowess seriously enough. We continue to believe that full employment is incompatible with price stability, despite claims to the contrary.

In the late 1950s the goal of full employment was formulated as the attainment of less than 5 percent unemployment. When Walter Heller, President Kennedy's economic advisor, publicly aspired to reach a full employment of 4 percent, he was chided for recklessness. As unemployment sank below even 4 percent in the mid-1960s, some began to wonder whether we had not previously underestimated our abilities and unnecessarily relegated millions of individuals to poverty. The public never became wholly convinced, however.

When the rate of inflation did spurt at the end of the sixties, it was concluded immediately that the rise in prices was due to our efforts to create full employment. Indeed, both the Nixon and Ford administrations argued repeatedly that "full employment" should be redefined as an unemployment rate of 5 or 5.5 percent. The Carter Administration formally adopted 4.9 percent as its definition of "full employment." The observation that we had earlier succeeded in attaining a much lower rate of unemployment for five or six years inspired precious few second thoughts.

But lack of resolution has not been the only obstacle to more effective aggregate demand policies. In the general euphoria of our discovery that we could manipulate aggregate demand, we have neglected some simple truths. The way in which aggregate demand is stimulated will have significant impact on the economy. A large reduction in interest rates, for example, will stimulate the housing and lumber industries, where interest charges are a major component of total cost. Investment credit allowances, on the other hand, will benefit manufacturers of steel, airplanes, and heavy machinery, with little impact on housing production. Indeed, every fiscal or monetary action will affect the distribution of output, as well as its volume. There really is no such thing as a neutral aggregate demand policy, that is, one that does not alter the proportional mix of output, relative prices, or the distribution of income.

What this suggests is that we might be able to do a better job of providing jobs for the poor if we examined the content of our aggregate demand policies more carefully. Some policies will provide more jobs for the poor, with little effect on prices, while others will do just the reverse. The trick is to find the right ones. This will require that policymakers explicitly incorporate antipoverty objectives into their aggregate demand planning and look more closely at the impact of alternative policy strategies. Unfortunately, the public's general apathy toward questions of race and poverty has permitted policymakers to ignore these requirements. Indeed, the general public believes that most poor people could find jobs "if they wanted to." As a result, policymakers tend to attribute their failures to the inherent unattainability of full employment rather than to their own errors of policy design and implementation. This syndrome has aptly been dubbed "blaming the victim."

However, even truly enlightened full employment policies will not provide decent jobs for all who need them. As unemployment levels drop it becomes increasingly difficult—and socially expensive—to reach those who still need employment. Accordingly, expansionary fiscal and monetary policies alone cannot wholly eliminate poverty among those who are presently or potentially in the labor force. But it is even more important to emphasize that without determined full employment policies all other efforts to eliminate poverty are rendered impotent. In 1975, for example, more money was spent on welfare, training, education, and other antipoverty efforts than in earlier years. Nevertheless, the number of people in poverty grew by 2.5 million because unemployment levels were allowed to rise. The demand for labor, especially labor provided by the poor, must be kept at high levels if the poor are to gain financial independence. All other efforts are secondary.

TRAINING POLICIES

While the necessity for maintaining a high level of demand for labor is clear, we must also recognize other approaches to full employment. One such approach is to train unemployed workers to fulfill unsatisfied demand. As every freshman economist knows, both supply and demand forces operate in the labor market. Hence, to many observers it seems as logical to adapt supply to demand as to proceed the other way around. Indeed, training programs for unemployed workers enjoy much greater acceptance than policies designed to expand and redirect labor demand toward the poor. What accounts for their popularity and how effective are they?

The potential of training programs to bring about greater employment is suggested by the observation that there are always job vacancies. Help wanted ads continue to appear even in periods of high unemployment. People move from job to job with great frequency, creating a kind of musical chairs situation in the labor market. In addition, there are always businesses either expanding or contracting, thereby creating or eliminating available jobs. Thus, at any point in time some jobs are vacant and employers must advertise that fact. How fast those vacancies are filled depends on how many workers are looking for jobs and what their talents are. Where millions of workers are unemployed (in 1975, for example), vacancies are quickly filled. In periods of lower unemployment (such as in 1967–68) employers must wait longer and look further before obtaining needed labor.

Almost as important as the number of available workers are the skills they possess. If employers are seeking skilled craftsmen, millions of unemployed day laborers will contribute little to the fulfillment of job vacancies. Skills possessed by job-seekers must bear some resemblance to the requirements of available jobs. Nevertheless, it should not be concluded that an existing mismatch of job requirements and skills of the unemployed constitutes an insurmountable barrier to full employment. On the contrary, rarely is a worker hired who is ready to perform his or her job with no orientation or training. Employers can and do provide available workers with needed skills. Government programs to train or retrain the unemployed can provide the same service.

Even though private employers frequently engage in some form of orientation or training, they seek to keep training expenses to a minimum. They much prefer to hire persons who are already skilled and experienced. That option is not always available. Those who are not yet hired are likely to possess fewer skills. The amount of training employers will have to provide thus varies inversely with the level of unemployment. If aggregate demand is strong, employers will incur the added expenses willingly.

Government programs to train the unemployed have a slightly different orientation. To some extent, they merely relieve private employers of the burden and expense of training. This may be done by providing training directly or by subsidizing the training efforts of private industry. But training programs directed at the poor have an additional objective: they seek to improve the competitive position of the poor in the labor market. Although the two training functions overlap, they have very different implications. Training designed to create skills in demand leads directly to increased employment; training designed to increase the competitive position of the poor serves to redistribute existing unemployment.

The first full-scale government training program was established in 1962 under the Manpower Development and Training Act (MDTA). Persistently high rates of unemployment in the period 1958–61 coupled with fears of advancing automation led many observers to conclude that a basic mismatch existed between people and jobs. The only way to approach fuller employment, it seemed, was to provide the unemployed with the new skills demanded by advancing technology. Accordingly, Congress provided for a national effort to retrain displaced and unemployed workers in new skill areas.

Recent Policies

In the years since the establishment of the MDTA program, the federal government has introduced and operated scores of training programs, including the Neighborhood Youth Corps (for high school students), the Job Corps (for high school dropouts), Operation Mainstream (for older workers), and the Concentrated Employment Program (for people in low-income neighborhoods). In more recent years, however, state and local governments have taken over most of the responsibility for providing training services. With the advent of revenue sharing, state and local governments obtained the financial ability to design and run their own programs. Moreover, many observers have argued that local officials are better attuned to the manpower needs of their community and thus more likely to provide the right kind of training. This conviction is expressed in the Comprehensive Employment and Training Act (CETA) of 1973.

The CETA Program

The basic intent of the Comprehensive Employment and Training Act (CETA) was to transfer responsibility for the design and administration of training programs to local governments. The federal role in training was to be limited to providing financial resources and technical assistance. The 451 prime sponsors (state and local governments) who receive CETA money tailor their employment and training programs to local needs. Hence, CETA both decentralized and decategorized the nation's employment programs.

The CETA program includes a broad range of employment and training services. In part, this reflects the decentralized nature of the program. Even more important, however, is the fact that CETA funds are allocated by Congress and distributed to the states under six different legislative titles. These include:

Title I: provides for a full range of employment and training services, including classroom and on-the-job training, work experience, job placement; counseling, supportive services, public service employment, remedial education; and so on. Title I provides Prime Sponsors with maximum program flexibility and was originally viewed as the principal component of CETA.

Title II: provides for a permanent program of public service employment (PSE) to assist individuals who have been unemployed for at least a month and reside in areas of substantial unemployment (i.e., areas with an unemployment rate of 6.5 percent or higher for three consecutive months).

Title III: provides employment and training services to "target" groups of special federal concern. These groups include youth, migrant farm workers, older workers, offenders, Indians, and persons with limited English-speaking ability. The federal government retains responsibility for administering these programs.

Title IV: provides for the continuation of the Job Corps program. The Job Corps provides educational and skill training to disadvantaged youth. Typically, this training takes place in residential Job Corps centers, and lasts for six months to a year.

(Title V creates the National Commission for Manpower Policy)

Title VI: provides for temporary public service employment (PSE) to provide jobs during periods of high national unemployment. Title VI is primarily counter-cyclical (i.e., it is expanded whenever national unemployment rates climb). By contrast, Title II PSE is more structural; it seeks to aid those who remain un-employed even when national unemployment rates are relatively low.

(Title VII specifies general administrative provisions of the Act)

Title VIII: establishes the Young Adult Conservation Corps (YACC). YACC is a year-round training and work experience program for unemployed youth. The work and training activities are located in forest and recreational areas.

The many titles of CETA authorize all kinds of employment and training activities. The distinction between titles also permits the federal government to retain considerable control over the content of CETA activities. Local prime sponsors must utilize federal funds for the purposes established in each separate title. In the years 1978–79, for example, President Carter vastly ex-panded federal funding of the activities, regardless of what different plans they may have had. Table 13.1 summarizes the distribution of CETA funds and enrollments for fiscal year 1978.

TABLE 13.1   CETA FUNDS AND ENROLLMENTS, BY TITLE, FY1978

CETA Title	Fiscal 1978 Funds	Number of Enrollments
Title I: comprehensive services	$1,910,400	965,100
Title II: structural unemployment; PSE	347,300	100,500
Title III: special target groups	1,438,800	1,204,000
Title IV: Job Corps program	376,500	48,900
Title VI: countercyclical PSE	1,861,200	555,800
Title VIII: young adult conservation corps	N/A	N/A

Source: Employment and Training Report of the President, 1979.

The WIN Program

A frequent criticism of CETA and other "mainstream" programs is that they fail to serve adequately the neediest individuals. The number of available training and employment slots is always less than the number of unemployed workers. Hence, some deliberate choices must be made about who to serve. Under these circumstances, program administrators often prefer to serve those individuals who are most job-ready. The least needy individuals are likely to provide the greatest "success" stories for program administrators. Unfortunately, this tendency to "cream" from the pool of potential program participants leaves many of the neediest job-seekers to fend for themselves.

The failure of "mainstream" training programs to provide adequate help to the neediest led to the creation of another major training program, the Work Incentive Program (WIN). What distinguished WIN from the outset was the fact that it serves only those who are receiving public assistance: program participation is specifically limited to adult recipients of AFDC assistance. Moreover, all adult recipients are *required* to register for WIN services, unless exempted for reasons of health or the care of preschool children. This provision resulted from the widespread conviction that welfare recipients seek to avoid employment (see Chapter 8). On a more positive note, the program attempts to provide the supplemental services necessary for successful program completion. These range from day-care services and work orientation to medical examinations, transportation allowances, counseling, and job placement. In addition, because of WIN's link to welfare, there are no financial barriers to program participation. WIN enrollees continue to receive the same public assistance they had prior to entry. Thus, the program offers a unified package of services designed to move people from welfare to employment.

Although WIN seemingly offered all the ingredients for successful movement into employment, the program has not been regarded as a success. This view of WIN was not based so much on demonstrated program outcomes—

WIN did achieve modest employment success—but more on the disappointment that WIN did not materially reduce welfare rolls.[1] In any case, the institutional training components of the program have virtually been scrapped. The emphasis in WIN is now on direct placement. What this means is that AFDC recipients are referred to employment counselors who try to find jobs for them immediately, rather than train them for jobs they might later fill. Such placement services can be valuable, at least to the extent that they improve communications between job-seeking welfare recipients and employers who might hire them. Unfortunately, the change in WIN was introduced just about the time national unemployment rates started soaring, leaving the employment counselors with little good news to report. Over the longer run, we cannot expect WIN to be very successful until unemployment rates fall and employers start looking for less qualified help.

PUBLIC SERVICE EMPLOYMENT

It was suggested in Chapter 9 that underdeveloped skills or education are not a prime cause of poverty. It was argued instead that education and training credentials simply render an individual more competitive in the job search. Credentials provide a person with early access to job vacancies, but they do not guarantee that such vacancies will exist. The experience with government training programs tends to support this view. For the most part, training programs are unable to place people in jobs unless labor market conditions warrant. If there are no jobs waiting when training is completed, the net effect of training is to create a slightly more skilled pool of *unemployed* workers. Training programs are not able to significantly increase employment, particularly when unemployment is rampant.

Frustration with the results of government training programs has led most observers to an obvious conclusion—that more jobs must be created. Expanded labor demand, not improved labor supply, appears to be the surest and fastest way to reduce unemployment and poverty. To a large extent, the government's responsibility to create jobs is recognized in the Employment Act of 1946 and again in the Full Employment and Balanced Growth Act of 1978. The government pursues this responsibility by implementing the fiscal and monetary policies necessary to expand aggregate demand. But manipulation of aggregate demand is not the only, or always the most efficient, method of job creation. An alternative is for the government to directly employ those who seek work.

Public service employment is a very special kind of job creation. It involves the government directly in the employment process. It gives the govern-

---

[1]For a description of WIN activities and outcomes, see Bradley R. Schiller, "Lessons from WIN: A Manpower Evaluation," *Journal of Human Resources,* Fall 1978.

ment explicit control over what will be produced and who will be employed to produce it. At times this control may be advantageous; public services are not well provided for in the market context. Even though all taxpayers anguish over the lack of sanitation, transportation, education, protection, and recreation services, few are willing to pay for them. Nor can these public services be provided and paid for on an individual basis.[2] Accordingly, there is an output void that can be filled only by explicit government provisions.

The control that public service employment bestows over the structure of demand can also be used to advantage. Generalized aggregate demand policies, such as tax cuts, have widespread impact, some of which may be undesirable. Public service employment programs, on the other hand, can channel new labor demand to those areas or population groups most in need. Hence, maximum impact can be achieved with minimum disruption elsewhere in the economy. This advantage is especially important when average unemployment rates are low and unemployment is concentrated among specific minorities or in particular areas.

Public service employment, then, may fulfill two objectives: it may provide needed services and expand employment opportunities. How well it fulfills these objectives depends on how much money is allocated for this purpose and how well those funds are spent. The Emergency Employment Act of 1971 provided for a maximum of 200,000 jobs over a period of two years. While that number was not insignificant, it represented only a small dent in the ranks of the unemployed, who, at the time, numbered over 5 million. The Works Progress Administration (WPA) of the 1930s employed about 2 million individuals at any given time. Even President Carter's expanded use of CETA public service employment appears modest by comparison.

It is unfortunate that the concept of public service employment instinctively produces an image of make-work activity. People continue to think of the WPA as a major leaf-raking force. Even members of Congress—themselves beneficiaries of public service employment—are prone to distinguish between "real" work and public service jobs. Yet, the WPA constructed 651,000 miles of roads, 16,000 miles of water lines, 35,000 public buildings, 11,000 recreation facilities, and much more. What relatively little leaf-raking did take place was the consequence of hasty implementation rather than a dearth of public needs. Today the situation is no different. There is an abundance of useful and needed work to be done, and well-designed programs can do it. We might start by cleaning up our air and water.

What is, perhaps, equally curious about the make-work accusations is that they are applied only to public service employment. Very few people wonder or care whether a stockbroker, psychologist, or college professor does

[2]This dilemma of public goods, or *externalities*, is discussed in most recent economics textbooks.

any "real" work. Indeed, we pay farmers enormous sums to avoid real work. Yet when the spotlight turns to the employment of poor persons, the public takes on a special concern for the nature and content of the work performed. Not only is such concern ill-founded, it also implies an inequitable double standard. There is no justification for subjecting the output of the poor to any more scrutiny than that to which we subject the output of the affluent.

Another misapprehension about public service employment is that it requires the government to do all the administrating. This was done in the 1930s, but it is not the only approach possible. Where the government perceives that a service can be provided usefully, it may contract with private firms to carry out the actual hiring and production activity. The federal government can just as easily pay the Boeing Company to build sewage treatment plants as to build aircraft frames. This approach cuts right across the distinction between public and private employment. It may also render public service employment programs more acceptable politically. The government can even channel public service funds through community organizations, thereby reaching a higher proportion of those in need.

Although the potential of public service employment is impressive, it has not won broad acceptance. CETA vastly expanded the use of public service employment, especially during President Carter's economic stimulus program of 1977–78. However, critics have argued that many of the jobs "created" by CETA simply substituted for state and local jobs that would have been funded with nonfederal revenues. In the most blatant cases, cities "laid off" workers one day and "rehired" them the next day with CETA money. In the process, no new jobs were created. When such "fiscal substitution" occurs, public service employment is simply a disguised form of general revenue sharing.[3]

Public service employment programs are also opposed because they enlarge the size of the public sector. When the government creates more public jobs, it acquires greater control over our economic decisions. Moreover, a larger public sector implies that fewer resources will be available for the production of private goods and services. Hence, even proponents of public service employment argue that such jobs should be temporary, with a planned transition to public employment. This transition is dependent, however, on adequate private-sector demand and some training while in public service employment. Neither expectation has been completely fulfilled.

[3]For a discussion and estimates of "fiscal substitution," see Michael Wiseman, "Public Employment as Fiscal Policy," *Brookings Paper on Economic Activity,* (Washington, D.C.: The Brookings Institution, 1976); George Johnson and James Tomola, "The Fiscal Substitution Effect of Alternative Approaches to Public Service Employment," *Journal of Human Resources,* Winter 1977; and Michael Borus and Daniel S. Hammermesh, "Estimating Fiscal Substitution by Public Service Employment Programs," *Journal of Human Resources,* Fall 1978.

FURTHER READING

CONGRESSIONAL BUDGET OFFICE, *CETA Reauthorization Issues.* Washington, D.C.: Government Printing Office, 1978.

LERMAN, ROBERT, "The Public Employment Bandwagon Takes the Wrong Road," *Challenge,* January 1975.

NATIONAL COMMISSION FOR MANPOWER POLICY, *CETA: An Analysis of the Issues.* Washington, D.C.: Government Printing Office, 1978.
———*Job Creation through Public Service Employment.* Washington, D.C.: Government Printing Office, 1978.

PERRY, CHARLES R., et al., *The Impact of Government Manpower Programs.* Philadelphia: University of Pennsylvania Press, 1975.

ULMER, MELVILLE E., "The Pitfalls and Promises of Public Employment," *Challenge,* January 1975.

U.S. DEPARTMENT OF LABOR, *Employment and Training Report of the President.* Washington, D.C.: Government Printing Office, annual.

14 EQUAL OPPORTUNITY POLICIES

Earlier chapters have documented the disadvantaged status of minority groups in America. Not only do such groups command fewer resources now, but they have less chance to acquire resources in the future. They have less opportunity to attain higher educational levels or even good quality schooling at lower levels. Even with appropriate educational credentials, they are not permitted to make maximum use of their attainments in the labor market. Such discrimination—both in schools and in the labor market— creates institutional barriers between people and jobs. Those barriers, in turn, alter both the size and composition of the poverty population.

In Chapter 11, a distinction was drawn among three different categories of discrimination. These were: present market discrimination; prior market discrimination; and nonmarket discrimination. Social policies may be directed toward the elimination of any one or all of these categories. At the same time, however, we must recognize that each form of discrimination may require a different kind of policy adaptation. Furthermore, the potential of each kind of institutional policy to reduce poverty varies considerably.

The necessity for adaptive policy is easily illustrated. Consider, for example, the alternatives of eliminating present discriminatory practices or eliminating the effect of prior discrimination. There is no way to forbid discrimination that has already taken place. Consequently, efforts to combat previous discrimination must focus on the effects of that discrimination. Such remedial policies may take many forms, including government

This dependence of the EEOC on individual complaints has several drawbacks. First, it is tremendously expensive and time-consuming to review and process each complaint; indeed, as of June 1977 the EEOC backlog of unprocessed complaints totaled 130,000, overwhelming its staff lawyers and constraining its effectiveness. Second, an aggrieved person has little incentive to report discriminatory actions. The complaint procedure subjects an individual to potential union or employer retaliation, costs him much time and money, and yields little practical benefit. At best, a complaining individual is apt to gain employment or promotion with a chastened and possibly resentful employer.

Much more effective action would be possible if the EEOC had the power to initiate broader investigations and seek more comprehensive resolutions. Realizing this, a former chairman of the EEOC, Lowell Perry, argued that "the one-to-one approach is not going to make a dent in our problem" and initiated investigations of "systemic" discrimination. What this means is that the EEOC would study the hiring and promotion policies of an entire company vis-a-vis minority groups, rather than just the experiences of individual complainants. In this way one action could bring relief or compensation to a much larger number of workers. In one of the first suits developed for this purpose, the EEOC was successful in persuading American Telephone and Telegraph Company (AT & T) to pay nearly $50 million in compensation to its female employees who had been denied equal job opportunities. Despite this early success, the EEOC has made limited use of this systemic approach. Although the EEOC has had over 300 attorney positions in its General Counsel office alone, the EEOC itself admits that only 30 to 40 percent of its attorneys have been sufficiently trained in trial work.[1] In addition, the EEOC has had to cope with its backlog of individual complaints and a continuing flow of 80,000 to 100,000 new cases per year. At the urging of President Carter, EEOC procedures were streamlined and given new leadership in 1977. These administrative changes improved EEOC performance, but gave it no new powers. Nevertheless, the EEOC was able to achieve a landmark "conciliation agreement" with General Electric in 1978. According to this agreement, General Electric agreed to spend $31.9 million to redress prior discrimination and provide improved job and training opportunities for minorities and women.

The OFCCP

Stronger powers of initiative and enforcement have always been available to the Office of Federal Contract Compliance Programs. The OFCCP may itself initiate investigations to determine whether discriminatory practices ex-

[1]U.S. Commission on Civil Rights, *The Federal Civil Rights Enforcement Effort—1977* (Washington, D.C.: Government Printing Office, 1977).

ist. It may also impose sanctions, such as contract termination, where discrimination is discovered. Furthermore, OFCCP may require employers to take "affirmative action" to remedy past discrimination. These sanctions may be applied to all businesses that sell or service products to the government. Thus, the potential power of the OFCCP is as vast as the government's position in the economy. As of 1979, all companies with more than 50 employees and selling at least $50,000 worth of goods and services to the federal government were required to negotiate affirmative action plans with the government.

While the potential power of the OFCCP to eliminate discriminatory practices and rectify past injustices is great, that power has been rarely used. Politics are partly to blame. An employer beset by the OFCCP always has recourse to other authorities. Should he command the attention and sympathy of congressmen or other executive offices, OFCCP sanctions may be suspended. Bureaucratic interests also undermine the OFCCP's power. The Department of Defense, for example, regards weapons procurement as more vital to its mission than guidelines for equal opportunity. Hence, it may devote relatively little attention to compliance with OFCCP edicts and may even inveigh against contract cancellations that threaten orderly procurement. Accordingly, the power of the OFCCP remains largely on paper. Until 1979, not a single contract had been terminated or cancelled to enforce equal opportunity, and very few firms have been barred from further federal contracts. In 1979, however, the Labor Department did impose a ban on further federal contracts with Uniroyal, the nation's third largest rubber manufacturer (which received $36 million in contracts from the federal government in 1978). The cut-off of Uniroyal contracts was based on the company's failure to cooperate with an OFCCP investigation of discrimination (begun in 1968!), not becase of discrimination per se. Nevertheless, the Uniroyal action signaled greater OFCCP enforcement action.

Quotas and
Guidelines

A more affirmative kind of action has been taken by the government with regard to the nation's labor unions, especially the construction unions. As we saw in Chapter 11, blue-collar unions have the potential to provide many black workers with immediate remunerative employment. In addition, the government is a major force in the construction industry, purchasing up to one-third of total output, and could exert considerable leverage to break down discriminatory barriers. In pursuing such an effort, the Nixon administration tried to establish guidelines for minority recruitment in the building trades. The first attempt, in Philadelphia, proposed to raise the proportion of new black recruits from 5 percent in 1970 to 25 percent in 1975. That attempt and later "Philadelphia plans" elsewhere have not been successful, however.

Unions have tremendous political strength and do not like interference. From their point of view, "plans" and "goals" look too much like quotas, especially when enforced by threats of contract termination. Furthermore, the slack economy of the early 1970s raised anxious questions about whose jobs would have to be sacrificed to make room for newly hired black workers, the same kind of "reverse discrimination" fear that later surfaced in other industries (including universities). Faced with the prospect of unemployment, union ranks solidify against the threat of increased competition. The government has also been unwilling to carry out threats of contract termination, which would also cause losses for employers.

While the short history of federal activity in the area of employment rights is not encouraging, it has not been wholly without impact. The enactment of legislation and the issuance of executive orders are important, even if they are not religiously enforced. They at least establish the principle that discrimination is not acceptable. They also lay the groundwork for stronger enforcement powers later. From this perspective, federal equal employment policies appear to be a timid beginning rather than an outright failure.

One of the most important side effects of federal legislation and pronouncements has been to stimulate private efforts, particularly legal actions against discriminatory employers. Federal action has established a legal basis on which private individuals can build. Accordingly, much of the responsibility for implementing and enforcing equal employment opportunity has been taken over by individuals and the courts. And in a score of cases— including the major EEOC suit against AT&T in 1974—individuals have won substantial sums of money from their employers to compensate for the income they were denied as a consequence of discriminatory practices in hiring and promotion. In the most controversial decision yet reached, a federal judge in Richmond, Virginia, ruled in January 1975 that workers at a tobacco plant who had been denied promotions because of race or sex discrimination could jump to the higher rungs of the company's job ladder, in the process "bumping" more favored workers down the ladder. That ruling (later appealed) is so drastic in its implications that it is sure to increase employers' efforts to dismantle discriminatory barriers.

Reverse Discrimination

The employment successes that have been achieved with various forms of affirmative action have not eliminated discriminatory barriers. They have been effective enough, however, to arouse growing hostility to any form of "special" opportunities for women and minority workers. Three-fourths of all Americans oppose "equal" employment opportunity programs that give special "preference" (quotas, guidelines, etc.) to certain groups. In large part, this hostility arises from the threat that affirmative action poses for already privileged positions. But this is not the only basis for decrying "reverse discrimination." Critics also point to the basic contradiction between "special" hiring preferences and "equal" opportunity. Others point out that the existence of affirmative action casts a shadow over the real achievements of minority workers. Such achievements are too easily dismissed as the outcome of affirmative action.[2] Such thoughts help explain why only a bare majority of minority and women workers favors "special" preferences.

The critics of affirmative action have taken their case to court. In one such complaint, Brian Weber, a white, male employee of Kaiser Aluminum, sued Kaiser and his union, the United Steel Workers, for reverse discrimination. Weber had been rejected by a craft training program that reserved half its places for minorities. In the absence of such a privileged "set-aside," Weber argued, he would have been accepted for training. Lower courts agreed with Weber, noting that Kaiser could not use racial quotas except as a remedy for past discrimination at Kaiser. Since Kaiser itself did not admit to such prior discrimination, there was no legal basis for the special quotas. In 1979, the Supreme Court overruled the lower courts, however, arguing that preferential access to training is permissible when used to remedy "manifest racial imbalance."

EQUAL EDUCATIONAL OPPORTUNITY POLICIES

Government policy in the field of equal educational opportunity is more difficult to characterize than in the field of employment opportunity. Politics and bureaucracy again take their toll, of course, and there is, again, much complacency and inertia. What renders this subject especially complex, however, is the degree to which equal educational opportunity responsibilities are shared by different levels of government. Educational policy has traditionally been a prerogative of the separate states. The federal government provides less than 10 percent of all educational expenditures and administers no schools. Consequently, it has less power to create equal opportunity in the schools. It cannot terminate contracts or open new job slots as it may do in the labor market. In general, it must instead rely on, and cooperate with, the states and the courts to abolish discrimination in the schools. Only in higher education, particularly among large, research-oriented universities, does federal grant money account for a significant enough share of total income to make direct federal action a more serious threat.

The most obvious form of discrimination in the educational system is school segregation. While discrimination can take place even in the absence of

[2]See Thomas Sowell, " 'Affirmative Action' Reconsidered," *Public Interest,* Winter 1976.

segregation, not even a pretense of equal opportunity is possible so long as segregated schools are maintained. The Supreme Court itself made this observation, as we saw in Chapter 10. To what extent, then, are governmental bodies endeavoring to abolish segregation?

de jure vs. de facto Segregation

A distinction is commonly made between two kinds of segregation. The first, *de jure,* refers to a situation where blacks and whites are legally constrained to attend separate schools. The second, *de facto,* refers to a situation where school segregation results, not from edict, but from circumstance. Such a case occurs where blacks and whites live in different neighborhoods, thereby making school integration difficult.

While the distinction between *de facto* and *de jure* segregations is often useful, it does have unfortunate consequences. It creates a distinction that few victims of discrimination can appreciate. As Judge J. Skelly Wright noted in a 1967 ruling on District of Columbia schools: "Racially and socially homogeneous schools damage the minds of all children who attend them . . . whether the segregation occurs in law or in fact." The distinction between *de jure* and *de facto* also gives rise to a false aura of innocence. *De jure* segregation is commonly seen as the consequence of evil intent, while *de facto* segregation is seen as the innocent by-product of socioeconomic forces—especially in the housing market. Such a view obscures the fact that government bodies can and do set the pattern for much *de facto* segregation. Segregation of the schools is rarely, if ever, a completely natural and unplanned circumstance.

Governments have two kinds of effects on *de facto* segregation. They may directly affect residential housing patterns, thereby enlarging or diminishing the foundation for *de facto* segregation; or they may alter the distribution of schools within established housing patterns, thereby facilitating or obstructing greater integration of the schools.

Housing Patterns

To a large extent existing residential patterns are the outcome of millions of individual housing decisions, but free choice is not the only force operative in the housing market. The government, through its building and loan programs, has also participated in the establishment of segregated neighborhoods, and thus, must bear a significant responsibility for the *de facto* school segregation that results from neighborhoods isolated by race and class.

The Federal Housing Authority (FHA) has been a major factor in the housing market since its creation in 1938. It had a particularly important role in establishing the housing patterns of the post-World War II housing boom, patterns that still predominate today. The power of the FHA to alter housing choices lies in its ability to insure or guarantee loans on residential construction. FHA support oftentimes determines whether a house can be purchased, at what location, and at what cost. A measure of its influence is easily grasped. In 1965 alone, the FHA, together with the Veterans Administration (VA), insured or guaranteed some $150 billion in mortgage loans, providing money for more than 15 million housing units. During the housing boom of the late 1940s and 1950s, the FHA helped finance one-third of all new housing. Today's suburbs are, in large part, the product of FHA financing.

Given the power of the Federal Housing Authority in the housing market, its ability to foster or contain segregation is clear. For the most part, it has chosen to encourage and extend rigid racial and class segregation. The FHA Underwriting Manual of 1938 declared that "if a neighborhood is to retain stability, it is necessary that properties shall continue to be occupied by the same social and racial groups." Agency valuators, considering whether or not to make FHA loans, were warned to protect against "inharmonious racial groups." The FHA even composed and distributed a model racially restrictive convenant, prohibiting "the occupancy of properties except by the race for which they are intended." The FHA deemed it necessary and proper that it create and maintain racially and socially homogeneous neighborhoods.

In 1962, President Kennedy issued an executive order on equal opportunity in housing, which brought to an end the explicitly segregationist practices of the FHA, but that order came too late and has too little force. The new FHA policy of nondiscrimination is limited largely to new housing. Thus, the established patterns of housing segregation are virtually unaffected. Furthermore, FHA loans now cover less than 20 percent of new construction. Of even greater significance is that the issuance of FHA guarantees still depends on the decisions of private lenders. FHA loan insurance is available only to those persons who are eligible to get loans from private banks. Thus, FHA policy reflects the racially and socially restrictive practices of most commercial lenders.

Poor families of whatever color are further handicapped by the FHA's focus on middle-class families. Because loan applicants must be eligible for commercial loans, FHA insurance and guarantees benefit few, if any, poor families. As a consequence, middle-class families get loans quickly and cheaply, while the poor are confined to overpriced and inadequate housing.

Federal efforts designed explicitly to improve the living conditions of the poor have likewise failed to promote residential integration. Public housing projects are a vivid example. Public housing is almost always located in the poorest areas and most often segregated by race. Thus, it tends to intensify racial and economic isolation. The U.S. Commission on Civil Rights reports that, of the quarter of a million public housing units built in the nation's twenty-four largest metropolitan areas, only seventy-six units have been located outside the central city. The result is not only residential segregation but *de facto* segregation of schools as well. The commission has cited some illustrations:

> *In San Francisco, for example, six projects totaling more than 2,300 units, each predominantly Negro, are grouped on one piece of land called Hunter's Point. The schools in the area that serve the housing projects all are more than 90 percent Negro. In Cincinnati, two nearby projects—Lincoln Court and Laurel homes—total almost 2,300 units. Together the projects are 99.7 percent nonwhite, and house 2,616 school-age children. Schools serving the development, many of them built specifically for that purpose, are all predominantly nonwhite.*

> *The most extreme example, perhaps, is Robert Taylor Homes, a project in Chicago. Opened in 1961–62, it contains 4,415 units, 75 percent of them designed for large families. Of the 28,000 tenants, some 20,000 are children. The entire occupancy is Negro and schools were built in the area to serve the project alone. Indeed, classes for lower grades are conducted in project units, by agreement between the school board and the housing authority, as a way to relieve overcrowding in the nearby schools.* [3]

While the federal government cannot be held responsible for all *de facto* school segregation, it is clear that its housing policies have encouraged racial and economic isolation. The government's housing policies have also intensified popular prejudice and fear, thereby further obstructing the attainment of residential and school integration.

School Patterns

While public and private housing decisions have created a foundation for school segregation, residential patterns alone do not maintain segregated schools. School authorities have broad discretion in defining the number and nature of school boundaries to be superimposed on residential patterns. Hence, local school authorities have the power to combat the segregation that exists in housing. Once again, however, this power has often been employed to intensify rather than to combat racial and economic isolation.

The power of local school authorities to encourage or resist school segregation is embodied in a variety of public decisions. Housing patterns

[3]U.S. Commission on Civil Rights, *Racial Isolation in the Public Schools* (Washington, D.C.: Government Printing Office, 1967), pp. 37–38.

alone do not define neighborhoods, much less school zones. Instead, the definition of a neighborhood is partly determined by the decisions of where and how to locate public schools. The number of schools to build, their size, and their geographic location are all decisions that help to shape neighborhoods. Building one large school between racially segregated housing areas, for example, does more to promote school integration than constructing two separate schools within racially homogeneous communities. Also important for the pattern of school integration is the number of grades to be served by each school and the actual specification of attendance zones. These decisions, too, can abet or overcome residential segregation.

To a large extent, of course, existing school patterns reflect historical, rather than current, decisions. This fact does not exonerate school authorities from responsibility, however. Residential patterns are continually changing and schools are continually being built or rezoned. Hence, school authorities have discretion to alter the distribution of pupils or facilities and to counteract past decisions. They have broad latitude to promote or impede integration as they see fit. Unfortunately, they have often chosen either to neglect the potential for integration or, worse still, to purposefully extend segregation. Local school authorities have used the following tactics successfully to achieve precisely these results.

Gerrymandering. Gerrymandering refers to the purposeful restructuring of school attendance zones to foster school segregation. It is the oldest, simplest, and most blatant tactic available to local school authorities. Its visibility, however, has led to a decline in its use, especially where legal suits have arisen. The Hawthorne Elementary School in Kansas City provides a rare illustration. There, black families began to expand westward into the school zone of the previously all-white Hawthorne School. School authorities managed, however, to keep integration just beyond the reach of black children, simply by moving school lines westward as fast as black families moved into the area.

More often than not, effective gerrymandering is accomplished in conjunction with new school construction. The Sawyer Junior High School in Cincinnati is a more typical case. Prior to 1962 two junior high schools, Ach and Withrow, served pupils in that city's western area. Ach was 92 percent black, Withrow 58 percent white. To relieve overcrowding, a third school, Sawyer, was opened in 1962. As Figure 14.1 illustrates, Sawyer Junior High was located at the boundary between white and black residential areas. While this location could have been utilized to expand integration, it was employed for opposite purposes. The attendance zone for Sawyer was designed to extend only to the west, incorporating only black residences. As a result, Ach ended up 99 percent black, Sawyer 98 percent black, and Withrow 83 percent white. Such is the power of school authorities to create *de facto* segregation.

—— Ach, Withrow attendance boundaries before Sawyer opened

——— Sawyer attendance boundaries

▓ Predominantly black area

☐ Predominantly white area

FIGURE 14.1   Gerrymandered School Zones
Source: U.S. Commission on Civil Rights, *Racial Isolation in the Public Schools* (Washington, D.C.: Government Printing Office, 1967), p. 49.

Optional Zones.   A tactic not far removed from gerrymandering is the use of optional attendance zones. An optional zone is a limited geographical area in which students are permitted to choose the school they will attend. In effect, optional zones are a more subtle and flexible tool to achieve either greater integration or segregation. Two illustrations cited by the U.S. Commission on Civil Rights convey the potential of this tool. In San Francisco an optional zone existed for two decades between the Geary Elementary School, predominantly white, and the Emerson School, predominantly black (see Figure 14.2). During that time, the residents of the optional zone were mostly white. By 1960, however, the great majority of the zone's residents were black. Continuation of the option thus threatened to enable black children to attend the white-majority Geary School. In 1961 the option was rescinded; residents of the zone were, thereafter, included in the attendance area of Emerson. Racial isolation was enforced.

In the South, *free choice* provisions are the counterpart of optional attendance zones. Students are permitted or required to state a preference for the schools they wish to attend. Priority is given to those preferences, however, that are based on residential location, established school ties, or other correlates of race. Just how free choice can operate as a subterfuge for purposeful segregation was illustrated in Atlanta. Its Kirkwood School was all-white but located in an area becoming all-black. Free choice provisions required that some blacks be permitted to attend Kirkwood. To forestall integration, however, the superintendent of schools sent a letter to the parents

1950

EMERSON

☐GEARY

1961

EMERSON

☐GEARY

[- - -] Optional zone

➤ Indicates which school children in this area could attend

☐ Predominately white neighborhood

■ Predominantly black neighborhood

FIGURE 14.2   Optional Attendance Zones

Source: U.S. Commission on Civil Rights, *Racial Isolation in the Public Schools,* (Washington, D.C.: Government Printing Office, 1967), p. 53.

of Kirkwood pupils, notifying them of the impending influx and reminding them of their free choice options. The parents responded promptly. Kirkwood, which had been all-white in 1964, was all-black when it reopened in 1965. All the white children had transferred elsewhere.

School Construction. As noted earlier, the selection of a school site can have tremendous impact on the pattern of school segregation. Schools located within all-white or all-black residential areas solidify racial isolation. Schools located in fringe areas have the potential—if not subsequently gerrymandered—of accelerating integration. Unfortunately, site selection all too often conforms to segregationist practices. Of the 371 schools newly constructed in sixteen cities from 1950 through 1965, over 80 percent opened nearly all-white or all-black.

San Francisco's Hunter's Point community has already been mentioned as an example of federally financed residential segregation. The same area illustrates another dimension of school construction that can be manipulated for racial purposes, namely, school size. The abrupt influx of families into the Hunter's Point area necessitated more classroom space. To acquire that space, three of Hunter's Point's predominantly black schools were enlarged to a capacity of 1,000 pupils each. At the same time, however, a new school, Fremont, was constructed within an adjacent white area. The Fremont school, however, provided space for only 450 pupils. Hence, it could not handle any of the overflow from Hunter's Point. The decision on school size reinforced existing segregation. Fremont retained its all-white character.

Grade Structure. Even when faced with established school locations and size, school authorities are not powerless to alter racial attendance patterns. One extremely subtle but very effective means for overcoming these obstacles is to redefine grade structures. Enlarging the number of grades a school will serve has the effect of shrinking its attendance zone. On the other hand, schools that serve only a few grades must reach out in all directions to include a sufficient number of pupils. The Meigs School in Nashville illustrates how the technique can be employed. Most Nashville schools are organized on a 6–3–3 or an 8–4 grade pattern. The Meigs School, however, is an exception. It is located in a small black area and is structured to serve grades one to twelve. It is the only school in Nashville so structured, and it was all-black in 1965. The Dunbar Junior-Senior High School in Lexington, Kentucky, and the J.N. Ervin School in Dallas have been structured similarly and for the same purpose.

The many options local school boards have for creating or restructuring school-attendance patterns greatly weaken the distinction between *de jure* and *de facto* segregation. In 1974, the federal courts explicitly noted the difficulty of maintaining this distinction in Boston. Boston had never been segregated by law. However, Judge W. Arthur Garrity, Jr. observed that in the purchase and construction of new facilities, the assignment of staff and students to individual schools, and the use of open enrollments, the Boston School Committee was "at all times displaying an awareness of the potential racial impact of their actions. . . . The defendants have, with awareness of the racial segregation of Boston's neighborhoods, deliberately incorporated that segregation into the school system."[4]

Busing

To reduce the segregation of Boston's school system, Judge Garrity ordered mandatory busing of pupils between white and black schools. In view of the extensive segregation of both neighborhoods and schools, busing was perceived as the shortest route to equality of educational opportunity. Proponents of busing argued that buses are the only sure access to equality of facilities and may help promote more complete social integration. The legal basis for using school buses to promote equal educational opportunity had been firmly established by the U.S. Supreme Court in 1971 (in *Swann* v. *Charlotte-Mecklenburg*).

[4]Opinion of Judge Garrity in *Morgan* v. *Hennigan,* cited in U.S. Commission on Civil Rights, *Fulfilling the Letter and Spirit of the Law* (Washington, D.C.: Government Printing Office, 1976).

The reaction to interracial busing in Boston and other cities was initially hostile and even violent. Visions of masses of white children being bused into black ghettos stir the fears of most white parents. Such visions obstruct an oftentimes reasonable and expedient solution to established segregation patterns. Anxiety is also expressed for the stamina of children who must be bused daily to their classrooms. What is seldom realized is that busing of children to school is a common phenomenon in the United States. In recent years, for example, over one-third of all public school children rode buses to school. Most are bused simply because such transportation is most convenient. Others are bused to distant schools to relieve overcrowding at schools nearer by. Still others are bused to extend and enforce racial segregation.

The cities of San Francisco and Cincinnati again offer convenient illustrations. The Anza Elementary School in San Francisco was built in a white area about eight blocks from the predominantly black Golden Gate Elementary School. At the same time, classrooms at Golden Gate were overcrowded and pupils were being bused fifteen blocks to another school. Yet, when Anza was completed, its enrollment was nearly all white. Black pupils from Golden Gate continued to be bused to the more distant Pacific Heights School.

Cincinnati school authorities were even more blatant. There, black students were bused out of a predominantly white area to a nearly all-black school 5.5 miles on the other side of Cincinnati. The explanation for busing focused on overcrowding, yet there was available space in closer schools, schools with predominantly white enrollments. The U.S. commission on Civil Rights asked local school authorities to explain Cincinnati's unusual busing pattern. The response is as illuminating as it is evasive:

> . . . the neighborhood—the concept of relationship of having children attend the school that is in the immediate proximity of the school, those closest to it. Now in this particular case all we did different from that is we picked them up and moved them some place else for a school, but in terms of parents we also tried to get the parents to maintain this relationship rather than dividing them up, into five different places and splitting them in five different spots. That's the only difference.[5]

In other words, the school board felt it necessary to keep all black students together, regardless of where or how they attended school.

The question of busing—especially when it is proposed for purposes of facilitating integration—touches a very sensitive nerve in most Americans. Three out of four Americans oppose mandatory busing, even

---

[5]U.S. Commission on Civil Rights, *Racial Isolation in the Public Schools,* p. 56.

though most still claim to support school integration. Indeed, the hostility to busing is so strong that many white families have fled the cities or schools where mandatory busing has been imposed.[6]

Why is the opposition to busing so fierce? In part, the opposition to busing reflects fears for the safety and stamina of children. As noted above, however, this fear may be exaggerated. A more important concern may be the expectation that the quality of education will decline when mandatory busing is imposed. In part, this concern may simply manifest latent racial prejudices. In addition, however, white parents realize that their children already have a monopoly on better schools. To share these limited resources with bused-in black students implies a reduction in education services. To be bused into a formerly black school implies an even larger reduction in educational services. Also, the turmoil and confusion that accompany the implementation of busing plans is almost sure to disrupt the educational process for at least some time.

Finally, busing is almost always perceived as a direct threat to the cherished notion of a neighborhood school. Even the Cincinnati school board felt obliged to defend its peculiar busing arrangement on the basis of the neighborhood school concept. It is worth reflecting for a moment, then, on what a neighborhood school really is and why it is so revered.

Neighborhood schools are usually deemed desirable for two reasons. They are close to home and thus conveniently accessible. They also serve to foster community cohesiveness. Children who reside close together and attend a common school have more opportunity to interact and are thought to establish more enduring relationships. These two benefits, proximity and social integration, are the mainstays of neighborhood school support.

What is curious about arguments for neighborhood schools is not their potential benefits but their historical perspective. Arguments against economic or racial integration usually proceed from the assumption that integration is destroying the neighborhood school. There are two problems with this perspective. First, children have, historically, traveled quite far to school and continue to do so. More proximate schools have resulted from increasing population density rather than from an increased awareness of any "neighborhood" benefits. One could also question whether this higher density actually has fostered better community and personal relationships. Second, we have already demonstrated that there is considerable flexibility in defining a neighborhood school. School attendance zones themselves can create neighborhoods, and deliberate manipulation of school zones can even affect residential choice. Families will want to live near the schools they know they can attend.

[6]See Charles T. Clotfelter, "School Desegregation, 'Tipping,' and Private School Enrollment," *Journal of Human Resources,* Winter 1976.

Neighborhood schools, then, are not historically sacrosanct. They may not even be the most desirable. As they are now conceived, they serve two specific goals. It would not be completely alien, therefore, to broaden our objectives. Schools could be structured to promote a sense of community in a larger and integrated society rather than to promote cohesiveness in a narrower and often isolated residential tract. Indeed, the narrow neighborhood concept has been repeatedly sacrificed to other social objectives. Every major city, for example, has at least one citywide school reserved for students of outstanding ability. In these cases, productivity and individual development are deemed more important than neighborhood cohesiveness. No one has argued that the attending students are in any way deprived. A high percentage of white parents send their children to distant private schools for exactly the same reasons. And finally, society has all too often demonstrated a willingness to subordinate neighborhood socialization to the goal of racial segregation in the schools. Neighborhood schools are deemed inviolate only when integration threatens.

The opposition to busing, then, is firmly based in both prejudice and privileged position. To overcome this opposition, school authorities would have to provide credible evidence that busing does not reduce the quality of education. School authorities may even have to "bribe" white students to stay in the public schools with improved facilities and programs. In other words, busing for desegregation purposes is most likely to succeed when school authorities recognize the origins of white opposition and respond to them in tangible ways.

To date, the experience with desegregation busing is mixed. There is no convincing evidence that either black or white students have materially benefited from desegregation, much less from forced busing. However, the kinds of benefits expected are both long-run and somewhat intangible. A major objective of the desegregation process is to reduce racial identities and barriers, to develop a more cohesive society. In the process, the quality of the broad educational experience is expected to improve. But none of these things happen automatically, or even very fast. Even under the best of circumstances—when political and financial resources are mobilized to implement desegregation smoothly— the gains from desegregation and busing may be slow to materialize.[7]

The continuing opposition to school busing has succeeded in limiting its use. Although the United States Supreme Court has decided that busing is an acceptable mechanism for achieving more equal opportunity *(Swann v. Charlotte-Mecklenberg Board of Education,* 1971), it is up to local ad-

---

[7]For a review of the experience with school segregation and busing in forty-seven school districts, see U.S. Commission on Civil Rights, *Desegregation of the Nation's Public Schools: A Status Report* (Washington, D.C.: Government Printing Office, 1979).

ministrators and courts to determine the extent and nature of its actual use. Moreover, the Supreme Court ruled in 1974 that school busing plans may not be imposed across school district lines unless it can be shown that the segregation was intentional and materially affected neighboring districts (*Milliken* v. *Bradley (Detroit)*, 1974). In addition, the court has recently emphasized (in Austin, Indianapolis, and Omaha cases) that all court-mandated desegregation must be based on *de jure* segregation Specifically, plantiffs must demonstrate that school authorities *intentionally* acted to segregate schools before the courts may impose desegregation remedies. The cumulative effect of these decisions is to restrict opportunities for desegregation (and busing in particular), especially where cities and their suburbs are racially and economically segregated.

Just how far we have progressed toward racial isolation across city-suburb lines is apparent in Washington, D.C. (71 percent black), Newark (54 percent), East St. Louis (69 percent), Atlanta (51 percent), Cleveland (59 percent), and other large cities. As a consequence, racial and low-income minorities are forced to confine their struggle for equal opportunity to the limited resources of their own school districts; one effect of this limitation has been to foster increased antagonism between inner-city minorities and adjacent low-income, white neighborhoods.

The U.S. Congress has also attempted to limit busing and other desegregation tactics. In nearly every year, Congress has sought to restrict the ability of HEW to provide funds for forced busing or to cut off any federal funds to school districts that failed to comply with desegregation orders. One such act was the Eagleton-Biden Amendment to the 1978 Labor-HEW Appropriations Act. This amendment forbids HEW to require, directly or indirectly, the transportation of any student to paired or clustered schools. This effectively prohibits HEW from cutting off funds to schools that refuse to bus students for desegregation purposes beyond their neighborhood school.

Fiscal Disparities

As we have observed, one of the arguments for school busing is that it will help reduce inequalities in educational facilities. Interestingly enough, the opponents of busing also argue that a more equal distribution of educational resources would eliminate the need for busing, and often offer to redistribute some resources, to provide "quality education for everybody," when pro-busing forces seem to be gaining strength. It seems reasonable to assume, then, that nearly everyone recognizes that educational resources are not equally distributed, that some children are provided with a lot more school resources than others.

Much of this problem derives from the way schools are financed. As we noted in Chapter 11, local communities continue to provide the bulk of their own school resources. In 1978 the federal government supplied only 9 percent of all educational expenditures and the state governments contributed 43 percent; local governments provided the remainder. This means that the quantity and quality of educational resources in a community depends largely on the ability of the local populace to pay taxes. In substantive terms this means that wealthier white enclaves in the suburbs can provide educational opportunities for their children that few cities can ever hope to match.

It is easy to see how such disparities arise. In the suburbs the ratio of property values to school age children is far higher than in the cities. Indeed, population density is ten times larger in urban ghettos than in surrounding areas. This means that residents of the city must support far more school children per square mile than people in the suburbs. Furthermore, the wealthier residents of the suburbs are better equipped to support public schools. They have the property and income on which school revenues depend.

The economics of local school financing encourages school districts to attempt to maximize their tax base while minimizing enrollment size. That is, they seek to include the wealthier and exclude the poorer, especially those with many children. The results are staggering. In California, for example, the poorest elementary school district had only $438 of assessed property per pupil in 1977. The richest district had over $2.4 million of property per pupil. This lead to a lower tax rate for those most able to pay, an outcome of great benefit to the wealthier but of great disadvantage to the poor.

Given the nature of school financing, suburban communities have a tremendous incentive to insulate their school systems from the poor. They have little desire to impose higher tax rates on themselves to provide more educational opportunity for others. In some communities wealthier neighborhoods may even seek to incorporate independent school districts to dispose of responsibilities they already share. This tactic has taken on special significance as the courts have ordered opportunities to be equalized within, but not across, school districts.

To some extent, state and federal governments attempt to equalize the educational inequalities between richer and poorer communities. The Elementary and Secondary Education Act of 1965 is an example of such an attempt. Under this act the federal government distributes approximately $2.5 billion a year to the poorest schools, but even this infusion of funds is inadequate. Over $150 billion was spent on education in the 1978–79 school year, and wealthier communities continue to command a disproportionate amount of those resources. The most absurd and distressing statistic of all is, perhaps, this: the wealthiest schools are more likely than the poorest schools to have subsidized milk or food programs. Many poor schools are denied such benefits because they cannot afford cafeterias, extra personnel, or their share of total costs.

The subject of school financing highlights several important dimensions of the educational opportunity issue. The localized nature of school financing, for example, provides an independent motive for segregation.Even persons who harbor few racial prejudices are not immune to self-interest. On the contrary, most people seek to minimize their tax burden while providing well for their own children. Thus, they seek to exclude poor children, many of whom are black, from their school systems. This exclusionist tendency illuminates again the close ties of racial and class discrimination.

The class discrimination inherent in existing patterns of school financing has recently become a major judicial issue. In August 1971 the California Supreme Court acknowledged that fiscal disparities between school districts "makes the quality of a child's education a function of the wealth of his parents and neighbors." Ruling that such discriminatory treatment violated the Fourteenth Amendment of the U.S. Constitution, the Court declared the state's entire system of financing public schools to be unconstitutional. However, the U.S. Supreme Court effectively overturned that decision in 1973 in a similar case originating in San Antonio, Texas. In its decision the Supreme Court admitted that the present basis for financing schools was "imperfect," but argued that it did not have the prerogative to interfere with the function of the legislative branch and overturn the wisdom and experience of state legislatures and educational administrators. Solutions to the inherent inequalities of school finance, the Court suggested, should be sought in state legislatures, not the courts.

Compensatory Education

An approach to equal education opportunity that has aroused relatively little hostility is compensatory education, the provision of added educational resources to children from poor or minority homes. Indeed, most of the federal money spent on elementary and secondary education is distributed to the lower-income school districts, either by federal statute (Title I of the Elementary and Secondary Education Act) or by allocation decisions made by the states that receive federal grants. The unspoken objective of these efforts is to improve the resources available to poor and minority groups without sharing those (via racial or class integration) available to upper-income groups. As we noted earlier, however, the total federal effort is small in relation to the size of the educational system.

Perhaps the most important form of compensatory education has been the preschool program, particularly Head Start. As the designers of Head Start observed:

> ... *the early years of childhood are a most critical point in the poverty cycle. During these years, the creation of learning patterns, emotional development and the formation of individual expectations and aspira-*

tions take place at a very rapid pace. For the child of poverty, there are clearly observable deficiencies in these processes, which lay the foundation for a pattern of failure, and thus a pattern of poverty, throughout the child's entire life.

To help such children get a more equal start in the education system, Head Start was created to provide educational, health, nutritional, and social services to disadvantaged children in their preschool years. Since its creation in 1964, over 8 million children have participated in Head Start.

Evaluations of Head Start have consistently documented its success in raising preschool children's capabilities, interest, and aspirations. At the same time, however, observers noted that the program's impact tended to be short-lived: after a year or two in their regular school systems Head Start children performed no better than their similarly disadvantaged classmates.[8] Critics of the program were quick to cite this as evidence of the basic genetic or cultural deficiencies of minority children. More sympathetic observers argued, however, that ghetto schools operated as levelers, that the higher motivation and aspirations of Head Start children were not being reinforced by their regular schools. Indeed, the realities of ghetto schools, combined with the increased awareness and ambition fostered by Head Start, might well inculcate an irrevocable sense of defeat. Accordingly, the Follow-Through program was created in 1967 to provide continuing services to Head Start children as they progress from kindergarten to the third grade. Unfortunately, the resources of the program have not been large enough to provide services to all needy Head Start graduates.

College Admissions

One very clear implication of our review of (un) equal opportunity in the pre-school, elementary, and secondary school systems is that minority groups will be less prepared than others to enter colleges and universities. Because they are not provided full and equal opportunities to develop their skills earlier, they will not exhibit the required skills at the time of admission to higher education. This will be manifest not only in grade records, but even more clearly in standardized college entrance exams (the SAT, for example) that are a major screening mechanism for admissions applicants. Accordingly, if all college applicants were treated equally, we would expect a much lower proportion of blacks and other minorities to gain entrance to higher education. The effect of such an "equal opportunity" policy would be to widen educational disparities between whites and blacks (and thus, as we shall note in the next chapter, to increase income inequalities as well).

[8]For a review of the Head Start evidence, see Burt S. Barnow and Glen G. Cain, "A Reanalysis of the Effect of Head Start on Cognitive Development: Methodology and Empirical Findings," *Journal of Human Resources,* Spring 1977.

The vestiges of prior discrimination thus raise very serious policy questions about our concept of equality and the appropriate role of educational institutions in fulfilling equal opportunity goals. On the one hand, it can be (and is) argued that equal treatment is the only objective of policy and that schools should not be expected to exceed that mandate. From this point of view, the overriding goal of higher education is to enhance society's productivity by concentrating resources on the most able. So long as all applicants are treated equally, then the goals of efficiency and equality are both fulfilled.[9]

As we have noted, however, this kind of admissions policy effectively "writes off" the talents of individuals who have been discriminated against in the earlier components of the school system. Hence, an alternative viewpoint stresses the importance of achieving equality of status between whites and blacks, while suggesting that black applicants will prove their worth (demonstrate their latent abilities) once they have an opportunity to catch up. Thus, it is argued, blacks and other minorities should be admitted to college and professional schools on a preferential basis (with lower test scores and grade-point averages), a policy that will not only hasten the achievement of status quality, but will ultimately fulfill our goals of efficiency as well.

Clearly, there is considerable merit to the above argument, particularly if the preferentially admitted students do indeed catch up. But the merits of the case are not likely to impress those who end up paying the costs of such a policy, in particular, those white applicants who are denied admission to make room for minority groups. Such students have worked hard to meet college admission standards and are naturally resentful when others with fewer "qualifications" take their place. Indeed, such students argue that they themselves are being denied equal opportunity—are the victims of "reverse discrimination"—and have sought appropriate relief from the courts. In one of the most publicized cases to date, a rejected applicant (Marco DeFunis) of the University of Washington Law School sued to gain admission on the grounds that he had outscored a number of admitted black and Spanish-speaking students on the Law School Admissions Test. The case ultimately reached the U.S. Supreme Court in the spring of 1974. Unfortunately, the Court was able to declare the case moot because DeFunis had been admitted on a provisional basis while his case was working its way through the courts and actually was graduating when his case reached the Supreme Court.

A more recent case concerns a rejected applicant to the University of California's Medical School at Davis. Under a special admissions program, sixteen of that school's one hundred admissions are set aside for minorities, a policy that has been attacked on the same "reverse discrimination" basis. A superior court judge in the county ruled that the program did violate the equal protection clause of the U.S. Constitution, the corresponding provision of the

[9]For a fuller discussion of this viewpoint see the symposium "On Equality" in *The Public Interest,* Fall 1972. or Arthur Okun, *Equality vs. Efficiency: The Big Trade-Off* (Washington, D.C.: The Brookings Institution, 1975).

California constitution, and Title VI of the U.S. Civil Rights Act of 1964. In June 1978, the U.S. Supreme Court agreed with Bakke. The Court noted that race could be considered as one factor in the admissions process, but ruled that rigid quotas based on race were too discriminatory.

There is no simple way to resolve these competing claims for educational resources; there is clearly some degree of merit to each argument. Only by making admission available to everybody (a policy initiated at City University of New York) can everyone's claim to admission be satisfied. But such a policy not only arouses serious concern for the quality of higher education, but puts severe pressure on school budgets. In the absence of open admissions, a delicate compromise must be struck between those claims to admission based on achievement and those based on denied opportunity (and thus potential achievement).

SUMMARY

Equal opportunity policies can help eliminate poverty in two ways: they may provide access to educational credentials; and they may dismantle artificial barriers between people and jobs. Access to educational credentials is important to the extent that it opens new employment opportunities or redistributes existing ones.

The federal government's effort to create equal opportunity in employment has not met with much success. Black workers continue to suffer inordinate levels of unemployment and to be relegated to undesirable jobs. A major reason for this continuing discrimination lies in the nature of government efforts. For decades the federal government has had the power only to exhort employers to create equal employment opportunities. It was not until the early 1960s that the government acquired some meaningful powers to enforce its proclamations. The Office of Federal Contract Compliance Programs may terminate contracts of discriminatory employers, while the Equal Employment Opportunity Commission may facilitate legal action. Those powers have been used rarely, however, and then mostly as a threat. Political, bureaucratic, and economic interests continue to impede the attainment of equal employment opportunity; what progress has been achieved is largely the result of private legal action, building on public legislation.

In the educational system, equal opportunity has been just as elusive. Local and state governments have not demonstrated a consuming ambition to open school doors to all. On the contrary, they have often employed a variety of manipulative techniques to forestall school integration for as long as possible. The localized nature of school financing also creates a tremendous incentive for wealthier and whiter communities to exclude poorer and blacker children from their schools. Federal authority to alter the pattern of segregation resides primarily in the power to bestow or withdraw funds under the Elementary and Secondary Education Act. But the amount of funds involved is relatively small and the political pressure to maintain their flow great.

FURTHER READING

CONGRESSIONAL BUDGET OFFICE, *Inequalities in the Educational Experiences of Black and White Americans.* Washington, D.C.: Government Printing Office, September 1977.

JENCKS, CHRISTOPHER, et al., *Inequality.* New York: Basic Books, Inc., 1972.

MOSTELLER, FREDERICK, and DANIEL P. MOYNIHAN, eds., *On Equality of Educational Opportunity.* New York: Random House, Inc., 1972.

NEWMAN, DOROTHY K., et al., *Protest, Politics, and Prosperity: Black Americans and White Institutions, 1940–1975.* New York: Pantheon Books, 1978.

PLATTNER, MARC F., "The Welfare State vs. The Redistributive State," *Public Interest,* Spring 1979.

SOWELL, THOMAS, *Race and Economics.* New York: David McKay Co., Inc., 1975, Chs. 7–9.

U.S. COMMISSION ON CIVIL RIGHTS, *Desegregation of the Nation's Public Schools: A Status Report.* Washington, D.C.: Government Printing Office, 1979.

U.S. COMMISSION ON CIVIL RIGHTS, *Toward Equal Educational Opportunity: Affirmative Admissions at Law and Medical Schools.* Washington, D.C.: Government Printing Office, June 1978.

SUMMARY AND CONCLUSIONS

15 DIRECTIONS AND PROSPECTS

According to official estimates, nearly 25 million Americans remain in poverty. Although these estimates themselves have been challenged, it is evident that millions of Americans are poor, either because their standard of living is below "minimally adequate" standards or because they depend primarily on public assistance (welfare) to maintain that poverty standard. Recognition of the fact that so many Americans remain poor has led to two simple questions: (1) Why are so many individuals poor? and (2) What policies will eliminate their poverty? The preceding chapters have provided much of the background material necessary to resolve these questions. This concluding chapter attempts to summarize the salient impressions of our inquiry and offer policy suggestions.

THE CAUSES OF POVERTY

The most popular diagnoses of poverty focus on the personal characteristics of those who are poor. The poor are thus viewed as less able, less motivated, overly reproductive, too aged or sick, or otherwise handicapped. By inference or declaration, they are thus assumed to be responsible for their own impoverishment. This Flawed Character view of poverty, as we have called it, is reinforced by conventional statistical profiles of the poverty population. Very high percentages of the poor *are* in families that are aged, or female-headed, or large, or prone to sickness and disability.

There are two critical weaknesses in these demographic theories of poverty, however. Not all of the poor fit one or another of the various categories of misfits. Indeed, the largest single demographic group among the poor consists of traditional male-headed families, most with a father working full time all year round. But the weakness of demographic theories involves more than just narrow horizons; these theories also suffer from shortsightedness. Even those poor families who manifest distinctive demographic traits, such as broken homes, are not necessarily poor because of those traits. On the contrary, for the most part the aged poor were poor before they were aged, broken poor families were poor before they split up, large poor families were poor when they were smaller, and sick poor families were poor even when they were well. Thus, theories of poverty causation that are based only on observations at a single point in time fail to perceive the dynamics of impoverishment. They confuse association with causality.

A broader, more dynamic perspective on poverty is achieved by focusing on the relationship of people to the labor market. For the most part, it is a person's relationship to the market that determines his economic, and even social, status. One immediate advantage of this perspective is that it draws attention to two critical questions: (1) What forces determine how many good income earning opportunities are available? and (2) What forces determine, who will obtain those opportunities? The myopic perspective of demographic theories of poverty encompasses only the second question. It assumes that good jobs are always available in sufficient quantity. But they are not, as history has repeatedly shown, and as we have again witnessed in the escalating unemployment rates of the mid-1970s. To understand why so much poverty exists at any point in time, we must consider and resolve the first question. The answer to the second question tells us primarily how that poverty will be distributed.

In seeking to resolve the first question, we have put a heavy stress on the importance of aggregate economic policies in determining the extent of poverty. We have suggested that the number of available jobs is a phenomenon over which individual members of society have very little control. Similarly, they have little control over what kinds of jobs will be available or where they will be located. These decisions are made, instead, by the interplay of labor market forces, among which government fiscal and monetary decisions are often the most decisive. Accordingly, we conclude that collective social decisions in the area of economic policy— especially those concerning the extent and structure of the demand for labor—are responsible for much poverty.

We should not conclude, however, that all available income-earning opportunities are taken. Even in relatively prosperous times, some families will break up, others will become sick or disabled, and some may even choose not to work. Hence, even with prolonged full employment, not all families will participate fully in the economy. Some disequilibria between the number of available jobs and potential workers do arise from demographic forces, and we must include them as independent causes of poverty where appropriate. Family breakup rates high among these factors, with age and disability slightly less important. Their cumulative importance at present appears to be relatively small, however.

The third general set of causes are those related to discrimination, both in the schools and in the labor market. Minority groups, the offspring of the poor, and women are deprived of an equal chance to acquire productive skills and use those skills in the labor market. Hence, racial, class, and sex discrimination have significant impact on both the distribution and extent of poverty. As long as discrimination persists, we may predict that the children of the poor, blacks, and female-headed families will dominate the ranks of the poverty population. Even in a relatively prosperous economy, discrimination tends to create artificial barriers between workers and jobs, leaving some individuals poor. We may estimate that discrimination is responsible for a significant share of all poverty and that it is the foremost determinant of the distribution of low incomes.

In assessing the causes of poverty, then, we may make the following generalizations: (1) labor market forces are primarily responsible for the extent of poverty, with demographic handicaps and discrimination of secondary importance; and (2) the distribution of poverty is determined by patterns of discrimination and demographic characteristics. Because available knowledge and statistics about poverty and discrimination are not complete, there is room for argument on the precise dimensions of each relationship. Nevertheless, the broad outlines of causality are clear enough to provide the necessary perspective for public policy approaches.

POLICY DIRECTIONS

An understanding of the causes of poverty gives clear direction to the formulation of required public policy. To eliminate poverty, we must first expand the number of decent job opportunities and their availability. Harry Johnson of the University of Chicago summarized the point well: " . . . in the absence of a policy of raising the demand for labor to the stretching point, ad hoc policies for remedying poverty by piecemeal assaults on particular poverty-associated characteristics are likely to prove both ineffective and expensive. The most effective way to attack poverty is to attack unemployment, not the symptoms of it."[1]

To reduce unemployment and poverty, the government has several options available. First and foremost, it must seek to maintain a high level of aggregate demand by the judicious use of fiscal and monetary tools. In addition, it must give special consideration to the structure of demand those tools stimulate. Aggregate economic policies have identifiable impact on different areas, industries, and labor market groups. Accordingly, it is the responsibility of government policymakers to select that mix of public actions that maximizes impact on the unemployed and poor, while minimizing dislocations, such as inflation, elsewhere.

Concomitant with the thrust toward full employment, government agencies must make a determined effort to equalize educational and employment opportunity. This will not only further reduce poverty and inequity, it will also make the attainment of full employment easier and less expensive.

Finally, the public must assume responsibility for those who are temporarily or permanently unable to participate in the labor market. Adequate income support must be available, both to alleviate hardship and to reduce intergenerational deprivation. Greatest priority should be placed, however, on reducing the need for public assistance to a minimum.

Viewed against this policy framework, recent public antipoverty activities do not appear well directed. Only rarely has there been a sustained and determined effort to reach full employment, and even at those times, policy decisions stopped short of considering the structure of aggregate demand thereby created. Instead, public antipoverty activity has, for the most part, been a bread and circus kind of affair. We have allotted— grudgingly, to be sure—huge sums of money to feed, clothe, and house the poor, in the hope, perhaps, of achieving social tranquility. At the same time, we have subjected the poor to a kaleidoscope of training and education activities, holding out false promises of job opportunity. Yet we have done close to nothing to create the job opportunities that are our most pressing need. Some recent experiences are worth reflection.

Welfare Reform

At the end of 1979 there were nearly 15 million individuals receiving, in the aggregate, nearly $45 billion of public assistance (cash and in-kind). Translated into tax dollars, this means that the average nonpoor individual in the United States contributed over $235 in 1979 to provide the poor

[1]Harry G. Johnson, "Poverty and Unemployment," in Burton Weisbrod, ed., *The Economics of Poverty* (Englewood Cliffs, N.J.: Prentice-Hall, Inc., 1965), p. 170.

with income maintenance. While these amounts are a small fraction (under 10 percent) of all government expenditures, they are large enough to stir public anguish. Indeed, the cry for welfare reform has been strident.

In Chapter 12, we reviewed the character of recent welfare reforms. Generally, they incorporate many important and necessary improvements in our system of income maintenance. However, there are two fundamental problems with recent welfare reform efforts. First, most reform proposals have been presented as comprehensive "solutions" to our welfare problems. They are not, nor can they be. At best, welfare reform can achieve a more equitable or efficient compromise between the conflicting goals of income adequacy, work incentives, and cost efficiency. The basic conflict between these goals will remain. Each time welfare reform is proposed, it is defeated when this realization sets in.

The second problem with welfare reform proposals is that they tend to capture all antipoverty attention. Because "welfare reform" is such an enticing prospect, it tends to receive high policy priority. The problem with welfare reform's high priority is that it threatens to impede more meaningful and permanent poverty remedies. Public interest in poverty issues dissipates easily. Welfare reform thus threatens to satisfy the need for action, to divert our attention away from more fundamental causes of poverty and inequality. There is grave danger that welfare reform will be regarded as a solution to the problem of poverty and that other remedies will be neglected.

Education and Training

Perhaps the second ranking area of public concern is the field of education and training. Administrative and congressional spokesmen continue to exhort the young to stay in school and the unemployed—especially those on welfare—to undertake further training. Appropriations to expand government training programs are rarely denied, and political support for educational outlays is easy to muster.

No general case against educational and training expenditures has been presented here. Again, the focus is only on the appropriateness of those expenditures as antipoverty tools. The issue is important because educational and training programs gather much of their support on the basis of their reputed antipoverty effectiveness. What we have sought to demonstrate is that this belief bears very little resemblance to the causal roots of poverty. Lack of training or education, by itself, is not a very significant cause of poverty. Thus, programs to provide more education and training are not particularly well suited to reduce the incidence of poverty. What impact they have is dependent on manpower policies generally. The limited potential of educational advancement to eliminate poverty has been underscored by a recent report of the U.S. Commission on Human Resources and Advanced Education: the commission found that 25 percent of all college graduates are already overtrained for the jobs available.

Employment Programs

Recent public actions in the area of manpower policy best illustrate the mistaken direction of current antipoverty efforts. The single most important observation of this book is the causal significance of aggregate demand policies for the incidence of poverty. High unemployment and sluggish economic growth are the most certain and forceful agents in perpetuating poverty. Nevertheless, public policy in the mid-1970s can be characterized as a deliberate return to the slower growth and higher unemployment rates that characterized much of the 1950s. Two recent decisions illustrate the direction of public policy.

From the first day it took office, the Nixon administration expressed grave concern for the movement of prices and the threat of accelerating inflation. To restore price stability, the administration curtailed growth in government expenditures and increased the cost of borrowing. The effects of these actions were soon felt. Unemployment rates jumped from a low of 3.5 percent in early 1969 to over 6 percent in 1971. The number of persons in poverty increased at the same time. The Ford administration contributed to this trend by declaring inflation to be "public enemy number one" and forsaking expansionary policies. As a result, unemployment rates continued to climb, reaching a peak of 9.0 percent in May 1975. At thr same time, an additional 2 million Americans fell into poverty. What is particularly distressing about this movement is that it was not necessary. The security of millions of individuals was hastily sacrificed without even considering viable policy alternatives, be they wage and price controls to curb inflation, selective measures to cushion the unemployment impact of anti-inflation policies, or even stepped-up public employment.

The Carter Administration initiated a much more expansionary policy. President Carter elevated the goal of full employment to highest priority and began in 1977 to stimulate aggregate demand. Unemployment rates fell steadily for two years, and the number of poor persons declined. In 1978–79, however, inflation accelerated, and the Administration's priorities switched from expanding employment to fighting inflation. Once again, the poor and unemployed were sacrificed to price stability, with relatively little consideration of alternative policies.

Equal Opportunity

Recent activity in the area of civil rights has been sufficiently publicized to require little restatement here. Basically, it has been a question of the courts leading and the executive branch timidly enforcing. We cannot yet claim that we have provided equal opportunity for all, white and black, rich and poor.

It is important to realize that even complete enforcement of civil rights legislation will not lead to equal status for whites and blacks. Even if all racially based barriers to achievement fell tomorrow, blacks would continue to be handicapped by past discrimination. Black school children would still be far behind their white peers in educational attainments. Equal opportunity to attend college would thus still exclude most blacks. In the labor market, too, the enforcement of nondiscrimination would be of relatively little use to a person who has been denied twenty years of training and experience. The elimination of racial discrimination would narrow racial differences in education and income, but the process would be excruciatingly slow.

To achieve equal economic status between whites and blacks, then, we must do more than enforce equal opportunity; we must also compensate for the heritage of previous discrimination. This means providing compensatory education and training. It also means providing preferential opportunities. Black school children with fewer attainments will have to receive special consideration, while job requirements, in terms of qualifications, experience, and credentials, will have to be set aside for many black workers. As we noted in Chapter 14, such extreme "affirmative action" inevitably conflicts with the claims of those whites who feel they have "earned" admission to desired schools or jobs and thus necessitates difficult and delicate compromises. But to forsake any such action is to perpetuate discriminatory status.

CAUSES, ATTITUDES, AND POLICY

While present policy directions are not well suited to achieve equality or eliminate poverty, there is some prospect for future change. Both the non-poor and the poor are becoming increasingly frustrated with policies that provide more income maintenance and fewer opportunities. A recent Harris poll showed that 80 percent of the American public regards our welfare problem as "very serious." They want more jobs provided for poor persons, and less welfare. If required, the necessary jobs should be guaranteed by the government.

Although public demands for less welfare and more jobs are persistent, an undercurrent of hostility and distrust remains. Over 80 percent of the public agrees that "too many people on welfare could be working" and that "too many people on welfare cheat by getting money they are not entitled to."[2] With respect to minority concerns, 41 percent of white America believes that black unemployment rates are high because blacks don't want jobs.[3] In addition, one out of four whites believes blacks have less native intelligence. Only 4 percent of all whites believe that job discrimination is a major barrier to black employment. White perceptions of Spanish-speaking minorities are comparable.[4] Finally, a majority of Americans opposes preferential access to jobs or schools for either poor people or minorities, preferring to let "merit" determine access to schools and jobs.

These perceptions of poverty and discrimination are major determinants of public policy. If we are going to eliminate either poverty or discrimination, public perceptions must reflect reality more closely. Then those perceptions must be reflected in public policy.

[2]Louis Harris survey of June 1976.
[3]CBS/New York Times poll of October 1977.
[4]Louis Harris and Associates, *A Study of Attitudes toward Racial and Religious Minorities and toward Women* (New York: National Conference of Christians and Jews, 1978).

INDEX